# Reinventing Liberty

Edinburgh Critical Studies in Romanticism
Series Editors: Ian Duncan and Penny Fielding

Available Titles
*A Feminine Enlightenment: British Women Writers and the Philosophy of Progress, 1759–1820*
JoEllen DeLucia

*Reinventing Liberty: Nation, Commerce and the Historical Novel from Walpole to Scott*
Fiona Price

*The Politics of Romanticism: The Social Contract and Literature*
Zoe Beenstock

*Radical Romantics: Prophets, Pirates, and the Space Beyond Nation*
Talissa J. Ford

Forthcoming Titles
*Ornamental Gentlemen: Literary Antiquarianism and Queerness in British Literature and Culture, 1760–1890*
Michael Robinson

*Literature and Medicine in the Nineteenth-Century Periodical Press:* Blackwood's Edinburgh Magazine, *1817–1858*
Megan Coyer

*Following the Footsteps of Deep Time: Geological Travel Writing in Scotland, 1750–1820*
Tom Furniss

# Reinventing Liberty

## Nation, Commerce and the Historical Novel from Walpole to Scott

Fiona Price

EDINBURGH
University Press

Edinburgh University Press is one of the leading university presses in the UK. We publish academic books and journals in our selected subject areas across the humanities and social sciences, combining cutting-edge scholarship with high editorial and production values to produce academic works of lasting importance. For more information visit our website: www.edinburghuniversitypress.com

Edinburgh University Press Ltd
The Tun – Holyrood Road, 12(2f) Jackson's Entry, Edinburgh EH8 8PJ

First published in hardback by Edinburgh University Press 2016

Typeset in 10.5/13 Sabon by
Servis Filmsetting Ltd, Stockport, Cheshire,
and printed and bound in Great Britain by
CPI Group (UK) Ltd, Croydon CR0 4YY

A CIP record for this book is available from the British Library

ISBN 978 1 4744 0296 5 (hardback)
ISBN 978 1 4744 2607 7 (paperback)
ISBN 978 1 4744 0297 2 (webready PDF)
ISBN 978 1 4744 1289 6 (epub)

# Contents

# Acknowledgements

An earlier version of the first part of Chapter 1 is to be found in 'Ancient Liberties? Rewriting the Historical Novel: Thomas Leland, Horace Walpole and Clara Reeve', *Journal for Eighteenth-Century Studies* 34.1 (2011), pp. 19–38, and some of the material on Jane West's *The Loyalists* in Chapter 3 also appeared in different form in '"Experiments Made by the Airpump": Jane West's *The Loyalists* (1812) and the Science of History', *Women's Writing* 19.3 (August 2012), pp. 315–32. I would like to thank Kate Mitchell and Nicola Parsons, editors of *Reading Historical Fiction: The Revenant and Remembered Past* (Palgrave, 2014) for allowing me to explore some earlier thoughts about Ellis Cornelia Knight in my piece 'The Uses of History' (pp. 187–203). I am very grateful to the Huntington Library for awarding me a short-term visiting fellowship; I would also like to thank Chawton House Library and the British Library as well as the Research Office at the University of Chichester, and our own librarians, particularly Wendy Ellison. For providing intellectual engagement, inspiration and advice my heartfelt thanks goes to colleagues Pamela Clemit, Benjamin Dew, Christina Davidson, Natasha Duquette, Gillian Dow, Jennie Batchelor, Porscha Fermanis, Hugo Frey, Matthew Grenby, Rebecca Probert, Fiona Robertson, Thomas McLean and Devoney Looser. I am also very grateful for the guidance given by my editors, Penny Fielding and Ian Duncan. Finally, I would particularly like to thank Benjamin Noys and my parents for their unfailing help, patience and intellectual support.

# Introduction

The British historical novel before *Waverley* (1814) is often seen as a minor and immature form. Measured against Scott, and presumed to be tediously antiquarian, works of historical fiction are deemed relative failures or, when more successful, re-categorised.[1] This critical narrative is inaccurate – there are historical novels of considerable complexity and importance in the latter half of the eighteenth century. In the work of Scott's predecessors historical tropes are exploited, recycled and distorted in a complex conversation about the problem of liberty. Worried about King George III's supposed absolutist tendencies, in the 1760s historical novelists began to re-examine the balance of parliamentary and monarchical authority. But their attempts to rethink the distribution of power were complicated: by a reluctance to undermine the parliamentary settlement achieved after the Glorious Revolution of 1688; by fears of abrupt change generated by the English Civil War; and by ancient constitutionalism, the key mode of thinking about legal and constitutional change in Britain in the seventeenth and eighteenth centuries. Historical novelists from Leland to Ann Radcliffe interrogated ancient constitutionalism, using the notion of a return to ancient liberty, first, to defend the prerogatives of the nobility against the Crown, and, later, to emphasise the prerogatives of the people. But their work made it evident that the myth of Anglo-Saxon liberty lacked flexibility. The fantasy of return to a pre-feudal past was inadequate in the face of the issues of national debt, inflation and taxation that emerged out of the American and French Revolutions.

A different way of imagining the unwritten constitution, of refiguring the relation of past to present, was urgently needed. Seeking such an alternative, historical novelists turned to stadial history. Understanding the past in terms of particular economic stages, accompanied by characteristic political and social forms, stadial history could allow for narratives of progress, of decline, and even of continuity. For Scottish stadial historian, William Robertson, for instance, the manners of the feudal past and the present were linked by the codes of chivalry. If the idea of an ancient constitution enshrining liberty was fragile, could the notion of 'chivalry' provide a benign civic imaginary, a way of understanding the respective roles – and prerogatives – of monarch, nobility and people past and present? Responding in part to Edmund Burke's nostalgia for chivalry in his *Reflections on the Revolution in France* (1790), radical writers, like Mary Wollstonecraft, Charlotte Smith and William Godwin were doubtful. Probing the idea of progress implicit in stadial history, they instead proposed historical narratives which would measure movement towards greater liberty in term of the economic well-being and political awareness of the people. In their turn, such narratives were adapted by historical novelists like James White to question the liberty of the colonial subject, and eventually contested and recuperated by more conservative novelists such as Jane West, transformed in the service of Union.

Despite its influence upon Scott, this conversation has been largely forgotten. In contemporary scholarship Scott problematises the Union; registers economic pressures; ends history and underpins the nation with the dubious legitimacy of romance. The idea of Scott as restorative has long been subject to criticism. Nonetheless, this motif, which emerged quickly and proved so persistent, played a role in rendering the historical novel before Scott invisible.[2] In the General Preface to the Magnum Opus edition of the Waverley Novels in 1829 Scott recounts how a period of 'long illness' threw him 'back on the kingdom of fiction', establishing the medicinal power of his work.[3] What is at stake in this restorative account becomes evident in Maria Edgeworth's 1834 novel, *Helen*. In this, Edgeworth's last novel, when her hero, Granville Beauclerc, is abused by the company for claiming he is 'glad' to 'have never seen' Scott, he defends himself from the charge of 'indifference'. Scott has 'medicined to repose the disturbed mind'; he is the 'Great and good enchanter' 'for in his magic there is no dealing with unlawful means'.[4] But Beauclerc still argues that meeting Scott in person would have been a disappointment. Via her character, Lady Davenant, Edgeworth insists that, on the contrary, Scott lived up to all expectations. His healing powers are connected with a manner that recalls the 'chivalrous courtesy of other times'. Based on first-hand evidence, this quality is as genuine as the signature of the 'gallant' Essex that begins the discussion of hero worship.[5] Elsewhere in *Helen* forged texts circulate, terrifying and irrepressible, in a manner that recalls the post-French Revolution debate. Against such distortions, Scott and his works stand as instances of authenticity, presenting a last word, a stable past. Clearly, Scott's implicit positioning of the Waverley Novels as a return to health is persuasive – not least because the recuperation the books offer is more than purely personal: Scott's 'kingdom of fiction' will presumably also facilitate political convalescence.

To extrapolate from Edgeworth's remarks, if her restorative Scott used no 'unlawful means', the earlier historical novel was presumably politically and legally disruptive, darker in its enchantments, more injurious to the social body than medicinal. Shared by other historical novelists including Anna Maria Mackenzie and Clara Reeve, this sense stemmed from the form's consideration, particularly after 1794, of mass political activity and economic inequality. Previously, the eighteenth century had been characterised by a fear of luxury and the moral and political discontent it might generate. The apprehension caused by the social mobility associated with capitalism is evident, for instance, in Reeve's own *Old English Baron* (1778), where she attempts to imagine an Old Whiggish past in which economic and social status – and the liberties supposedly accompanying that status – are fixed. But when radical historical novelists used stadial history to focus on the economic suffering and well-being of the masses, they opened the way to other imaginaries of the commercial realm. What Ernest Gellner calls 'an enormously complex transformation' was necessary to create the modern British commercial nation: the historical novel before Scott was a site of the 'artifice' and 'invention' that shaped this 'unique' yet globally influential event.[6] In the opening decade of the nineteenth century more moderate writers like Edgeworth herself were able to suggest there were forms of exchange and social mobility that did not threaten abrupt political breakage.

As such, the historical novel is an important site in the development of the gradualist myth of modern British national identity – the myth that in Britain political change takes place incrementally and judiciously, against an implicit backdrop of safe commerciality. In the second *Waverley* novel *Guy Mannering* (1815) the lawyer Mac-Morlan replaces the 'deplorable' garments of Dominie Sampson 'judiciously' by 'degrees'; despite the violent transitions that form the substance of Scott's novels, here Scott imagines that the alterations necessary for commercial modernity proceed peacefully, aided by the law.[7] Above all, Abel retains only an 'indistinct and embarrassing' consciousness that 'metamorpho[sis]' has taken place.[8] Were even the mild Dominie to notice the changes his superiors decree, resistance might follow. To avoid this threat, to allow the new to be accepted as the old, history needs to be rewritten. As a result of historiographic work performed by, amongst others, Elizabeth Hamilton, Jane West and Jane Porter, national culture was reshaped: the emphasis on political and economic freedoms for the individual was transformed into the idea of a struggle for the liberty of the nation. Thus, while a moderated form of 'liberty' was retained, in one influential strand of discourse the very idea of (another) revolution became un-British.

While these novels claim the notion of gradual political change for the parliament and monarchy, they also testify to an intense struggle and uncertainty regarding the British future, imagining and reimagining the processes and possibilities of transition. Even though, like Scott, these novelists engage with shifting feudal and commercial social imaginaries, their works register deep anxiety regarding the changing nature of modernity: the economic present can be dangerous, disruptive and potentially cruel. Hence, instead of foregrounding inevitability, they champion intervention. As such, these works speak to the present moment – a moment in which, Fredric Jameson suggests, it is easier 'to imagine the thoroughgoing deterioration of the earth and of nature than the breakdown of late capitalism'.[9] Uneasy about the increasing dominance of the market, or sometimes about the distortion of primogeniture on that market, Scott's predecessors try to find alternative sources of political and social value.

In Karl Marx's 'Eighteenth Brumaire of Louis Bonaparte' (1852), the philosopher suggests that at the moment of revolution, the attempt is made to borrow costumes and masks from the spirits of the dead. Change is clothed in the language of the past. This is the first step in the creation of a truly 'new language', which can only be assimilated when the speaker 'moves in it without recalling the old and when he forgets his native tongue'.[10] Such total construction of the new is, though, challenging, as Sanja Perovic's work on the earlier revisions to the French Republican Calendar suggests.[11] Frustrated with the narratives of the past available to them, British historical novelists before Scott did not directly adopt a 'new language'. Instead they sought to rewrite the past itself: as 'artist[s] of the historical process', they would forge a new grammar by which the past was to be understood.[12] The Waverley Novels complete this movement. Scott's narratives confirm the creation of an innovative history to replace the 'tradition of all dead generations'.[13] Nonetheless, Scott's writing is deeply marked by the tension that characterises the work of his predecessors.

## The Invisible Novel

Usually mentioned only briefly in surveys of the historical novel as part of the genre's prehistory, the historical novel before Scott is a surprisingly elusive form.[14] Most frequently, individual historical novels have come into view when considered in relation to other genres. A tendency to interpret the early British form primarily as an offshoot of the French tradition was begun by James R. Foster's 'The Abbé Prévost and the English Novel'.[15] Foster's study benefitted certain works, most notably Sophia Lee's *The Recess* (1783–5), but it also foreshadowed the trend of positioning such works as 'gothic'.[16] In accounts of the development of the gothic, the marginal presence of historical fiction is usually signalled by the inclusion of Horace Walpole's *The Castle of Otranto* (1764), Clara Reeve's *The Old English Baron* and Sophia Lee's *The Recess*, that is, two works that explore the discourse of ancient con- stitutionalism and a third which rejects it. It is because the narrative of ancient constitutionalism is always concerned with the decline of liberty, constantly haunted by the spectre of (Jacobite) royal absolutism, that these works are so easily read against the gothic novels of the 1790s, in which the imagining of feudal oppression takes its most vivid form. In addition, in their rejection of the (entertaining) tyrannies of previous times, gothic novels of that revolutionary decade implicitly invoke the Whiggish narrative of progress that is critiqued in Lee's work. However, Lee and her fellow historical novelists probe the past with a suspicious historiographic eye that distinguishes them from their later gothic coun- terparts. Far from serving a straightforwardly patriotic agenda, the early historical novel re-examines the way the past is constructed, querying the nature of 'progress' in order to engage in a sceptical reappraisal of the economics of the present.

In these novels, the writing of history rehearses and thus reveals the operations and fantasies of power. While initially the genre focuses on political representation and judicial fairness, the issue of the composite nature of Britain and Ireland rapidly becomes a central preoccupation. It is for this reason that the 'historical fiction' has had a liminal presence in criticism on the national tale.[17] In *Bardic Nationalism*, for instance, Katie Trumpener fills the 'blank' of a Scotland, 'neither a nation or a province', that Edwin Muir had, in 1936, suggested Scott was writing into.[18] To do so, she draws on a vast range of sources (including the earlier historical novel). Her focus is on how 'in Britain Anglo-Scottish and Anglo-Irish cultural revivals partly offset a process of cultural centralization'.[19] In respect to this project, as Trumpener allows, the early historical novel is ambiguously placed. It can be used to support nation-building (although uncomfortably the nation in question is often a Union) yet it also exposes the weaknesses in any such project. When the history of the genre itself is examined, what becomes apparent is nationalism's duality. In *The Scottish Chiefs* (1810), for example,

Wallace's fight against Edward I is not used simply to promote the liberties of the ordinary people, or to plead for Scottish independence; instead, Jane Porter redirects nationalist sentiment to the British efforts against Napoleon. Even whilst nationalism apparently allows the small nation to fight exploitation in the historical novel it ultimately facilitates the dissipation of progressive political energies.

Partially visible through the lens of the gothic and the national tale, often awkwardly positioned in relation to discourses of commercial progress and of Union, the early historical novel has also in the past suffered as a result of the low status of eighteenth-century historiography: 'scientizing' developments in nineteenth-century historiography led to a tendency to dismiss or undervalue the period's history writing that persisted into the twentieth century.[20] Along with Karen O'Brien's *Narratives of Enlightenment* (1997), Mark Salber Phillips's *Society and Sentiment: Genres of Historical Writing in Britain, 1740–1820* (2000), began to correct this situation. Drawing attention to the generic diversity of eighteenth-century historical discourse, Phillips's work has led to a re-examination of the diversity of history writing and the representation of the past, as, for example, in Ruth Mack's *Literary Historicity* (2009).[21] Yet, despite this interest in the eighteenth-century presentation of time, the British historical novel remains oddly neglected. In his wide-ranging *The Historical Novel in Europe, 1650–1950* (2009), Richard Maxwell, for example, draws on James R. Foster to argue that the French historical novel influences Scott and Scott influences Europe. However, the eighteenth-century British historical novel falls largely outside his scope. And while Anne H. Stevens's *British Historical Fiction before Scott* (2010) is an honourable exception to the tendency to underestimate the predominance of the genre, adapting Franco Moretti's 'quantitative' approach to focus on print culture, Stevens's title suggests a certain discomfort with the label 'historical novel'.[22]

Such critical unease is a lingering result of Georg Lukács's influential definition of the form. In *The Historical Novel* (1937) Lukács raises the possibility of an eighteenth-century historical novel only to foreclose it. Walpole's *Castle of Otranto* (1764) is the 'most famous "historical novel" of the eighteenth century' but it is a piece of 'mere costumery'.[23] Walter Scott is the first historical novelist because he registers a sense of history as a force linked 'in its national element [. . .] with problems of social transformation', a sense which Lukács primarily connects with the French Revolution, and, across Europe, with the 'Napoleonic Wars'.[24] As such, Scott 'fathom[s] historically the whole of English development to find a "middle way" for himself between warring extremes' – the extremes of feudalism and capitalism. In tracing this path, Scott 'exonerate[s] nothing in the development of capitalism' and, despite his acute sense of sympathy, 'display[s] no violent opposition to the features of the new development'.[25] In other words, for Lukács, Scott's work correctly diagnoses the breakage represented by the French Revolution. Additionally, (through their realism) these works contain the kind of revelations of commercial political life that Lukács saw as a necessary stage on the road to political enlightenment. To draw out the logic of Lukács's argument, whereas the Waverley Novels finally ask the reader to leave the world of feudal romance for that of commercial modernity, earlier historically themed fictions presumably rehearse no such generic shift.

Lukács's own political perspective, his notion that transformation is necessary and inevitable, means he has a restricted notion of how change should be figured in the historical novel. His implicit narrative, from feudalism, to bourgeois and then to proletarian culture, contains an assumption of progress but, Murray Pittock warns, the (Whiggish) idea of history as progress is one to which it is easy to 'surrender', particularly where the historical novel is concerned.[26] As the work of Miranda Burgess and Ian Duncan on romance has suggested, other, less 'Whiggish' paradigms are possible.[27] The historical novel before Scott sometimes refuses and often probes the value and meaning of progress. The ancient constitutionalism so important to the genre relies on the idea of return. Even when the genre draws on stadial history, the acceptance of the 'new development' Lukács finds in Scott is lacking. Comparing geographically and chronologically distinct social formations, the early historical novel instead offers choice: primitivism, a return to a state of nature in which social relations can be reconstituted (a possibility raised in the anonymous *Arville Castle* [1795]), or a commitment to Roman Republicanism (as in Ellis Cornelia Knight's *Marcus Flaminius* [1792]) are, for example, investigated as a solution to British constitutional difficulties.

In line with this doubt over the nature of progress, in the early historical novel the relationship between the feudal and capitalist, or between the aristocratic and the commercial, is (appropriately enough for late eighteenth-century Britain) less clear than Lukács's account suggests. This is evident in Charlotte Smith's *Desmond* (1792). There, the French aristocrat and revolutionary sympathiser Montfleuri complains of the 'the imposts levied at the gates of every town', burdens imposed on the poor 'because they were poor', not 'noble'.[28] In *ancien régime* France history ensured that aristocratic vested interests blocked individual self-determination and social mobility. Then again, similar obstacles exist in British commercial modernity. Lord Newminster is (as his name suggests) only second-generation nobility – his father has bought the title – yet the young man is idle, arrogant and intolerant to the poor, assuming all the traditional privileges of his newly adopted class. The system of oppression reproduces itself. In these fictions, feudal and capitalist extremes can be imagined, but they are tightly intertwined, sometimes in struggle, sometimes in support. It is also noticeable that, in this intricate debate, attempts to think through the relation between capitalism and feudalism rarely lead to the moderation of tone 'middle way' suggests. Even the Shandyesque whimsicality of Ann Yearsley's *The Royal Captives* (1795) operates to deliver radical sentiment. More often, the novels stage violent scenes of political conflict. In Louis de Bruno's *Lioncel* (1803) demagoguery leads to robbery and bloodshed. Such conflict still echoes in *Helen* through the 'loud voice of universal execration' that follows Granville's declaration of his happiness at not seeing Scott; historical fiction itself becomes the site of controversy.[29] Finally, Scott's own tone of moderation was studied; it did not, Richard Cronin states, reflect political neutrality.[30]

Once the emphasis on progress and the moderation of the 'middle way' is removed, a new way forward emerges. Historiographic awareness is the key to the form. It is the interrogation of the subject matter, methodology, purpose, manufacture and reception of history, broadly understood, that constitutes the historical novel. When this is understood, it becomes evident that there is an eighteenth-century British historical novel of considerable historiographic and political complexity. The historical novel before Scott registers history as a 'mass experience' of transformation from the inception of the Revolution but it also engages with another crisis less central to Lukács's original account of the genre – a crisis that emerged out of the particular circumstances of mid-to-late eighteenth-century Britain.[31]

## British History and Crisis

Admittedly, in terms of discovering such a sense of crisis, the British eighteenth century initially looks rather unpromising – insufficiently marked by conflict. First, for historians 1688 (connected with the 'Glorious' Revolution in which James II was replaced by William III and Mary II) is seen as a key transitional moment in British history. Consequently, as J. C. D. Clark puts it: 'the "eighteenth century" is . . . coupled to an industrial-democratic engine of change and drawn off into "the future"'.[32] His metaphor suggests the strange kind of passivity often conferred on the period – if it belongs to modernity, it does not get there under its own steam. Second (but not altogether inconsistently), the British eighteenth century is often seen as a time of political stultification: after 1688, 1832 is seen as the next significant landmark in British parliamentary reform.[33]

This uneasy sense of political stultification was registered in contemporary historiography. In *An Historical and Moral View of the French Revolution* (1794) Mary Wollstonecraft writes that, following the 'revolution' of 1688, Englishmen were 'with reason, proud of their constitution'. However, she argues, the revolution itself 'soon introduced ... corruption'; 'noble pride' 'degenerated into arrogance' as 'its cause [English constitutional superiority] became less conspicuous'.[34] Although Wollstonecraft's radical agenda is one with which many of her more conservative contemporaries would have disagreed, hers is a narrative of conjectural history in which progress has stalled: liberty is being eroded. On the one hand, 'arrogance' in relation to the constitution is a symptom of the difficulty of thinking about further political change. On the other, this very 'arrogance' indicates a context in which there is continued commitment to the notion of liberty – a commitment that might eventually require action. The self-satisfaction which Wollstonecraft identifies as a retardant to political 'progress' in the eighteenth century is neither straightforward nor unmixed. As J. G. A. Pocock suggests, the notion of the balanced constitution that emerged from the events of 1688–9 allowed for considerable dispute throughout the century.[35] While Wollstonecraft's initial mention of 'corruption' is probably a reference to Sir Robert Walpole's use of royal patronage during his period of political dominance (from around 1721 to 1745), her narrative seems to place the period of actual 'arrogance' later. Significantly for the historical novel, disquiet about the constitution became particularly acute following the accession of King George III in 1760. At this point, although the possibility of a Stuart restoration seemed largely at an end, the anxiety concerning a return to royal absolutism resurfaced.[36]

Even as the seeming intransigence of the monarchy generated concern, however, the issue of imagining political change remained a thorny one. Writing after the Civil War and 1688, Scott's precursors knew very well that political transition could become revolution: the stress placed throughout the eighteenth century on 1688 as the return to original political purity (as implicitly opposed to the events of the mid-seventeenth century) attests to that general anxiety. Hence a suspicion of political breakage marks the form. Yet, at the same time, the works of these historical novelists also bear witness to a prolonged sense of a society on the threshold of crisis. Both the conventional constitutional smugness and the actual sense of unease are evident, for example, in the anonymous *Edward de Courcy* (1794), set in the reign of Richard II. Essentially describing romance blocked by priestly machinations (and rival contenders for the throne), the novel begins on an appropriately Whiggish note, asserting the 'flourishing condition' of religious and civil liberties 'at the end of the eighteenth century' before emphasising how the '*line of the Brunswick*' is linked with this development.[37] In opposition to this, though, the work also suggests that 'millions of intelligent beings' are 'equal by nature'.[38] Initially, the anonymous author's anti-Catholicism seems to sit safely with King George III's resistance to Catholic emancipation. Nevertheless, fears of Catholic oppression could also be used to drive a progressive agenda which that monarch would have rejected utterly. As *Edward de Courcy*'s mention of equality suggests, this was not only a period in which the meaning of revolution shifted, but one in which other revolutions continued to impact on British political life. It was also a time of growing anxiety about possible tensions between commerce and the existing British political system. The Scottish historian David Hume, for example, suggested that the beginnings of the shift towards commerciality had already proved a factor in the downfall of the Stuarts.[39] Although this is, then, in one sense, in the British context, a post-revolutionary period, for Scott's precursors and arguably for Scott himself, in terms of an imaginatively felt sense of political stability the post-revolutionary era refuses to be born.

The British historical novel of the late eighteenth century struggles to create this sense of stability by examining the meaning and possibility of liberty. As Wollstonecraft's remarks in *An Historical and Moral View* indicate, the concept of 'liberty' was a key one in eighteenth-century English (and British) political discourse. According to the discourse of ancient constitutionalism, liberty had emerged from the distant Saxon past. In this historically inflected narrative, liberty was at once connected with the idea of political stability and with recurring threats to that stability: it was vulnerable, in need of defence. This narrative of supposed national freedom was convenient when it came to discussing depopulation of the countryside and enclosure (writers often collapsed the Charter of the Forest [1217] into the Magna Carta) and it could be employed (as Viscount Bolingbroke had in the 1730s) to argue against changes in the commercial and banking sector. However, it was more difficult to use in favour of modernisation. For such change to be managed, the concept of liberty would have to be rewritten. The expansion in the genres of history writing in the eighteenth century arguably stemmed in part from this need to reshape the historically grounded understanding of national life.[40]

Given the popularity of history-based publications in the eighteenth century, for Anne H. Stevens the amount of historical fiction can in part be explained in terms of commercial good sense.[41] Yet there was more at stake. As the way history was written became subject to challenge, the historical novel became a space of political and historical experimentation. Modern (as opposed to classical) history was still not formally taught;[42] however, the eighteenth century saw changes in the subject matter of history and disputes over philosophical and antiquarian approaches, both of which arguably destabilised the use of history as political exemplar. The traditional historical focus on military and political and military subjects was also difficult to align with the developing interest in economics and the new emphasis on 'manners' that stadial history writing demanded. Narrative allowed these relations to be reimagined. Elizabeth Hamilton's *Memoirs of the Life of Agrippina, the Wife of Germanicus* (1804), for example, (not a work of 'fiction', Hamilton insists) imaginatively applied the stadial approach to fill out classical history.[43] In *Feudal Events; Or, Days of Yore* (1800) the less historically serious Anna Maria Mackenzie notes that while it would be fruitless to suggest she has found an ancient manuscript preserved like 'asbestos', she is indebted to an unpublished historian 'who has made it his peculiar study to examine the private memoirs of ancient families, for events of a domestic nature; anecdotes of which, (for their minuteness) have been over-looked by more voluminous writers'.[44] Such domestic (but wholly fictional) material could cast provocative sidelights on official history. As a result of such relative flexibility, the historical novel became a space in which the form, content and purpose of history writing could be explored. The implications of history writing for contemporary life could be re-examined in the genre's pages: the past and its liberties would be reimagined in order to reshape the present.

Historical novelists began to interrogate the notion of desirable continuity between past and present that was so endemic in legal and political life. If John Wilkes, editor of opposition paper *The North Briton* (1762–3), 'or the people concerned with *The Monitor*', did not see the connection between that 'great prince' and legislator, Alfred the Great, and George III but instead suggested some less prestigious historical parallels, after 1762 the historical novel, sometimes inadvertently, magnified such doubts.[45] The manipulation of such historical parallels led to a growing suspicion of the performance of history, of tradition, ceremony and courtly set pieces, which sometimes recreated the past in the present in order to enshrine the political status quo. Sophia Lee's *The Recess*, for example, undercuts Queen Elizabeth I's pageant at Kenilworth; the anonymous *Lady Jane Grey* (1791) contrasts the actual crown with the 'glorious crown' the 'Redeemer' can confer;[46] and *Desmond* agrees with the National Assembly's abolition, in June 1790, of hereditary titles. This concern spills out of the historical novel. Wollstonecraft's *Historical and Moral View of the French Revolution* rejects the artificiality and theatricality of shows of power more generally. By 1810 the conservative Jane West registers a more general preoccupation with the performance of history for political purposes in *The Refusal*. Rather like the eponymous heroine of Madame de Staël's *Corinne* (1807), the Italian Paulina shows a 'genius as flexible as her form' when she embarks on a series of historical impromptus: 'Thus the delighted spectator sometimes gazed on the sober charms of Octavia, beheld Agrippina weeping over the urn of Germanicus, or Cornelia devoting her sons to the service of their country.'[47] But Paulina seduces a politician. The radical critique of the performance of history is ultimately redirected against radicalism itself.

Against this background, historical novels begin to investigate the reification of the historical, engaging with the antiquarian. Antiquarian approaches to history were often the subject of dispute in the eighteenth century, sometimes supposed to be inimical to the philosophical or stadial accounts of other historians, sometimes positioned as providing vital evidence in support of such accounts. Moreover, antiquarians often struggled with the narrative frame into which their data was to be inserted. As Walpole, himself an antiquarian, was well aware, historical objects could prove curiously intractable. In *Castle of Otranto* such objects are foregrounded (perhaps generating that suspicion of 'costumery'). Items that should be static, the huge helmet, the giant suit of armour, and the grandfather's portrait become uncannily animated. When the hereditary principle is undermined, and exchange begins to happen in a different way, objects resist their removal out of the line of descent. In Sophia Lee's *The Recess* the resistance posed by objects is potentially even more contentious. Secret documents challenge historical set pieces; the meanings of miniatures, portraits and history paintings fluctuate; and the casket documents used by Queen Elizabeth against Mary Queen of Scots are supplemented and challenged by private letters. The selection of different objects, Lee hints, can lead to the construction of a different history in which the excluded and marginalised become central.

Here the antiquarian has a potentially difficult role to play. In Ann Radcliffe's *Gaston de Blondeville* (1826) the collector Willoughton enjoys the aestheticisation of the past yet the manuscript he uncovers suggests the disharmony that underlies feudal performance of civic unity. His nostalgic mediation of the fragments of history finally fails to convince. In the colonial context, the situation is worse. If, as the historical novelist James White suggests, bards and minstrels distort history (in *Earl Strongbow* [1789] the two groups, one Celtic, one Norman, are in competition), antiquarian evidence is equally subject to appropriation. It could (particularly in relation to Ireland) be destroyed or distorted in order to dispossess, or, alternately, be used to challenge such dispossession. In *The Blind and Blindness in Literature of the Romantic Period* (2007) Edward Larrissy suggests that the bard may act as a kind of vanishing mediator between ancient and modern.[48] The antiquarian performs a similar bridging function but, like the countless supposed editors and discoverers of lost manuscripts that populate the prefaces of historical novels, he fails to disappear. Susan Manning proposes that the antiquarian is a key figure in the Scottish Enlightenment's struggle to deal with 'the problematics of empiricism' – the 'ridicule attached to antiquarianism' was a way of dealing with the weakness empirical data posed to the stadial project.[49] The historical novel demonstrates that another potential response was trepidation. The antiquary operates as a disturbing reminder of the material traces of past and present political conflict.

The historical novelists of the 1780s and 90s used stadial history to resist the celebration of both chivalric artefacts and the material traces of history as instantiated in the wealth and status of the nobility. In the process, works like Godwin's *St Leon* (1799) provided a shift in the empirical focus of history, redirecting attention to the suffering and the political fate of the people. The resulting 'rational' literary historiography, the historiography of the 'mass' (as Wollstonecraft might have imagined it), was transformed by conservative novelists into narratives of history as folklore and romance or as science.[50] In Porter's *The Scottish Chiefs* Luckie Forbes, Scottish peasant woman, told 'of the wonderful deeds of William Wallace' but 'never omitted an opportunity of mingling a pious allusion with her narrations'.[51] The tales of the common people are rendered unthreatening in the hands of the historical novelist. Equally, in Scott's *Antiquary* Oldbuck hears the tale of Elspeth Mucklebackit and collects her (individual) words. Yet as a neutraliser of past narratives his effectiveness is more doubtful, given Scott's late attempt to neutralise the spirits of past ages in *Letters on Demonology and Witchcraft* (1830). The idea of history as science, on the other hand, usually associated with the German historian Leopold von Ranke, became the dominant historical model in the nineteenth century. It led to the dismissal of eighteenth-century historiography as the work of dilettantes and amateurs – a dismissal which rendered the eighteenth-century historical novel even more invisible. Perhaps ironically, this partial deletion also indicates the success of more conservative British historical novelists. For their recuperative project to work, the very debate about the nature of history had to be forgotten.

## The Truths of History

Particularly post-Scott, the works under consideration here appear unfamiliar as historical fiction and unconvincing in their historicity. A reader of Scott's *Ivanhoe* (1819), for instance, connects the Normans with chivalry and its corruptions but also with necessary progress. Encountering the Saxon Gurth, 'the born thrall of Cedric', and his slave collar, in the opening pages of Scott's novel such a reader might assume that any liberties associated with the Anglo-Saxon past have been greatly exaggerated.[52] Scott is both alluding to and adapting a major trend in the eighteenth-century historical novel. In the anonymous *Edwy, Son of Ethelred: An Historic Tale* (1791), for instance, Anglo-Saxon England is the home of liberty and a kind of improved chivalric behaviour. Yet this is not an instance of historical inattention on the writer's part. Rather, the unknown author is attempting to distinguish (waning) English virtue from Danish and Norman vice. She is considering the often-mooted possibility of a return to ancient political liberties – and finding it unlikely. At the same time, however, her portrait of Norman corruption also throws doubt on the Whiggish narrative of history as progress. This is a narrative of history as decay which Walter Scott will later complicate.

Even when such narratives of ancient constitutionalism begin, in the 1790s, to be displaced by works influenced, like Scott's, by the stadial historians of the Scottish Enlightenment, the results appear unfamiliar. The title of Ellis Cornelia Knight's 1792 novel *Marcus Flaminius; Or, a View of the Military, Political, and Social Life of the Romans: In a Series of Letters from a Patrician to His Friend* emphasises the author's scholarly seriousness and her knowledge of contemporary trends in history writing. Yet Knight also exploits the comparative tendencies of stadial history to startling effect, simultaneously exploring the classical world and the causes of the French Revolution. In this narrative, impelled by luxury, the inhabitants of ancient Germania desire 'universal equality'.[53] Knight's past appears unfamiliar in part because it offers a warning: luxurious modernity neither assures liberty nor represents progress. Still, the novel's comparison of first-century Germania and revolutionary France remains, historiographically speaking, quite bizarre.

Critical concern regarding the form's promiscuous nature dates back almost to its inception. Although Leland's *Longsword* (1762) did not arouse critical anxiety (its reviewer found 'the beauties of poetry, and the advantages of history' 'happily united'), with the advent of *The Recess*, disquiet regarding the mixture of fiction and history grew.[54] While in 1783 the *Critical Review* is still apparently untroubled by the mixture of romance and history in Lee's work (the 'wonderful coincidence of history' and the discovered manuscript which she speaks of are 'subterfuges which no longer surprise or deceive us', he writes), by 1786 the case is altered.[55] The reviewer for the *Monthly* finds that in Lee's work fiction is combined *'too lavishly* with fact'.[56] Lee's attempt to examine the distribution of emotion in historical writing breeds excess. The implicit worry is about the potential political confusion of reader: by rewriting the past, these works might cause disorientation in the present. In the 1790s the political agenda of such criticism becomes clearer. In the preface to *Memoirs of Sir Roger de Clarendon* (1793) (Clara Reeve's second attempt to stiffen the British historical backbone with her vision of chivalric social immobility), the author suggests that an accurate history of the great men of Britain has an important role to play. Such a history will correct the 'levelling principle[s]' of the 'new philosophy of the present day'. Yet to her horror she finds that: 'many attempts have been made of late years to build fictitious stories upon historical names and characters'.[57] Although Reeve implies that poor historical fictions collapse like poor constitutions, in the meantime, she suggests, they threaten to contaminate young minds – minds as yet untouched by 'vile indolence, effeminacy and extravagance of modern life and manners'.[58] Here historical fiction is dangerous because it is connected with radicalism, modernity and luxury. Ironically, though, Reeve herself could not escape criticism for her use of history and fiction, which, the *Critical Review* suggests, causes only 'double inconvenience'.[59]

Occasionally, such distinctions between fact and fiction also trouble contemporary critics. Toni Wein, for example, suggests that historical fiction can be distinguished from the gothic because the former admits that fiction has been added to history. Leland, Wein argues, acknowledges in *Longsword* that 'liberties' have been taken 'by enlarging and altering the accounts': Leland is 'scrounging in the bin of history'.[60] However, Leland is not simply a dishonest adulterator of our knowledge about the past. Set in the reign of Henry III, *Longsword* praises King George III but also, through its exposure of Henry's favouritism towards Hubert de Burgh, acts as a warning: a balance of power is necessary between parliament and the king if corruption is to be avoided. When

Leland describes his narrative as a transparent stream, not 'deep' but 'clear', he is claiming a particular kind of authority for his exploration of ancient political liberty.[61]

The presence of truth claims in titles and subtitles is also a potential source of misunderstanding. The popularity of the genre and its historical and political complexity meant that the writers employed a number of generic labels – 'a tale of other times', 'private history', 'an historical novel', 'a historical romance' and so on. Yet, although subtitles and prefatory material were, as Anne H. Stevens notes, used to 'advertise the basis of the novels on real events', such titular claims are frequently generically misleading.[62] *William of Normandy* (1787) is, for example, subtitled 'an historical novel', but instead of being entertained with a tale of William I's military prowess (or, more typically for historical novels of this period, his 'despotism and tyranny') one finds a rather slow-moving love story.[63] At the end of the novel the reader is left with the feeling that the author is surprised: either the number of allotted pages or the publisher's patience has been unexpectedly exhausted. In contrast, Ann Yearsley's four-volume novel *The Royal Captives: A Fragment of Secret History* (1795) is not, as might be assumed, a *roman-à-clef*. Rather, the work is another version of the tale Alexander Dumas later tells in *The Man in the Iron Mask* (1850–1). It is also one of the post-French Revolution historical novels that fictionalise history in order to emphasise the inter-reliance of the classes. Subtitles provide little guidance to the degree to which works use the 'the gleanings of historical anecdotes' or draw upon contemporary historiography.[64]

In relation to such confusion, it is also worth remembering that, despite Scott's choice of ''Tis sixty years since' as the eventual subtitle for *Waverley*, critics persist in using the generic label 'historical novel' to refer to the books in the Waverley series.[65] And this would hardly have surprised Scott. When he suggests in the introductory chapter to *Waverley* that subtitles 'pledg[e]' 'the author to some special mode of laying his scene', his use of chivalric vocabulary to refer to a largely commercial relation suggests any such guarantee is often belied. Such subtitles may thus be understood as a process of often troubled negotiation with audience expectation. Scott hints that this is particularly the case when political change is under discussion: the post-French Revolution debate can render even the 'general denomination' of a work controversial, doomed to connote either hereditary English loyalism or French-inflected, modern sensibility.[66] Generic difference signifies political difference, leading to a level of complication where the late eighteenth-century historical novel is concerned.

## The Meaning of Progress

As I explore in Chapter 1, the historical novel emerged in the 1760s as a form which at once employed and interrogated the dominant political narrative of 'ancient liberties'. The notion of ancient constitutionalism allowed proposals for reform or for limits on monarchical power to be seen as attempts to ensure stability or, at most, (in the case of the theory of the Norman Yoke) to return to political origin. Yet for Walpole ancient constitutionalism seems at times a troubled jest; Reeve senses that the motif desperately needs reinforcement; and after the more radical uses of the theory of the Norman Yoke by the Society for Constitutional Information in the 1780s and 90s, Radcliffe considers it a frozen fable. Haunted by the spectre of the divine right of kings and hence implicitly by the English Civil War itself, in such works the narrative of tradition ultimately proves an insufficient underpinning for the constitution. The American Revolution might have seemed to offer some kind of alternative, an escape into a pre-social state of nature, a historical blank, in which society could be constructed upon utopian lines, or an egalitarian constitution shaped. However, in the work of historical novelists, alternative communities that shelter in the pre-social space of the woodlands frequently fail – even constitutional agreements are capable of being undermined, as in *Montford Castle* (1795). Economic corruption disrupts the outlaws' paradise; their constitutions are often as weak as those supported by tradition. The time for a new language has not arrived: the effort to obliterate the past will fail. Attempts at such repression in the British (and in Susanna Rowland's *Reuben and Rachel* [1798] even in the American) context miscarry spectacularly, particularly following Sophia Lee's *The Recess*. By 1802 the confused, compressed *Children of the Priory; Or, Wars of Old* seems to have more characters emerging from underground than are actually living on the surface: the past is inescapable.

Imagining the threat of a (somehow) unmediated past colliding with the present, the British historical novel suggests that if the past cannot be ignored, it must be rewritten to generate a space for political and economic alteration. It is this rewriting and its effects on the recent past and political present that is examined in Chapter 2. In the 1780s Sophia Lee and her followers begin to draw on sentimental and stadial history to experiment with the political uses of sympathy. Radical writers, like Charlotte Smith and William Godwin, propose a shift in sympathy and historical attention from the aristocracy to the people. As Wollstonecraft suggests in her *Historical and Moral View of the French Revolution* (1794) and as Smith's *Desmond* implicitly argues, if the chivalry and courtly behaviour that stimulated historical sentiment were examined more critically, a new, more rational historiography and a better understanding of the purpose of government would emerge. The relationship of the rulers to the people would be taken into account and progress would be the result.

Smith and Wollstonecraft were proved right, but only in part. At first adapted by moderate writers, elements of radical historiography would ultimately be recuperated, reclaimed for the nation. During the French Revolutionary and Napoleonic Wars reformist novelists began to historicise the present. Drawing on stadial history to analyse the causes of Revolution, they gradually came to see economic inequality and mass political activity as inevitably connected. In order to avoid this (as they saw it) disastrous connection, they adjusted the radical approach to sentiment in historical narrative. They suggested that sympathy should be felt on behalf of both the lower ranks and the aristocracy – and that it should be used to bind them. Employing stadial history's link between economy and manners, a number of works from the anonymous *Charles Dacres* (1797) to Louis de Bruno's *Lioncel* (1803) to Edgeworth's 'Madame de Fleury' (part of *Fashionable Tales* [1809–12]) explore the possibility of a form of exchange that would be at once sympathetic and economic. In reply, Frances Burney's *The Wanderer* (1814), recalls the social stages of conjectural history, only to emphasise the inherently painful nature of labour whatever the point of social development.

With the possible exception of Burney's more pessimistic work, historical novels of this period, in acknowledging the interdependence of the lower and upper ranks, also implicitly suggest the need for the workers to be safely politicised. Here the idea of the nation is potentially key, providing a focus for political energies that might otherwise be turned against the ruling classes. Yet in the British context the nation itself was a troubled concept. Whilst an Act of Union had joined England and Wales in 1536, it was only in 1707 that England and Scotland became 'one united kingdom by the name of Great Britain', and not until 1800 that the 'United Kingdom of Great Britain and Ireland' was created. Hence, as Chapter 3 explores, historical novelists drew upon the comparative potential of stadial history, trying to reimagine British liberty in relation to the competing nationalisms of the sister kingdoms and the empire. As novelists like Ellis Cornelia Knight, Maria Edgeworth and Jane Porter realised, such competing nationalisms would have to be carefully balanced, shaped by new historical narratives, if national feeling were not to be as threatening to the emergent state as class identity.

However, in the years leading up to the publication of *Waverley*, I argue in Chapter 4, historical novelists recuperate the radical and reformist readings of history that had emerged during the post-French Revolution debate. While remaining attentive to the political differences between the writers considered here, it is possible to trace two overlapping strategies of reclamation. First, the radical emphasis on (non-chivalric) sensibility becomes an emphasis on chivalric morality. This shift is seen in the work of Anna Maria and Jane Porter and in the novels of Sarah Green. As Porter's *The Scottish Chiefs* (1810) most clearly demonstrates, within this paradigm of Christian feeling, the 'mass' of the people could identify, not with the struggle for political rights, but with national romance. Second, the radical emphasis on rational historiography was co-opted. Elizabeth Hamilton's associationist historiography reflects this tendency. Yet it is Jane West who most clearly incorporates radical rationality into a narrative of history as science (where all the evidence of the past supports the need for subordination). This absorption of reformist and radical energies into more conservative or cautious historical fictions facilitated a myth of modern gradualism against a background of secure commerciality; this myth would be problematised in Scott's production of Scotland as 'an idea negotiated through signs', literary, legal and financial, and his mediation of that nation's place within the Union.[67]

Yet both reformist and conservative novelists still expressed unease with the commercial present. The final chapter examines how Scott would finally be unable to erase this unease. Having attempted to calm the post-French Revolution debate concerning history in *The Antiquary*, in *Ivanhoe* Scott is unable to escape its tropes, giving a coded response to ancient constitutionalism; to the call for the redistribution of sensibility; to radical readings of stadial history and even to the more conservative narrative of history as a kind of scientific medicine for the national body. Moreover, as he responds to previous points of historiographic and political tension, his sense of the inherent violence of commerce and its fit with governmental structures grow. In *Nationalism and Irony* (2004) Yoon Sun Lee suggests that Scott displayed the anomalous nature of national identity, even while producing a feeling of national wholeness.[68] This chapter investigates how Scott built on earlier historical fiction to accentuate and rearrange such anomalies, interrogating ameliorative models of sentimental and political circulation. Analysing *St Ronan's Well* (1823) (a novel in which the transitions of modern commerciality are themselves seen as violent), I explore how Scott negotiates the historiographically shaped economic apprehensions of his predecessors.

In his *Rights of Man* Thomas Paine famously asserts: 'A constitution is not a thing in name only, but in fact. It has not an ideal, but a real existence; and wherever it cannot be produced in a visible form, there is none.' Paine goes on to suggest that Burke, despite the 'bulky' nature of his book, has 'declined the only thing that was worth while to write upon'. He has done so because in fact the 'people have yet a constitution to form'.[69] The historical novel performs the imaginative work of supplying that constitution, which remains, however, diffused in fiction, notional rather than real. Whether interrogating the sublime of monarchy, proposing history as a space of experiment, or transforming the past into medicine, the genre attempts to cure the country's political condition. Yet, in the process, it reveals the very malaise it sets out to heal.

## Notes

1. For an example of the former see Rooney, *The French Revolution Debate* (2013), p. 1.
2. See Fiona Robertson, *Legitimate Histories*, pp. 21–67.
3. Scott, *Waverley*, p. 350.
4. Maria Edgeworth, *Helen*, 1: 265–7.
5. Maria Edgeworth, *Helen* 1: 258, 1: 268.
6. Gellner, *Nations and Nationalism*, p. 19; for a discussion of 'artifice' and 'invention' see Hobsbawm, *Nations and Nationalism*, p. 10.
7. Scott, *Guy Mannering*, pp. 104–5.
8. Scott, *Guy Mannering*, p. 105.
9. Jameson, *The Seeds of Time*, xii.
10. Marx, *Survey from Exile* p. 147.
11. Perovic, 'The French Revolutionary Calendar', pp. 1–16.
12. Brown, *Walter Scott*, p. 3.
13. Marx, *Survey from Exile*, p. 147.
14. See, for example, MacQueen, *The Rise of the Historical Novel*; de Groot, *The Historical Novel*.
15. See James R. Foster, 'The Abbé Prévost', pp. 454–9. See also Richard Maxwell, *The Historical Novel in Europe*; Angela Wright, *Britain, France, and the Gothic, 1764–1820*.
16. James R. Foster, 'The Abbé Prévost', p. 443.
17. Burgess, 'The National Tale', p. 40.
18. Trumpener, *Bardic Nationalism*, p. 129; Muir, *Scott and Scotland*, pp. 11–12.
19. Trumpener, *Bardic Nationalism*, xi.
20. See Mark Salber Phillips, *Society and Sentiment*, xi.
21. Mack's *Literary Historicity* does not examine any historical novels apart from Walpole's *Otranto*. Instead, like Kasmer's *Novel Histories*, it examines the construction of the past across a number of other genres.
22. Stevens, *British Historical Fiction*, pp. 12–13; Moretti, *Graphs, Maps, Trees*, p. 4.

23. Lukács, *Historical Novel*, p. 19.
24. Lukács, *Historical Novel*, p. 25.
25. Lukács, *Historical Novel*, pp. 32–3.
26. Pittock, 'Scott as Historiographer', p. 146.
27. Burgess, *British Fiction*, Ian Duncan, *Modern Romance*, passim.
28. Charlotte Smith, *Desmond*, pp. 97–8.
29. Maria Edgeworth, *Helen*, 1: 265.
30. Cronin, *Paper Pellets*, p. 27.
31. Lukács, *Historical Novel*, p. 25. According to Lukács's account, the Enlightenment history that prepared the way for the French Revolution was particularly strong in France itself. In Britain, although the 'greatest transformation', that is, 'the creation of the economic and social preconditions for the Industrial Revolution', is taking place, the 'really dominating economic theorist' is Adam Smith; 'James Steuart, [sic] who posed the problem' historically was 'soon forgotten' (p. 21). This underestimates the importance of British historical discourse, including fiction, in thinking economic and political change.
32. Clark, *Revolution and Rebellion*, p. 3.
33. See, for example, Seaman, *Victorian England*, p. 63.
34. Wollstonecraft, *Works*, 6: 17.
35. See Pocock, *Virtue, Commerce, and History*, p. 228, for example.
36. See Monod, *Jacobitism and the English People*, p. 297.
37. Anon, *Edward de Courcy*, n.p., 2: 25
38. Anon, *Edward de Courcy*, 2: 58.
39. For Hume's belief that the 'rise of commerce' led to the greater power of the Commons see David Hume, *History of England*, 6: 406.
40. See Mark Salber Phillips, *Society and Sentiment*, xi. For Phillips, this expansion in eighteenth-century history writing has in part been obscured by the privileging of the novel in literary criticism. However, the early historical novel itself was also neglected.
41. Stevens, 'Tales of Other Times', p. 2.
42. Looser, *British Women Writers*, p. 11.
43. Hamilton, *Memoirs*, 1: x.
44. Anna Maria Mackenzie, *Feudal Events*, 1: iii–iv.
45. See Anon, *The Monitor*, p. 28. David Hume, *History of England*, 1: 90.
46. Anon, *Lady Jane Grey*, 2: 98.
47. West, *Refusal*, 2: 318.
48. See, for example, Larrissy, p. 48.
49. Manning, 'Antiquarianism, the Scottish Science of Man, and the Emergence of Modern Disciplinarity', p. 57. For a detailed account of antiquarian activity, see Sweet, *Antiquaries*. For the importance of antiquarianism to Romanticism see also Yoon Sun Lee, *Nationalism and Irony*; Ferris, 'Scott's Authorship and Book Culture', pp. 9–21; and McCracken-Flesher's *Possible Scotlands*.
50. Wollstonecraft, *Works*, 6: 18.
51. Jane Porter, *Scottish Chiefs*, p. 728.
52. Scott, *Ivanhoe*, p. 29, p. 27.
53. Knight, *Marcus Flaminius*, 1: 103.
54. Review of *Longsword*, *Critical Review*, p. 252.

55. Review of *The Recess*, *Critical Review*, p. 233.
56. Review of *The Recess*, *Monthly Review*, p. 134.
57. Reeve, *Memoirs*, 1: xvi, 1: xx.
58. Reeve, *Memoirs*, 1: xxi.
59. Review of *Memoirs of Sir Roger de Clarendon*, *Critical Review*, p. 281.
60. Wein, *British Identities*, pp. 4–5.
61. [Leland], *Longsword*, 1: 4.
62. Stevens, 'Tales of Other Times', p. 4
63. For such despotism see Caroline Maxwell, *Alfred of Normandy*, 1: 40.
64. Review of *Memoirs of Sir Roger de Clarendon*, *Critical Review*, p. 281.
65. For Scott's doubts concerning the conceptual distinctions between history, romance and novel, see, for example, Chase, 'Walter Scott: A New Historical Paradigm', p. 102.
66. Scott, *Waverley*, p. 3
67. McCracken-Flesher, *Possible Scotlands*, p. 112
68. Yoon Sun Lee, *Nationalism and Irony*. For sentimental circulation in relation to issues of social justice see Regina Hewitt, *Symbolic Interactions*.
69. Paine, *Political Writings*, pp. 81–2.

# Chapter 1

# Ancient Liberties

In *A Dissertation upon Parties* (1733), the politician and political philosopher Henry St John, Viscount Bolingbroke, argues that 'If liberty is a delicious and wholesome fruit, the British constitution is the tree that bears this fruit':

> our constitution is a system of government suited to the genius of our nation, and even to our situation. The experience of many hundred years hath shown, that by preserving this constitution inviolate, or by drawing it back to the principles on which it was originally founded, whenever it shall be made to swerve from them, we may secure to ourselves, and to our latest posterity, the possession of that liberty which we have long enjoyed. What would we more? What other liberty than this do we seek?[1]

Bolingbroke's remarks indicate the centrality of liberty in eighteenth-century English political discourse, its connection with both the 'nation' and the people.[2] In this discourse, liberty is historically inflected, having its basis in the ancient constitution. For Bolingbroke, at least, (there were other varieties of ancient constitutionalism) liberty originated with the Saxons and had been maintained (albeit with struggle) ever since.[3] Typically in relation to this trope, the tone of the narrative expresses at once bullish certainty and underlying anxiety. In the struggle for liberty, one key moment, Bolingbroke suggests, was the Glorious Revolution: the 'progression from a free to a slavish constitution of government' (a government in which royal prerogative was too dominant) was 'stopped at the revolution'.[4] But the need to continue the struggle remains.

Bolingbroke's use of the ancient constitution and his praise for the Glorious Revolution is strategic. He had supported the 1715 Jacobite Rebellion against King George I, only receiving a pardon in 1723. Ten years later the statesman was prepared to evoke a consistent tradition of liberty and to imply his support for the Hanoverian dynasty which had prevented James Francis Edward Stuart's return. But as he praises the 'drawing back' of the Glorious Revolution, he undermines the king's first minister, Sir Robert Walpole. The minister's use of political placemanship and closeness to the monarchy is, Bolingbroke suggests, threatening liberty once again. The former Stuart supporter also uses the discourse of ancient constitutionalism to register alarm over the growth of 'banking, credit and capital facilities' and their influence on politics.[5] Bolingbroke's use of the narrative of ancient constitutionalism demonstrates its malleability. It provided a convenient way of attacking the supposed corruption of political opponents. However, it also had an inherently uneasy relation with the political implications of economic change.

In *The Historical Novel* (1937) Lukács's agenda impels him to favour a narrative of abrupt social and generic change as most progressive. Nonetheless, for eighteenth-century political commentators continuity rather than breakage was frequently positioned as presenting the best chance of preserving freedom. As J. G. A. Pocock notes, 'throughout the seventeenth and eighteenth centuries, every major piece of either historical or legal thinking involved, if it did not consist in, the adoption of an attitude towards the "ancient constitution"'.[6] While ancient constitutionalism emphasised continuity, it could also be used to argue for reform. In the seventeenth century the jurist and politician Sir Edward Coke, for example, stressed the continuity of the constitution from Anglo-Saxon to Norman times through to the present. When he asserted that that Common Law was superior to the Royal Prerogative, he antagonised the Stuart monarch, King James I, implying a restriction on James's divine right to absolute authority. Later, Bolingbroke uses a similar tactic against Robert Walpole under George II: in order to restrict Walpole's freedom of manoeuvre, Bolingbroke implies that the first minister and implicitly the king are moving along the path toward absolutism. In the 1760s opponents of George III's administration again adopted the strategy. Wishing to confirm parliamentary rather than monarchical power, they too argued that a return to ancient constitutionalism was necessary to restrain the king's (supposed) absolutist tendencies. However, in the 1780s and 90s the idea of the Norman Yoke (the notion that the Normans had deviated from the ancient constitution) was used to argue for wider reform. Too much power had been given to the nobility and monarchy; King Alfred had understood that the law functioned for all the people equally. In reply Edmund Burke reversed Sir Edward Coke's narrative of continuity in order to defend the monarchy – he argued that the monarch, as well as the people, has certain privileges. Yet in all versions of the narrative, what was emphasised was not breakage but return to origin, a 'preserving' or 'drawing back': even those who desired political reform frequently justified it by labelling it a reversion to past practices.[7]

Ancient constitutionalism – or the interrogation of it – shaped the historical novel before Scott. In particular, for the historical novelists of the 1760s and 70s – Thomas Leland, Horace Walpole, and Clara Reeve – and their followers, the notion of inherited liberties was as important as any narrative of progress.[8] Here Lukács's description of Horace Walpole's *Castle of Otranto* (1764) as the 'most famous "historical novel" of the eighteenth century' becomes relevant.[9] While Scott had praised Horace Walpole as an important influence, Lukács's use of inverted commas suggest a certain ambivalence. Walpole's use of the past is not, as Lukács suggests, 'mere costumery'. Rather, Walpole was connected to and yet ambivalent about ancient constitutionalism because of its use against his father. When the importance of this narrative of 'ancient liberty' is understood, it becomes evident that Walpole and his contemporaries are, like Lukács's Scott, also exploring the distribution of power within the state.[10] With the end of the Jacobite threat, the historiographic dispute that had run so fiercely in the ten years after Bolingbroke's *Remarks on the History of England* (1730) and his *Dissertation* eventually spilled into the more flexible realm of fiction.

As the first part of this chapter explores, for Horace Walpole and the historical novelists of the 1760s, the transition from Stuart to Hanoverian rule eventually made possible by the Glorious Revolution was the event that shaped historical fiction. But the movement of ancient constitutionalism from history writing to the historical novel also indicates the increasingly problematic nature of the discourse. In the absence of the divine right of kings, the metaphysical underpinnings of the constitution – of justice and of correct inheritance itself – seemed weak. In the late 1780s and early 1790s it was also evident that the narrative of the Norman Yoke, as well as that of ancient constitutionalism more generally, could be used to argue for a more radical political reform, as *The Son of Ethelwolf* (1789) suggests. However, it was Edmund Burke's response in *Reflections* to such radical formulations of the trope that led (even amongst moderate thinkers) to sustained criticism of the notion of 'ancient liberties'. Queries were generated concerning both the present-day relevance of such supposed freedoms and the monarchical virtues on which they were based. In the anonymous *Edwy, Son of Ethelred*, for example, the moment of the perfect Anglo-Saxon constitution recedes into the political past: even in Anglo-Saxon England liberty is in decline. When Ann Radcliffe responds in *Gaston de Blondeville* to Burke's vision of constitutional continuity, what she emphasises is a continuity of discord. These works expose the static nature of ancient constitutionalism – an awkward fixity given the perceived mobility of consumer society.

## Ruling with Liberty? Leland, Walpole and Reeve

In what came to be known as the Whig version of history the Glorious Revolution was necessary to ensure political progress. However, in the first half of the eighteenth century both the Old Whigs and the Jacobites remained unconvinced. Disinclined to equate the events of 1688 with national advancement in any straightforward way, instead, like Bolingbroke, they argued for a version of history in which the ancient constitution had enshrined certain liberties – liberties that Sir Robert Walpole, the king's first minister, was undermining. By the 1760s, this rhetoric could be employed by discontented Whig aristocrats against the ministers, Bute and Grenville, and George III.[11] Supposed fear of absolutism and struggle for parliamentary power led to the use of 'gothic' political rhetoric once familiar to the Old Whigs. In such narratives, it was the absolutism supposedly connected with George III that was the newer political paradigm, threatening rupture with the past. Drawing upon this Old Whig approach, the novels of Leland, Reeve, and (more equivocally) Walpole show an awareness of absolutism as a threat that might generate abrupt political change and for this reason avoid a model of history as permanent breakage. Rupture is evoked only to be contained.

While discussions of Horace Walpole's *Castle of Otranto* and Clara Reeve's *Old English Baron* have frequently emphasised the gothic rather than the historical, examining these two works in relation to Thomas Leland's *Longsword* (often a point of cursory comparison) allows a new understanding of how and why such novels might be related to the genre of historical fiction.[12] In *Longsword* (a historical romance supposed to make 'straightforward' use of history) inherited liberties provide a way of avoiding the rupture threatened by the political corruption of absolutism.[13] Nonetheless, Leland struggles to imagine the survival of constitutional liberty without the guarantee afforded by the divine right of kings. It is this struggle (rather than similarity of plot, as usually assumed) that connects *Longsword* and *Otranto*. Reading Walpole's novel alongside Leland's, it becomes evident that *Otranto*'s tonal inconsistencies arise not only, as Toni Wein and others have suggested, as a result of Walpole's dislike of Grenville's political manoeuvring, but because of his vexed attitude to absolutism and the Old Whigs.[14] The resulting combination of Old Whig and Jacobite allusions found in *Otranto* is what distresses Clara Reeve. Her Old Whig sympathies and suspicion of *Otranto* are well known.[15] Less evident, however, is the way in which Reeve adapts the political motifs available in both *Longsword* and *The Castle of Otranto* in order to argue that the Old Whigs' model of the distribution of power could survive the burgeoning capitalist economy. Originating not from the context of the French Revolution but from ongoing constitutional struggle, these Whig anxieties become enduring concerns of the British historical novel.

Once the paradigmatic status of the French Revolution on the form of the historical novel is interrogated, Thomas Leland appears a more significant figure in the genre's development.[16] Irish historian and classical scholar, the Reverend Leland came to the notice of the Whig politician James Caulfeild, Earl of Charlemont, on the publication of a Latin translation *The Orations of Demosthenes* (1756). Caulfeild, described in *A Catalogue of the Royal and Noble of Authors* as a true patriot 'unwarped by party spirit, and untainted by venal views' and 'a nobleman of taste and literature', was perhaps impressed by the work's timeliness.[17] In 1752 David Hume argued for Britain's role in keeping the 'balance of power' within Europe, by suggesting the classical precedent of Demosthenes' orations to the Megalopolitans.[18] Two years later, coinciding with publication of Leland's translation, the issue of such balance was extended outside Europe with the start of the French and Indian War (1754–63), which drastically reduced French possessions in North America. Leland seems to have watched the British attitude to the conflict with alarm. In his Preface he comments on the Athenians' initial lack of political will when confronted by Philip:

> Although the Athenians were possessed with delicacy and sensibility, and entertained magnificent ideas of virtue and its duties, yet they wanted application, constancy, and perseverance. The good qualities which had long been the boast of that people, were now disappearing, while their faults increased. Hence it was, that they easily suffered themselves to be lulled into a false security.[19]

Here Leland uses eighteenth-century British interest in the Athenians' sea-faring empire in order to promote determined self-defence: any reluctance to pursue the French, Leland argues by analogy, stems from the decline of civic virtue.

Discontented Whigs who used the language of classical civic humanism to criticise contemporary politics also often appropriated Britain's own past in support of the cause. Hence, like the *Orations*, Leland's *Longsword, Earl of Salisbury; An Historical Romance* is appropriate to its political moment, a moment in which the need to preserve the balance of powers outside the state led to doubts over the distribution of power within Britain. When George III came to the throne in 1760 his inaugural speech to the Privy Council, written by the Earl of Bute, emphasised the need to bring an end to the conflict: 'as I mount the throne in the midst of a bloody war, I shall endeavour to prosecute it in the manner most likely to bring an honourable and lasting peace' – before, that is, William Pitt altered the wording.[20] When France then entered into negotiations with Spain, Pitt argued that Britain should declare war against the Spanish monarch, King Charles III. His uncompromising approach led to Cabinet opposition and he was forced to step down in October 1761; subsequently, the First Lord of the Treasury the Duke of Newcastle resigned on 26 May 1762 and was replaced by the king's favourite, John Stuart, third Earl of Bute. Given Bute's Stuart connection, this raised alarm over George III's attitude to the role of the monarchy. As Pocock remarks: 'It has many times been shown that the king was acting within the normal conventions of politics and had no thought of acting otherwise, but the fact remains that he was denounced, and that language was available to denounce him, for acting outside Whig rules.'[21]

The resultant concerns with favouritism, monarchical absolutism, and the French threat to empire are reflected in *Longsword*. Insisting on a parallel between virtue and certain forms of political behaviour, Leland's novel uses the reign of Henry III, when territories had just been won in Gascony, to warn George III about the dangers of favouritism and absolutism. In the first volume of this politically didactic romance, set largely in France, William Longsword, Earl of Salisbury, is shipwrecked and kidnapped, his presumed death threatening his English inheritance. Here the behaviour of the dishonest French nobleman Count Mal-leon represents the danger of corrupted values should Britain fail to keep the balance of power in Europe. Crossing back over the Channel to England, the second volume refines the lesson, revealing a threat to inheritance and civic peace from the king's favourite, Hubert de Burgh, and his follower Raymond. Leland's plot thus exploits the belief that 'French contamination had been an evil since the Norman Conquest and could be thrown off now only by Britons becoming more moral and more united.'[22] Britain, the novel argues, can only keep the balance abroad if the distribution of power at home is correct. The need for domestic political probity is further reinforced by an inset story referring to the Barons' Revolt in the reign of King John. Admittedly, Leland's warning remains politically cautious. In both main and subplot, the possibility of political rupture is present but ultimately avoided: William Longsword battles corruption and regains his inheritance; King John (extra-textually) signs Magna Carta. Nonetheless, by directing the 'clear' stream of history, he has heavily underlined the importance of politically moral behaviour – a vital weapon, he suggests, in the struggle to maintain civic peace and imperial strength.

The drift of Leland's ethico-political message in *Longsword* recalls the Old Whig suspicion of political corruption. For Leland, problems with the balance of power abroad and its distribution at home relate to excessive personal ambition of the kind associated with Sir Robert Walpole's government. Hence, in this narrative, while a desirable balance between aristocratic autonomy and monarchical authority is guaranteed by drawing upon ancient liberties and well-established codes, problems with such authority are caused by an (implicitly) modern and individualistic attitude to wealth, position and power. Worse still, discontent spreads from ambitious aristocrats to the lower ranks. Early in the novel, for instance, Leland sets up a contrast between the honourable Les Roches and the corrupt Count Mal-leon as well as between the 'brave and generous sons of honourable war' and their 'sullen', financially motivated counterparts.[23] No longer protected by the objectivity of convention, these ambitious members of the lower ranks, like their leader, Mal-leon, feel dissatisfaction with their class position. Here the concern about the replacement of a more feudal economy with an apparently more mobile capitalist one meets the preoccupation with the proper way to distribute power within the state and Europe.

Leland offers his clearest alternative to such individual political ambition in his inset tale. Here honour is linked with having a confident non-servile sense of social place – and such independence it seems can only come from ancient liberties. This is demonstrated by the story of the peasant Edmund, whose fiancée is attacked by a courtier. Edmund kills the nobleman and is taken before King John where he 'acknowledge[s] the crime, and with decent boldness declare[s] himself resigned to the punishment'.[24] Edmund is 'modest but not abject' – in other words, he has a sense of his lower social place but he does not, to use Shaftesbury's words, 'idolize the next in power above [him]' (as Shaftesbury suggests the French do).[25] Instead, as that almost oxymoronic phrase 'decent boldness' suggests, Edmund corresponds to an Old Whiggish fantasy of the behaviour of the lower ranks: named after the Christian king of East Anglia, St Edmund (c. 841–70), Leland's peasant is able to act without servility because he is a representative of a society supposed to possess ancient liberties. His difficulties arise only because he does not find himself in such a society but under Norman rule at the very moment when the barons are rebelling against King John.

In fact, despite Edmund's good political antecedents and William's final success, counter-examples to honour and 'decent boldness' proliferate in *Longsword*. Leland finds that it is insufficient to argue that antiquity legitimates and ultimately protects good political practice. Instead, it seems he wants to argue that what he construes as politically virtuous behaviour will succeed simply because it *is* virtuous. To do so, he first hints (as he does in his Preface) that language is a transparent medium through which virtue and vice can plainly be perceived, making right action easy. In *A Dissertation on the Principles of Human Eloquence* (1764) he proposes that passion generated by 'intercourse with mankind' 'naturally and unavoidably produce[s] an elevation or vehemence of speech'; this eloquence is a guarantee of sincerity.[26] However, the rhetorical evidence of passion can be 'counterfeit', and not only the 'ignorant and turbulent' crowd but 'a person of the greatest refinement' can be deceived.[27] Exposing such deceit is the challenge faced by William and Les Roches when they try to confront Mal-leon for attempted murder. When one of the corrupted soldiers is called forward to 'reveal' Les Roches's supposedly rebellious schemes, 'falling upon his knees and lifting up his eyes towards heaven, he called on every saint to bear witness to his innocence'.[28] The soldiers believe this perjury and the only recourse for William is to attempt to contradict the count by meeting him in single combat. Tellingly, though, this option, which in medieval society offers civil justice a divine underpinning, is in *Longsword* successfully avoided by political evildoers, whether French or Norman-English. Leland might like to assert the transparency of language and the interpretability of evidence with Enlightenment optimism but his own practice and knowledge of the world dictate otherwise.

Given the difficulty of distinguishing truth from falsehood in any immediate way (even in a society that accepts the efficacy of trial by combat), Leland insists on the importance of justice. Yet this too may be undermined. When William believes he has been usurped, he decides to go to court to appeal to the king. Here, the court of England is momentarily presented as a place where disinheritance and oppression are reversed. This royal fairness, William suggests, is as much due to the other nobles at court as it is a result of the 'justice of young Harry'. Nonetheless, this status quo is still threatened by the presence of the favourite, Hubert, as the knight Randolph suggests: '"Alas," said he, "little can thy honest heart conceive of that craft and wily insinuation with which this courtier hath wound himself to the heart of his easy Prince ... the remotest corner of the realm feels his pernicious influence".'[29] In *Leland* both justice and the distribution of power are guaranteed by the conduct of the monarch – and yet his behaviour is no longer legitimised by the divine right of kings and is likely to be undermined by internecine strife. Thus, although, as Toni Wein notes, *Longsword* compliments the youthful George III, this work also admonishes him.[30] Avoiding unconstitutional favouritism, George III must, Leland suggests, behave so that he is 'dreaded by the enemies of justice and his kingdom'; the alternative is political chaos.[31]

Leland concedes that there is a potential weakness at the heart of British government. The mixed constitution of eighteenth-century Britain is not underpinned by the rhetorically superb defence of the divine right of kings. This anxiety provides the point of connection between *Longsword* and *The Castle of Otranto*. Admittedly, in forty-eight volumes of correspondence Walpole fails to mention the earlier historical romance and the two novels are markedly different in terms of their tone and treatment of morality. Reflecting this difficulty, comparisons between *The Castle of Otranto* and *Longsword*, while commonplace, are often based merely on superficial similarities of plot.[32] Nonetheless, Walpole and Leland share an interest in the distribution of power: both works examine the threat of absolutism and hint at the possibility of a return to something similar under George III. Walpole, however, has a more ambivalent attitude to the notion of ancient constitutional liberty. Although he disliked absolutism, he acknowledges the political ambiguity of the 'gothic' myth – a myth that had been used against his own father. Walpole's work represents a humorous exaggeration of the contemporary political concerns expressed by Leland: for Walpole, a return to the absolutism formerly associated with the Stuarts seems at once terrifying and unlikely.[33]

*The Castle of Otranto*'s origins in the political events of 1763 and 1764 are familiar.[34] As Mowl recounts, on 25 April 1763 Wilkes's anti-establishment journal the *North Briton*, formerly used to attack Bute, alleged that 'the King had been tricked by his ministers into telling lies'; George Grenville 'in an action more Stuart than Hanoverian', issued a general warrant. When the warrant's legality was debated in parliament, Walpole and his cousin Henry Seymour Conway disagreed with the government.[35] Like Leland, then, Walpole was aware of the suggestion that George III was trying to alter the political structure, allegedly encouraged by the Stuart Bute towards a return to absolutism. But whereas Leland is coy about the ideological weight of his fictionalised history, Walpole's novel is playfully explicit regarding the political implications of his narrative. It is a critical commonplace that the ambiguous subtitle to the second edition, 'A Gothic Story', refers both to antiquarian interests and to the gothic tradition of political commentary which enjoyed considerable popularity during the late seventeenth and most of the eighteenth century.[36] This 'gothic' rhetoric (employed by Leland) had also been exploited by the Jacobites in order to gain credit with disaffected Whigs.[37] In a cunning piece of rhetorical reversal, the Jacobites suggested that the divinely sanctioned rule of the Stuarts had been supplanted with an arbitrary monarchy likely to threaten ancient English constitutional liberties. This rhetorical ploy was familiar to Walpole. Many of his fellow antiquarians were Jacobites, a matter of amusement for Walpole when writing to Richard Bentley in September 1753. 'My love of abbeys', he remarked, 'shall not make me hate the Reformation till that makes me grow a Jacobite like the rest of my antiquarian predecessors.'[38]

Despite his sceptical awareness of the links between gothic and Jacobite rhetoric, in *Otranto* Walpole follows Leland in retaining traces of the opposition between ancient virtue and modern vice. Although Manfred is not a tyrant, he shares the characteristics of Leland's political villains – like Mal-leon, he avoids trial by combat through dishonest means; like Raymond, he sees sexuality and brute force as a route to power. Manfred parallels the supposed absolutist tendency in British politics, while, on the other hand, Theodore, displays 'vigour . . . decently exerted'.[39] With his roots in the ancient political order, Theodore's self-worth recalls Leland's Edmund. Nonetheless, Walpole's awareness of Jacobite rhetoric gives this Old Whiggish opposition between ambitious, dishonourable tyranny and 'decent boldness' a new dimension. In this 'gothic' context Walpole's tale of a usurping family who hold power for three generations before the fourth generation (Conrad) is killed appears suspiciously close to the drama of Jacobitism: as the Stuarts had wished, the usurper's dynasty is finally threatened by the return of the rightful heir. Theodore's nobility is immediately perceptible in a way that is reminiscent of the manner in which Charles Edward Stuart's exploits, after the Jacobite Uprising of '45, were mythologised.[40] Like Theodore, Charles Edward was portrayed as personally courageous but, equally, he was supposedly caught up in the 'divinely ordained cycle of events' which was to lead to Stuart restoration and which 'required no human intervention'.[41] Similarly, Walpole's protagonist, although brave, is unusually passive for a romance hero. His return to power is ensured by ghostly intrusion. The giant suit of armour, a symbol of rightful rule, contrasts with the humanity and potential vulnerability of Theodore as the divinely ordained body of the Stuart heir contrasts with his human form. Theodore's emergence (apparently though not actually) from peasant stock, corresponds to Stuart rhetoric. According to Benjamin Bird, Theodore is a 'proto-democratic figure',[42] reflecting popularist Jacobite propaganda which argued the Stuarts, rather than the Hanoverians, were the true representatives of the people.

This combination of political rhetorics (the Old Whiggish emphasis on virtue alongside the motifs of Stuart propaganda) means that Walpole has the resources to further Leland's analysis of constitutional power. Having found the motif of ancient constitutionalism an insufficient justification, Leland had been forced to various inadequate fallback positions. In contrast, Walpole deftly exacerbates the sources of weakness identified by Leland. In his work both the transparency of virtue and the operation of justice appears uncertain. Consequently, he hints (as Leland never does) of the attractiveness of divine sanction for the ruler, while simultaneously satirising any such Jacobite solution. Walpole sets up the contrast between virtue and vice as strongly as Leland, leading Samson to suggest Walpole saw 'religion as a powerful counterforce' to tyranny.[43] However, this is optimistic: to an even greater extent than his predecessor, Walpole suggests the difficulty of distinguishing between good and evil. Despite Theodore's 'grace and humility', Manfred needs very little cause to accuse him: 'Villain! Monster! Sorcerer! 'tis thou hast slain my son!', he exclaims, and he is swiftly followed by the mob who 'caught the words from the mouth of their lord'.[44] As William and Les Roches had discovered, the mass of listeners are unreflecting and emotional, making truth hard to distinguish from falsehood. Walpole underlines the point: even the efforts of Father Jerome seem likely only to perpetuate injustice, while Theodore, unlike his predecessors William and Edmund, is cheerful about telling necessary lies. If Leland wants to assert that virtue will triumph on its own merits, Walpole's treatment of Theodore suggests doubt concerning its efficacy.

And if the direct power of virtue seems uncertain to Walpole, the fallback mechanism of the law appears equally fallible. In *Longsword* it initially seems as if William only has to appear at court to establish his rights. In contrast, Theodore possesses some of the most emphatic proofs of parentage provided in eighteenth-century fiction: he has a birthmark, writings around his wrist, and evidence of his grandmother's marriage. Nonetheless, when Manfred accepts the truth he does not do so because of empirical confirmation but because 'the horrors of these days, the vision we have but now seen, all corroborate thy evidence beyond a thousand parchments'.[45] Supernatural (even sanctified) aid is necessary to ensure the operation of law. Yet this guarantee is ultimately unconvincing, as Alfonso's final appearance suggests:

> The moment Theodore appeared, the walls of the castle behind Manfred were thrown down with a mighty force, and the form of Alfonso, dilated to an immense magnitude, appeared in the centre of the ruins. Behold in Theodore, the true heir of Alfonso! said the vision.[46]

Here Walpole retains the tendency seen in Leland to insist that even disruption supports continuity: Alfonso breaks the walls of the castle but, because of his interference, the true heir will be able to inherit. Hence the continuance of an old political order (an order connected with the fair-mindedness of Theodore) is safeguarded. But this position is complicated because such continuity is ensured by divine agency. The parallel is to the Jacobite suggestion, made to co-opt the Old Whigs, that the Stuart dynasty was linked to the supposed liberties of the political past. Given this combination of political rhetorics, the literal rupture of the castle walls appears threatening. On the one hand, it suggests the dangers of a return to absolutism. On the other, even more worryingly, it hints at the pointlessness of recovering (or seeming to recover) the past for political purposes. Leland had struggled to use history as warning and compliment, arguing simultaneously for its ideological neutrality and its ethical power: history is deep and clear. In contrast, Walpole is very aware of the use and dissection of history (whether text or antiquarian object) in the service of political rhetoric. History is searched for motifs and devices to serve a political turn, dismembered for an ideological purpose, becoming as fragmentary as Alfonso's armour.[47] Yet the final episode of *Otranto* suggests that, when these tropes are forcefully reassembled, the result is more threatening to existing political structures than might have been anticipated.

These political ambiguities generate the work's tonal uncertainty. For Leland, the operation of law is finally guaranteed by proper kingship; in *Otranto* the only guarantee of right rule is a supernaturalism that Walpole finds ridiculous. The supernatural tale is, according to the 'translator' William Marshal, perhaps only designed to 'confirm the populace in their ancient terrors and superstitions'.[48] As a coercive device, the idea that the ruler is backed by divine authority, once so politically persuasive, is now an outdated failure, connected with a defunct Catholicism and represented bathetically by the interference not of God himself but of the 'dilated' Alfonso. As when the servant Diego sees the 'foot and part of [a] leg' of a 'giant' (or 'Satan' or a 'ghost'), absolutism is terrifying to the participants who cannot free themselves from the chains of superstition, but ludicrous to those who are more detached.[49] Yet Walpole's work makes a darker point, implying that neither the appeal to the past nor the supposed transparency of political virtue seem likely to ensure correct rule, while the resurrection of the idea of a divinely guaranteed political order is farcical. The post-1688 mixed constitution lacks even the appearance of a firm ethical basis.

*Otranto*, then, shares its broad political themes with Leland's *Longsword*, but whereas Leland argues against the political and domestic consequences of tyranny, Walpole at once displays and undercuts them. It was this political and generic flamboyance that Clara Reeve disliked. Hence in *The Old English Baron* she borrows from the narrative of political virtue present in *Longsword* to correct the threat to the rhetoric of constitutional stability found in Walpole's *Otranto*. However, this is by no means a dismissal of Walpole's inventiveness in relation to political tropes. In Reeve's work the transparency of truth and equity of the law espoused with limited success by Leland are reinforced with a version of Walpole's divine intervention, purged of Jacobite associations. Reeve employs Walpole's technique because, as she sees it, the rise of moveable capital and increase in luxury radicalise the threat of usurpation: it is no longer a matter primarily for aristocrats but may occur at any social level. This increased danger to the mixed constitution leads Reeve's narrative of political virtue to be more emphatic than Leland's. The ambiguities introduced into the historical romance by Leland and exaggerated by Walpole are minimised; what narrative tension there is comes (as in Reeve's later novels) from repetition. In *The Old English Baron*, the possibility of rupture is persistently raised and persistently dismissed because anxiety over aristocratic titles and property has become a broader fear regarding brand legitimacy in a mobile, commercial society.

In his *Lives* Scott includes a letter in which Reeve emphasises the influence of her father, an 'Old Whig' who 'used to make [her] read the Parliamentary debates', which, she says, 'fixed [her] principles once and for ever'.[50] Rather than supporting a brand of Whig thought allied to court or commercial interests, Reeve's father objected to Sir Robert Walpole's closeness to court, which was perceived to weaken an English liberty originating with the Goths, Anglo-Saxons, or Normans[51] – a political stance also reflected, Reeve suggests, in his reading.[52] Reeve's own critical work, *The Progress of Romance* (1785), continues this literary project, notably emphasising that political corruption under the Hanoverians is a result of the spread of luxury. Published eight years before the *Progress*, Reeve's most well-known and successful work, *The Old English Baron* (significantly first published a year earlier entitled *The Champion of Virtue*) combines the Old Whiggish thought reminiscent of sections of *Longsword* with a concern over the transfer of wealth.

That *The Old English Baron* is, like Leland's novel, concerned with the relationship between the distribution of power and ethical probity is immediately evident. Both novels are set in a period when momentarily successful English claims to France are under threat – in Reeve's case, during the minority (1422–37) of Henry VI. The later reign of Henry VI was, as Gary Kelly notes, 'used by eighteenth-century opponents of the government, especially during the War of American Independence, as an analogy for misguided leadership, political factionalism and civil strife, and resulting loss of empire'.[53] Notably, though, in concentrating on the early years of his reign (rather than the particularly troubled period after 1553) Reeve points to a time of precarious relative success before territories are lost. In this early period, England, having claimed a right to impressive territories in France, found these gains in dispute – Henry VI had been crowned King of France in 1431, a claim Charles VII (son of the previous French monarch) challenged. In relation to the loss of colonial territory, the situation thus loosely parallels the position during the Seven Years War, when the French challenged British holdings in America. It also recalls Leland's concern that this perennial enemy be dealt with firmly, a possibility that Leland felt depended upon political morality at home.

Like Leland, Reeve sets up a strong moral opposition but her suggestion is that usurpation is not merely an aristocratic pastime. Hence, while the crimes of Reeve's central usurper Sir Walter generate the plot, the determination of the middle and lower ranks to improve their position without the currency of merit occupies most of the narrative. Edmund's chief enemy, the cadet Wenlock, an aristocratic hanger-on, has the excessive ambition of Count Mal-leon, but his crimes are worse. To preserve his comfortable position, Wenlock lays a plot that, if successful, would have involved his country in losses in their war against France. Lower down the social scale, Twyford fills the role of discontented peasant, adopting Edmund in anticipation of undeserved gain. Here Reeve's anxiety exceeds that of Leland, who, in a brief narrative moment, gestures towards the dangers of political vice in the lower ranks – his dishonourable soldiers are encouraged by the bad example of Mal-leon: 'be assured of the favour of our Count', one says to the other.[54] Twyford, however, has independent ambitions unsanctioned by any aristocrat.

Like Leland, Reeve constructs an emphatic alternative social paradigm in which such individualistic ambition is defunct. Protesting at his willingness to stay with the humble Wyatts, the champion of virtue, Sir Philip, remarks: 'I am sorry . . . you should think me so dainty; I am a Christian soldier; and him I acknowledge for my Prince and Master, accepted the invitations of the poor, and washed the feet of his disciples.'[55] In its codified austerity, such behaviour at once looks back to Old Whiggish values and anticipates the service-orientated image of the aristocracy emergent during the Napoleonic Wars. Reeve's selection of the name 'Edmund' for her hero heightens the emphasis on sturdy independence – for Leland, the narrative of the Saxon Edmund had been an aside: his hero was William Longsword – a bastard Norman. Thus, in an act of implied resistance to the French, Reeve argues for the need to return to a gothic origin supposedly connected with liberty. Predictably, then, like his namesake in *Longsword*, Edmund speaks 'with equal modesty and intrepidity'; he is 'humble but not servile to his patron'.[56] The point is reinforced in relation to the lower-ranking Wyatts. In parallel with Leland's Edmund, Wyatt's son, John, shows a mixture of modesty and intrepidity. His father volunteers him for Sir Philip's service but doubtfully remarks 'I fear he is not brought up well enough', in response to which John 'could not forbear speaking', a linguistic boldness seen by Reeve as a marker of honesty.[57]

Significantly, too, this enhanced narrative of Old Whig political virtue has an even stronger emphasis on financial probity than in Leland's work. Sir Philip's Christian charity stands in opposition not only to Sir Walter's greed but to the supposed spread of luxury under the Hanoverians, while the peasant Wyatt asserts his freedom from the contamination of consumerism by putting moral qualifications before economic ones: 'I am an honest man, though a poor one', he says.[58] Indeed, it is Reeve's attitude to the peasantry that proves the link between her fear of luxury and her emphatic promotion of political virtue. In adopting Edmund, Twyford embarks on a risky capitalist speculation which may improve his financial and social status considerably. Tellingly, however, Reeve does not allow Twyford's gamble to succeed. As in her later novel *Destination* (1799) (where the protagonist suffers from repeated attempts to steal his business name), Reeve is concerned to prevent the social mobility that might arise from trading on another's identity.

Reeve provides an alternative route to personal success. When John is given the opportunity for advancement, his father finds it unnecessary to 'make . . . terms' for him with Sir Philip. [59]A negative view on this is offered by Abby Coykendall, who argues that Reeve has 'transform[ed] the mutually binding, albeit flagrantly unequal, contractual labour of the Enlightenment era into the unpaid fealty and abject bondage of the middle ages'.[60] However, it is worth moderating this slightly. The contrast, between speculative, money-orientated service and feudal loyalty is not infrequent in eighteenth-century literature (witness the contrast between Spalatro and Paulo in Radcliffe's *The Italian* [1797] or between the scene painter and the carpenter Christopher Jackson in Austen's *Mansfield Park* [1814]) but Reeve uses her Old Whig background to argue that the feudal servant is not only more loyal but, paradoxically, more independent. Although historians including Hume had argued that the growth of trade from the sixteenth century on had created greater self-determination, for Reeve, capitalism and the consumer economy are equated with a social mobility that generates disloyalty; in contrast, a fixed social order is linked with ancient liberty. In contradistinction to Coykendall's suggestion, in this fantasy the Wyatts are emphatically not made 'abject', by their willingness to trust Sir Philip – Wyatt, Reeve states, is the 'master of [his] house'.[61]

However, even in the 'amiable' genre of 'Romance', Reeve struggles to recruit support for her stable society, repeatedly turning to the dubious constitutional supports employed by Leland.[62] As her predecessors had done, Reeve repeatedly finds both the transparency of truth and the efficacy of the law lacking. Edmund, she states, is 'frank and unreserved' but these markers of Old Whig political probity are insufficient – Wenlock too has the 'appearance of candour'.[63] True, Edmund's achievements in France mean that 'Not a tongue presumed to move itself against him; even malice and envy were silenced.'[64] Nonetheless, only a few pages later, the lies of the 'cabal', like water 'wear[ing] away a stone', contaminate Edmund's patron, the Baron.[65] Faced with such forceful epistemological erosion, Reeve, like Leland, attempts to shore up the truth by the process of law. Brought before the Baron to justify remarks made about the family, Edmund 'demand[s] [his] trial'; yet again, however, this position is weakened as he immediately admits that his enemies' 'artifices' make the outcome uncertain.[66]

Neither truth nor the law is ultimately effective in ensuring the correct descent of property. This, however, is unacceptable to Reeve. Hence, while *Longsword* suggests that law depends on the probity of the king, Reeve attempts to underpin her legal system even more firmly, suggesting it is divinely guaranteed. Initially, Edmund's mother had asserted she would never 'cease complaining to God, and the King', a dual appeal Edmund repeats when tried by the Baron: 'if . . . your Lordship should be induced to think me guilty, I would . . . appeal to another tribunal [Heaven]'.[67] As for Edmund's mother (and the Stuarts), however, direct heavenly intervention is not immediately forthcoming. Hence Reeve shifts the scene: Edmund's trial by ordeal in the abandoned wing of the house includes, in another departure from standard legal testimony, the divinely guaranteed statements of his ghostly parents, statements subsequently leading to the discovery of tokens of empirical proof. The same types of evidence that reinforced Theodore's claims are present, but brought within Reeve's definition of probability. Shoring up Leland's narrative of political virtue, these are indeed, as Walpole puts it, 'tame ghost[s]', meant to provide divine guarantee of correct succession without either Walpole's element of farce or the shadow of

Jacobitism.[68] A similar manoeuvre can be traced when Sir Philip avoids legal confusion by challenging Sir Walter to trial by combat. Sir Philip becomes, in Reeve's formulation, God's 'instrument to do justice on the guilty' – Walpole had had recourse to the threat of Alfonso's leg; more conventionally, Sir Philip's 'arm' becomes a 'minister of justice'.[69] The British political system and the correct transfer of property has been underpinned by a strange combination of Old Whig morality and the faint echo of the divine right of kings, here present as God's direct involvement in ensuring political virtue.

For Leland, Walpole and Reeve the terror of usurpation (arguably the key anxiety in late eighteenth-century gothic) indicates an underlying doubt about ancient constitutionalism. Legal structures do not seem sufficient to guarantee ancient liberties; the transfer of the constitution – and of property – from generation to generation is vulnerable. For Walpole (jokingly) and for Reeve (with deadly seriousness), the maintenance of property and power relies on the dead past being believed to manifest, divinely aided, in the present. The divine right of kings that was drawn upon by the Stuarts must now be transformed, its energies diffused to guarantee not only the monarchy but the constitution. Imagination invokes supernatural power to support the status quo. However, as these works testify, this political imaginary was under increasing pressure: how could a monarch keep the appearance of sublime virtue in the midst of commercial modernity?

## Saxon Experiments and Radcliffe's *Gaston de Blondeville*

In its paranoid insistence on ancient constitutionalism, Clara Reeve's *Old English Baron* inadvertently testifies to a shift in relation to the Old Whig notion of 'ancient liberties'. In Reeve's work, the appeal to past political behaviour remains, but she is also preoccupied by the possibility of increased social mobility in a commercial society, particularly as it affects the lower orders. Reeve stresses that, like their superiors, those of the lower ranks should also have a kind of liberty but one which involves no essential change in their condition. In other words, Reeve's desire to police the narrative of ancient liberties testifies to the increasing radical use of the paradigm in the late eighteenth century. According to the 'Norman Yoke' theory of the Society for Constitutional Information set up by Major John Cartwright and John Jebb, the invasion of William the Conqueror had obliterated the structures and political freedoms found in Saxon modes of government. Thomas Paine (a member of the Society) put the argument in its strongest terms, suggesting that if the 'succession' from William 'runs in the line of the conquest, the nation runs in the line of being conquered, and it ought to rescue itself from this reproach'.[70] Significantly, this particular narrative of a return to political origin did not only involve a readjustment between the monarch and ruling class, but between the government and the people. This new emphasis on the economic well-being and political protection of the people is present in the historical novel of the period, as Anne Fuller's 1789 novel, *Son of Ethelwolf* demonstrates. It is to the radical potential of this variety of ancient constitutionalism that Burke responds in his *Reflections on the Revolution in France*. Yet Burke's account further problematises the trope – and the resultant difficulties are evident both in the 1791 novel, *Edwy, Son of Ethelred the Second: An Historic Tale* and Radcliffe's *Gaston*.

Anne Fuller seems to have enjoyed a degree of success despite her early death in 1790. What is generally accepted as her first novel, *Alan Fitz-Osborne* (1787) was translated into French, while her second novel, *Son of Ethelwolf*, was given a favourable write-up in the *Monthly Review*.[71] In 1796 it was still in the mind of the theatre critic for the *Monthly Mirror*, who berating the drama 'The Magic Banner', advises the writer to read Fuller's novel: 'a very interesting and not undramatic attempt to expand the history of Alfred'.[72] The author's fame even spread as far as the *Allgemeine Literatur-Zeitung*, which praises the work but seems to find it only too historical: more could have been done with Alfred's character, the writer suggests.[73] That Fuller's interest in history was coloured by ancient constitutionalism is further suggested by the fact that *Alan Fitz-Osborne* (1787) is sometimes compared to *The Old English Baron* (ostensibly because both works contain a ghost). Yet *Son of Ethelwolf*, while still drawing on ancient constitutionalism, is decidedly more radical in tone than Reeve's Old Whiggish narrative. Rather than focusing on liberty within a fixed social structure, Fuller's work emphasises how Alfred's lawgiving propensities benefit the ordinary people.

Fuller begins the work with a dedication to the Prince of Wales, as she suggests, by permission. This dedication makes reference to the Regency Crisis of 1788–9, when, during the king's illness, there was a fierce debate over the powers and necessity of a regent. Celebrating George III's recovery, 'Heaven', Anne Fuller says, has restored to the prince a 'father, to England a sovereign, worthy of the tears that were recently shed for him, and of the happiness that his recovery now inspires.'[74] Her use of the passive construction to describe such conventional grief was perhaps wise. Both the Prince of Wales and his ally, Charles James Fox, a proponent of parliamentary reform, had seemed self-interested in the rush to institute a regency during the king's illness. These were reformers willing to assert (along with Burke during this crisis) the importance of hereditary succession in a way reminiscent of the seventeenth century. Read in this context, Fuller's laudatory dedication to the prince seems (like that given by Leland to George III) to be ambiguous. The Prince of Wales, one suspects, might have something to learn from the habits of that great lawgiver, Alfred.

Anne Fuller's novel opens in a peasant's hut, where the servant, Edbald, comes in late from the storm and is reproved by Winefreda, the herdsman's wife, 'for his awkwardness in domestic offices'. The scene is set, it is gradually revealed, in the aftermath of the Danish attack on Chippenham in 878 and the incompetent servant is Alfred himself. In this opening episode, Alfred's forbearance and his praise for the 'tranquillity' of the 'humble' (and, crucially, unambitious) existence of the people strike a fairly conventional note, but the peasant Dunwolf's bravery, military service for his country and subsequent neglect are rather less usual.[75] In his own travails, Alfred is beginning to learn how the separation between the king and the people prevents justice, a theme which becomes more explicit in the second volume. There, Alfred is again given hospitality by peasants but when he compliments them on their 'cheerful' looks, they make it plain that it is only a 'semblance of mirth': in actual fact the Danish oppressors have carried off their grain.[76] To them, even the return of Alfred, the 'good and just' would, they tell him:

> be . . . productive of no material alteration. We should change our masters, but we should not be freed from oppression . . . subject to the deprivation of a hard earned property at the will of an imperious superior.[77]

A regime change has little effect on those lower down the social scale who still suffer from excessive taxation. When Alfred (whose identity is unknown to them) asks why they could not 'carry to [the king] their complaints', they reply that 'our cries cannot penetrate to the throne, for it is surrounded by persons whose interest it is not to suffer them to be heard'.[78] Unjust taxation is accompanied (as the American colonists had found) with a lack of political representation. This is a situation Alfred vows to correct and such correction implicitly involves rejecting 'flattery' (something the Prince of Wales is warned about by the 'freeborn people of England' in the dedication).[79]

However, in this novel it proves too difficult (it is unclear whether on literary, historical or political grounds) to show Alfred ending the oppression of taxation. Rather, Fuller contents herself with remarking on the connection between law and commerce: supported by peaceful legality, commerce 'pour[s] the products of far distant realms into

[Alfred's] dominion'.[80] The reader is left to assume that, with Alfred restored, the peasantry presumably enjoy their share of prosperity along with the rest. Meanwhile, since depicting tax reform is so awkward, Alfred's clearest act of justice takes place in the sexual arena (thus foreshadowing the thematic link between political and sexual health in the novel of ideas in the 1790s). The peasant Adelfrida has been taken by the nobleman Siward who has promised to marry her – a promise which he fails to fulfil. Alfred intervenes and sends Siward back to the girl's grandfather, who angrily claims he will turn to Alfred for justice. From the elder's perspective, Siward may be a noble and Adelfrida's family peasants but they still have the right to appeal to the law. On hearing this, Alfred is not, as Siward expects, 'offended':

> 'Offended,' returned Alfred, 'offended at what makes my pleasure, my pride, my happiness! The words of Adelfrid are my best eulogium. Did Guthrum [the Danish ruler] fill my place, the old man had not trusted to the power of the laws; – he has more confidence in Alfred: – he knows that *he respects* them.'[81]

Instead of feeling pride solely in his superior status, Alfred acknowledges the law as an external force, one that applies to all people no matter what their rank. In this emphasis Fuller reflects (albeit in seemingly loyalist terms) the changing use of the narrative of ancient liberties in the late 1780s. Whereas in *Longsword*, *Otranto* and *The Old English Baron* ancient constitutionalism had been used in relation primarily to the rights of the upper ranks (even the peasants Theodore and Edmund turn out to be aristocrats), Fuller's narrative is more radical. Here it is the people rather than a class of political intermediaries that should be the primary beneficiaries of the narrative of ancient liberties. Yet equally clearly, as in the earlier fictions of 'ancient liberty', the law that should maintain freedom is still vexingly dependent on the monarch's character.

In the *Reflections* Burke responds to this growing emphasis within the discourse of ancient constitutionalism on the liberties of the people rather than the aristocracy, arguing that the 'legal hereditary succession of the crown' is considered by the English people 'as among their rights, not as among their wrongs'.[82] For Burke, the constitution forms a kind of 'artificial infinite', a sublime construction which includes the monarchy.[83] Significantly, even when he is forced to discuss political rupture, he stresses the importance of camouflage. Considering the Glorious Revolution (1688), Burke notes that Lord Somers, who drew the Declaration of Right, used 'address' to keep 'this temporary solution of continuity' 'from the eye'. According to Burke, this moment of breakage only exists to ensure stability – the Declaration 'settled for ever' the future of the monarchy.[84] Contra the theory of the Norman Yoke, Burke argues that there is a direct line from Anglo-Saxon legal structures to the present day. There is no need for a return to purer origins: the current arrangement is the one that benefits the people.

However, the use of ancient constitutionalism in the *Reflections* is necessarily rather different from those found either in the seventeenth century or in parliamentary circles in the 1760s. Burke cites the opinion of Sir Edward Coke on the 'oldest reformation' of the monarchy – according to Coke, Burke suggests:

> the antient charter, the Magna Charta [sic] of King John, was connected with another positive charter from Henry I and that both the one and the other were nothing more than a re-affirmance of the still more antient standing law of the kingdom.[85]

In this standard narrative of ancient constitutionalism both the 1100 Charter of Liberties (also known as the Coronation Oath of Henry I) and Magna Carta (1215), which placed restrictions on the power of the monarchy, are seen to date from the earlier structures of Anglo-Saxon law. When Coke made this argument, in the seventeenth century, as Ivo Kamps notes, 'the practical consequences . . . were that historically James I's royal prerogatives did not originate from the king himself and were therefore circumscribed by law'; at that period, 'historians like Spelman took a line more favourable to James when he argued that parliament post-dated the Norman Conquest'.[86] In the 1760s the debate had centred on the same (alleged) fear of royal absolutism and the erosion of parliamentary power.

After the Regency crisis and at the first moment of the French Revolution, however, the case had altered, as had the political valence of the narrative of the Norman Yoke. Although Burke had been a keen supporter of limitations on monarchical power, in 1790 he was concerned to argue against later, more radical uses of 'ancient liberty'. Hence Burke employs ancient constitutionalism to restrict the rights of the *people*. The 'old fanatics of single arbitrary power', Burke argues, 'dogmatised as if hereditary royalty was the only lawful government in the world, just as our new fanatics of popular arbitrary power, maintain that a popular election is the sole lawful source of authority'.[87] Burke suggests that, as well as restricting monarchical power above, the narrative of ancient liberties also prevents its spread below. In Burke's narrative royalty is not the enemy: the royal behaviours that made Magna Carta necessary are temporarily overlooked and the period 'after the conquest' is seen not in terms of breakage but as a time in which key liberties were enshrined. The more radical narrative of the

Norman Yoke that the Society for Constitutional Information used is overwritten.

Burke reinforces this argument with one of the shifts in perspective that his opponents found so annoying. Speaking at large about those who followed Coke, he writes:

> In the matter of fact for the greater part, these authors appear to be in the right; perhaps not always: but if the lawyers mistake in some particulars, it proves my position still the more strongly; because it demonstrates the powerful prepossession towards antiquity, with which the minds of all our lawyers and legislators, and of all the people whom they wish to influence, have always been filled.[88]

The argument, first based on legal authority and the 'fact' of historical precedent, is now a matter of opinion, intention and emotion. Moreover, for Burke, the radical suggestions of the Society for Constitutional Information not only deviate from properly understood versions of ancient constitutionalism but also fail the commercial test of modernity. The political books circulated by the Society 'might' otherwise 'lie on the hands of the booksellers'.[89] In this account, the present-day monarch and the market are discretely allied, rendering the spread of political knowledge an act of unwanted charity.

Although the narrative of ancient constitutionalism (in various forms) proved persistent, there were, as Burke's careful manoeuvres suggest, significant and growing difficulties with the notion of 'ancient liberties'. The first was the fit of such ideas with commercial modernity. When Burke implies that it is the Society rather than the monarch which is out of tune with the market, for instance, he does so indirectly: the monarch of a commercial society is an inglorious figure in chivalric terms. In fact, ancient constitutionalism performed little imaginative work when it came to positing the relationship between the monarchical and constitutional sublime and the market. For instance, whilst in *Waverley* Scott is able to imagine a benign Hanoverian monarch reigning over commercial Britain, in *Ivanhoe* (published in 1819 and most directly pertinent to the narrative of ancient liberties) the monarch Richard I has to be absent for most of the text in order to remain free from the vicious entrepreneurialism of the Norman barons. By 1823 in *Quentin Durward* matters are still worse. The monarch who presides over the transition to the modern French state is himself a figure of commercial corruption: Louis XI 'resembled the merchant or shopkeeper of the period' and the uncomplimentary nature of this is evident since he can also be mistaken for a 'decoy duck' working for a 'murderer'.[90] Although the market may itself be seen as infinite, in its day-to-day manifestations it is less than morally glamorous. The monarch of a commercial state is a far less sublime figure than that evoked by Burke's artificial infinite.

In addition, the appeal to custom was equally intellectually fragile. Back in 1767, in an *Essay on the English Constitution*, Edward King had queried the tendency to defend the constitution on the grounds of antiquity alone: 'One would suppose,' he remarks, that the constitution could be:

> defended on no other principles, than those of its having been established in nearly the same form wherein it now exists, for ages immemorial. A fact which some have with great labour and difficulty endeavoured to render probable; but of which there is much reason to suspect the truth.[91]

The constitution, King argues, is not static. On the contrary, he suggests, the 'ancient constitution . . . was *such* as we may reasonably suppose to have been most fit and expedient for the Nation at those times'.[92] In this account, the ancient constitution becomes something that evolves according to society's stage of economic development. King moderates the narrative of ancient liberty so much that it becomes stadial history. After the publication of *Reflections*, unease with the legitimatising force of custom increased: radicals like Wollstonecraft saw no reason to join Burke in 'reverenc[ing] the rust of antiquity'.[93] The situation was further complicated because (particularly given what Pocock notes is the fictive status of ancient constitutionalism) the original moment at which the ancient constitution was in operation was hard to trace.

These difficulties with the sustaining force of custom and heritage, particularly in relation to luxury, are evident in the 1791 novel, *Edwy, Son of Ethelred the Second: An Historic Tale*. The work maintains the fiction of a return to political origins, suggesting that 'the AUGUST family who now possess the *English* Crown are *Saxons*'.[94] This, then, is a kind of reversion, presumably to ancient liberty, yet the novel's attitude to the Saxons themselves is not entirely positive, modifying the compliment. Although the final chapters of the book evoke the theory of the Norman Yoke by suggesting the tyranny of William the Conqueror, most of the narrative is concerned with the failure of Saxon rule and Saxon morality. Here, Anglo-Saxon decline follows the iniquity of Edgar in killing Athelwold and marrying Elfrida. The corrupt nature of Elfrida's son, Ethelred (commonly known as the 'Unready'), supposedly leads to the murder of his elder half-brother Edward the Martyr, to several generations of Danish rule and to the defeat of Edmund II ('Edmund Ironside', King of Wessex). Although Edmund challenges the Danish ruler to single combat to decide the fate of England (in a way rather reminiscent of the single combat proposed by William in

*Longsword* and carried out in *The Old English Baron*), the attempt fails and Edmund is eventually assassinated. Matters are no better under Edward the Confessor: it is his indecision about his successor that leads to William of Normandy's invasion.

While the book concentrates on this narrative of decline and dispossession, it also shows some passing concern with the resultant economic state of the country. It is clear to the author that Anglo-Saxon poverty (following the oppressions of the Danes) is as unsatisfactory as (supposed) Danish luxury. Yet a prosperity which avoids luxurious corruption is hard to achieve. Whilst the rule of law would, the book implies, aid commercial and moral probity, the Anglo-Saxon kings are unable to guarantee the order that would allow trade. Meanwhile, under Danish rule taxation impoverishes the original inhabitants of the country; and matters deteriorate further after the Norman Conquest, an event which leads to the depopulation of the once prosperous communities of the New Forest. As such, this novel transforms Reeve's worry about the relation between inherited wealth and power and the ambitions of the lower ranks: here the fear is that the failure of rule will generate, not working-class immorality, but widespread economic disruption. Meanwhile, Edwy, the central character, spends much of the narrative bemoaning his loss of his inherited position (a doubly dubious habit by eighteenth-century mores since he has been born out of wedlock). A rather unsympathetic narrator who listens to the stories of others while mostly remaining sheltered from events, he still finds time to condemn increasing Anglo-Saxon lethargy. His constant lament is for the 'Unhappy race of *Ethelred*!'[95] Edwy is, as the author admits, a 'perfect blank' to history (although 'all historians agree' he existed) and also a largely inactive onlooker in the novel – far more so even than Scott's Waverley.[96] Even in the midst of a struggle for liberty, action proves hard to take.

If, in contrast to Burke's sublime of succession, *Edwy* suggests that the ancient constitution was threatened before the Normans, for Ann Radcliffe the idea of liberty after the Conquest appears equally fraught. Apparently responding to Burke, Ann Radcliffe's last and largely neglected novel *Gaston de Blondeville* (published in 1826 but said to have been finished around 1803) suggests that the tale of (English) constitution is not one of continuity but of constant disruption. Radcliffe is of course most famous for her gothic novels of the 1790s and the reverberations of the Old Whiggish narrative of ancient liberties in such writings are considerable, albeit not always recognised. In fact, as Radcliffe's own writing makes clear, in part late eighteenth-century gothic can be seen as a comment on feudal (that is, post-Norman) iniquities (although any direct relationship to the notion of the Norman Yoke is weakened by the foreign settings often used in such works). Typical here is *The Italian* (1797) where if hereditary power is to survive, it must be updated.[97] In particular, Radcliffe suggests, in order to avoid the perils of tyranny, the structures of authority supported by primogeniture need to become less autocratic and superstitious. Representative of the new generation of rulers, Vivaldi, the hero, is not perfect but he is better than the other (implicit) representatives of state and church in the novel – that is, his proud, unfeeling aristocratic father and his vicious, unnatural, and Catholic mother. Radcliffe, then, espouses a limited form of progress without wishing to break with inherited forms of property and power. Yet the feeling evident in Radcliffe's work that the past is certainly no more a place of liberty than the present puts her in a good position to reply to Burke.

In noting *Gaston de Blondeville*'s similarity to William Godwin's *Things as They Are; Or, the Adventures of Caleb Williams* (1794), Claudia Johnson implies the work's relevance to the post-French Revolution debate.[98] Like Godwin's Caleb, the protagonist of Radcliffe's novel, Hugh Woodreeve, is in possession of information which his social superior, Gaston, does not want revealed. This is a narrative of misused authority: when Woodreeve accuses Gaston of being involved in the murder of his kinsman, Reginald de Folville, a plot is carried out by Gaston and the corrupt Prior to prevent him receiving justice. Worse still, King Henry III is unwittingly complicit in this planned miscarriage of justice. However, the novel's concern with the balance of power and the intervention of a supernatural agency (the murdered de Folville himself) also mean it can be placed in relation to Walpole, Reeve, Leland and ancient constitutionalism.[99] Radcliffe's work deepens the doubts present in those earlier novels: the Crown is corrupt and the tensions between the aristocracy, clergy and people uncontrollable. In short, the descendants of the Conqueror are as iniquitous as radical eighteenth-century theorists of the Norman Yoke might desire. However, the consistent corruption of the monarchy is such that any narrative of ancient liberties begins to seem unlikely. Whereas Burke had created a kind of sublime of tradition to support the monarchy and constitution, here the use of history, ceremony and custom to control the past seems vulnerable. Most disturbingly, this novel is so filled with observers and their comments that it seems impossible to achieve an accurate interpretation, not only of history, but of any narrative, image or event.

In *Gaston de Blondeville* scepticism about the 'sacred' institution, monarchy, is immediately evident. In the frame narrative two contemporary travellers, Simpson and Willoughton, discuss Queen Elizabeth's reign, reflecting on the duty and ability of past monarchs to protect 'the wayfaring part of his Majesty's liege subjects'. The protection provided by past monarchs seems dubious given that the 'thick and gloomy woods' through which loyal subjects had to travel were also the 'home of the doubtful fugitive'.[100] The moral conduct of those who wear the crown is also open to critique. When the more poetic antiquarian Willoughton asserts that Elizabeth's 'wisdom partook too much of craft' and her 'cruelty to poor Mary is a bloody hand in her escutcheon', Simpson suggests his companion is 'too ardent … much may be said on her conduct on that head': morality and statecraft are two different things.[101] Mary's execution, the imprisonment of Edward II at Kenilworth (he is subsequently murdered) and even the death of Charles I (too traumatic to allude to directly but present through the allusions to Cromwell) all haunt the opening pages of this text, much as Elizabeth's ghost is said to occupy the ruins of Kenilworth. In the works of Leland, Walpole and Reeve concern about the usurpation of power is frequently displaced onto the aristocracy. Radcliffe is more forceful. Here the unbroken monarchical succession which Burke boasts of seems nothing more than a constant '[dis]solution of continuity'.[102]

By setting her narrative in the reign of Henry III Radcliffe underlines this state of disruption. Coming to the throne in his minority, Henry III had confirmed Magna Carta of King John but, like his father, he attempted to renege, claiming he had been coerced. In suggesting that Henry 'never' practised 'such cruel means of extortion as did his father, King John', the fictional writer of Radcliffe's manuscript, is actually highlighting this unpleasant consistency.[103] Further, Radcliffe, via Willoughton, recalls the civil strife this prompted, remembering 'Montfort, on whom [Henry III] had bestowed Kenilworth, and who added ingratitude to treason, by holding the fortress against his benefactor and liege lord'.[104] As John had faced the Barons' Revolt, Henry had triggered the Second Barons' War in which Simon de Montfort had played a leading part, attempting radically to reform parliamentary representation in the kingdom.

Perusing an ancient manuscript, the travellers are initially confronted with the past as a series of the images, static yet still redolent of instability and unease. Like all of the novel's chapters, 'The First Day' begins not with a drawing but with a description of a drawing: the fictional past is already doubly mediated.[105] Evidence is constantly distorted. Although the image's epigraph describes the 'King and Queen, with their train, passing under the towers of Kenilworth', the picture also captures an instant in the life of the ordinary people, an instant signalled by the past progressive – when the soldiers lean forward to view the king, 'the cap of one . . . was falling on the multitude below'. For the 'man pressing through the crowd, with eager gesticulation and a wild countenance', this is an instant as much of disquietude as amusement.[106] What the picture underlines is the distinction between what Wollstonecraft calls the 'cumbersome brocade of ceremony' with its sense of unbending permanence, and the exigencies, discord and class tensions of the political moment.[107] Radcliffe's narrator uses an equally politically suggestive metaphor, comparing the spectacle of the court's arrival to the sublime ruin of the aqueduct at Rome, 'grander in its sweep than it might have shown when' complete, all the greater because it requires imagination to reconstruct.[108] Yet, the narrative emphasises, imagination will fail: the governing structures of this country are emphatically not the ordered whole, receding in grand perspective, which Burke's sublime of tradition suggests.

Disharmony continues in the body of the chapter. The French queen's 'Mynstrells of Music' drown out the 'bells of a village' and the noise of the 'proud trumpeters' triumphs over the 'merry bugles' of the forest-ers.[109] Competition is also present on the social level. The castellan is displeased by the monks' attempts to present themselves to the king, whilst the monks become glad to 'follow in [the king's] train' because, on his appearance, 'the crowd was forced back'.[110] In this ceremonial welcome, then, the effete court and the religion and feelings of the people; the country and the military power of the king; the civic and religious authorities; and the king and the people, are all in aggressive and damaging rivalry. Further, the hostility to the French favourite and French queen represents more than traditional international enmity or knee-jerk Francophobia. According to the narrator, 'The walls and turrets, thronged with faces, seemed to be alive and to shout, as with one voice, "Queen Eleanor! long live Queen Eleanor!" – but some few were heard to shout, "Away with the foreigners! – away with all foreigners!".[111] Recalling Marie Antoinette's initial popularity with the Parisians and their subsequent hostility to *l'Autrichienne* (as her opponents called her), this uncanny anthropomorphism (the very walls cry out) strikes a particularly grim note. The fear of 'French contamination' that Leland had played upon becomes a way of suggesting that this is a discontented and potentially revolutionary society.

Moreover, the imagery hints that responsibility for this discontent lies with monarchical authority and its failure to control the competing interests of the three estates: church, people and nobility. In reference to Henry's (documented) decision to have a mural of the Anglo-Saxon saint and monarch, Edward the Confessor, painted on the wall of his bedchamber, Radcliffe has Henry decorate the chapel at Kenilworth 'with the story of . . . the Confessor, giving the ring off his finger to a poor stranger'.[112] Yet there is no continuity with Anglo-Saxon charity (or presumably with Anglo-Saxon legal structures) here. Moreover, the adoption of King Edward as role model is dubious: for the author of *Edwy* his behaviour led to the Norman Conquest. In any case, Henry is hypocritical. Although Henry in life is said to have copied the plainness of Edward's dress, Radcliffe's monarch is less ascetic. The narrator-monk, Grymbald, remarks that with the 'dignity of [Henry's] carriage there was mixed good humour': this lack of emotional austerity is gradually connected to a lack of self-control.[113] By the time the monk narrates 'The Seventh Day' he is willing to be more direct. Driven by 'sorrow and remorse' at Gaston's death, the king 'with the intention, as he persuaded himself, of preventing further evil, was about to execute an act of injustice and stern cruelty'.[114] The reversal of meaning here – in which justice becomes injustice – reflects the Enlightenment concern with accurate representation found in *Longsword*. But it also recalls the frequent post-French Revolution struggles over signification.[115] Here it is 'passion' that causes such reversal and opens the king to the plots of 'designing men'.[116] Despite Henry's fondness for decorating his walls with 'the noble achievements of his ancestors and others' (Richard the Lionheart, 'Merlin, King of Britain', 'the sailing of William from Normandy' – but also the siege of Troy), he lacks what Adam Smith calls 'the great, the awful and respectable, the virtues of self-denial' – and this prevents his effective rule.[117]

The self-indulgence of king and court has, Radcliffe indicates, pernicious social and economic effects. Even as Radcliffe depicts the court hunting and feasting in the forest, she undercuts the vision of pastoral social order. Encountering 'three hundred foresters, who feigned to be outlaws of the forest, presenting Robin Hood' and company, the 'noble company' itself 'feared not' and were 'nothing daunted'.[118] The very denials suggest the repressed fears of the nobility: sordid and threatening reality is turned into romance. Still, though, the court disregards the state of the country. The hunting expedition recalls the post-French Revolution unease over the French and British game laws. In *Edwy* William I's creation of the New Forest as a hunting ground is seen as an act of tyranny which destroys the communities that were settled there and the motif is repeated in Charlotte Smith's *Desmond* and Wollstonecraft's *Vindication of the Rights of Men* (1790).[119] Representing sport and pleasure for one class of society at the expense of another, reflecting the depopulation of the countryside during the agricultural revolution, the woodland causes crime. Radcliffe also alludes to the post-French Revolution fascination with woodland as alternate social space – not only in *Caleb Williams* but also in the anonymous *Arville Castle* and *Montford Castle*, the forest allows outlaws to enter into their own social contract. Radcliffe is undoubtedly aware of this tradition but for her the alternative social order represented by Robin Hood and his men is no more than a space of fiction. Instead of nurturing an ideal community, the 'dark thickets' are the 'home of outlaws', damaging the health of England.[120] And while in *Arville Castle* the reader finally discovers that it is the dispossessed aristocracy who are running a failed and corrupt alternative space, Radcliffe is more direct. Gaston de Blondeville, the corrupt favourite, and the Prior are responsible for the murderous woodland robbery which generates the plot.

Under corrupt rule it is not only the displaced peasant that suffers. With a Norman first name and a surname that combines Anglo-Saxon etymology with a reference to *The Old English Baron*, Hugh Woodreeve is a merchant. *The Old English Baron*'s fixation with the effect of trade on social mobility and personal identity is reinvented by Radcliffe – the trader is witness and victim of crime. Even on the first day the crowd misinterprets Woodreeve's quest for justice, believing he 'has assailed the life of our good King'. Their 'roaring' with 'women brawling' the loudest (recalling the fishwives' march on Versailles) temporarily drowns out vital information: the king is alive; there is no crime.[121] Commerce is believed to threaten monarchy but, Radcliffe suggests, the reverse is true. When Woodreeve manages to speak directly to the king, the king initially asserts that 'justice should be done upon the guilty' but his attitude changes when he discovers that the accused is his favourite Gaston.[122] If Woodreeve goes 'farther', the king threatens, he 'must be taught what it is to dishonour a gentleman and a knight'.[123] This naïve equation of moral worth and title leads to Woodreeve's unsympathetic cross-examination by the king, in which an often comic feature of Radcliffe's earlier fiction, the interrupted digression, becomes reinterpreted. Stories told by obscure narrators are easily written over by those in power.

While the king dismisses the possibility of an extrajudicial solution (a 'sentence by other modes') and rules out 'trial by ordeal', both options suggest Woodreeve's vulnerability.[124] Equally, Radcliffe stresses that the powerful can manipulate evidence. The Prior insists that it is:

> extraordinary, that, if the calamitous adventure, related by the merchant, had occurred so near Kenilworth, and so few years back, it should not be generally known ... the name of Reginald de Folville [Wooodreeve's murdered relation] not being found in the cemetery-book of the Priory.[125]

Yet this gap in the historical records has been constructed by the Prior himself (who has erased the inscription on Reginald de Folville's tomb).

Even trial by jury is flawed by threats of jury-tampering or the possibility of a retrial. Accused by the people, interrogated by the king, judged by the monks of St Mary's Priory, experiencing two formal trials and condemned out of hand by the king after the death of Gaston de Blondeville, Woodreeve is one of the most persistently questioned petitioners for justice in literature.

Woodreeve's case is also punctuated by an unusual number of supernatural appearances. In *The Old English Baron* Reeve had rejected the divine right of kings, instead suggesting that the state is supported by a more general providential order. Her use of the supernatural emphasises the point. Radcliffe undermines this position. The appearances of the murdered Reginald de Folville suggest that the demand for justice will recur, even after the threat has apparently been laid to rest.[126] However, such reappearances are subject to misinterpretation and even distortion. Hence when the drops of blood on Gaston's robe spread (in line with the medieval belief that the blood of the victim flows to accuse the murderer), the prisoner is accused of 'sorcery' – and is condemned to death for a magical plot against the Prior's life.[127] Evidence, even of a supernatural variety, is co-opted by power. Further, while in *The Old English Baron* Sir Philip is able to participate in trial by combat, becoming the 'minister of justice', in Radcliffe's narrative the ghost of Reginald de Folville has to defend his own cause. Even the spectre's victory makes no difference to Henry, who continues with Woodreeve's execution. Only when the apparition directly threatens the king, saying 'if he [Woodreeve] perish for my sake he shall not fall alone. Be warned', will the king listen.[128] Despite Woodreeve's ultimate vindication, *Gaston* portrays a sense of justice in crisis that is greater than its predecessors. This is a corrupt social order that not only lacks supernatural underpinning but also refuses any idea of providential intervention.

After suggesting the extent of judicial corruption, *Gaston* exaggerates the repetitive aspects of the fictions of ancient liberties, adding a sinister sense of paranoia. What initially seems inert or dull becomes, by the end of the narrative, curiously troubling. The book's static quality comes not only from the description of the images which head each chapter but from the pedantry of its clerical narrator and the court ceremony it contains. However, all this is ominously undercut by the apparent impossibility of historical and cultural representation. The king and queen try to control their artistic environment but fail. On the third day the ornate ceremonies of marriage and feast are interrupted by a mysterious, untraceable 'figure'.[129] Interruption and misinterpretation are followed by unauthorised spectral representation on a grand scale.

At the banquet, the Crusades are re-enacted to stirring martial music, unexpectedly followed by images of de Folville's murder. The food is doctored: the 'suttletie' showing 'archers in the forest' designed to complement Gaston's new wife, Lady Barbara, includes an odd detail: 'At a distance, within the shadow of the trees, stood an aged man alone, wringing his hands' but 'what this might mean none knew.'[130] Music without minstrels; a cast of thousands with no actors; and wedding fare with moving perspectival pictures all indicate that representation is uncannily out of control.

The number of commentators only increases this sense. In this novel the feeling of mass observation – of the very turrets and walls becoming animated – reflects the growing post-French Revolution awareness of the people as a political force. Rumour and counter-rumour flourish, making accuracy impossible. The actions of the king and queen, innocuous or doubtful, are all subject to criticism ('many there thought the King too hasty in this').[131] *Gaston de Blondeville* suggests that constitutional struggle seems both inevitable and perpetual. Power attempts to project continuity by presenting static images of past traditions, but, amongst the mass of observers, each individual tries to shape his own interpretation of events. As a result, the political threat is barely contained. Although *Gaston* can be read in relation to *Caleb Williams*, it also seems (despite its supposed date of composition) like a darker rewriting of *Ivanhoe*. Trade and the political classes are in fundamental conflict; luxury is pitted against criminalised poverty and the crowd has a threatening capacity for action. The sense of a disrupted and paranoid society lingers.

The revival of Old Whig rhetoric in the 1760s meant that Leland, Walpole and Reeve felt the constitutional past as a historical force acting upon the present: the gothic has both historical and political meaning. Even in the 1780s and 90s ancient constitutionalism continued to be a focus for political debate: while Burke posited a smooth continuity from past to present (or at least suggested that such a fiction should be maintained), more radical writers drew upon the notion of the Norman Yoke to position their demands for reform as a return to political origins. Consequently, as *Edwy, Son of Ethelred* and Radcliffe's *Gaston de Blondeville* show, ancient constitutionalism came under pressure. Such novels focus on continuity or, at the very least, a return to political origins, rather than rupture, but they find such continuity an increasingly implausible motif in relation to the political present.

One of the key problems for the novelists considered here is social mobility – a mobility that ancient constitutionalism promises, but does not manage, to limit. Thus it is that, despite his desire to protect ancient political virtue by distinguishing it sharply from ambitious vice, Leland finds virtue hard to guarantee. Political parasitism undermines the system from the top and the lower ranks follow the corrupt aristocracy in choosing money over honour. Leland suggests that the probity of the monarch is crucial; however, when a paean of praise to George III slides into a warning, the chances of this seem slim. Walpole's novel suggests that the correct line of succession can be hard to maintain. Combining allusions to Old Whig and Jacobite thought, he not only mockingly hints that divine intervention (of the kind favoured by the Jacobites) would be necessary to underpin the rule of law, but he also indicates the perils of manipulating a distended and dismembered past for current political gain. If the novel suggests that the threat of absolutism may be read as either ludicrous or terrifying, *Otranto*'s actual spectre – the lack of underpinning for the post-1688 mixed constitution – is far more genuinely dismaying.

For Reeve, who contemplated the added pressures of consumerism and the movement of capital upon the social structure, Walpole's critique of the British political system was unacceptable. Yet her attempt to control the spread of consumerism by appealing to a divinely underpinned gothic past makes her an anathema to Scott and condemns her to the generic troubles of her predecessors: Reeve's concern regarding the threat of social usurpation means that the moment of rupture is perpetually revisited. Reservations about the usefulness of ancient constitutionalism as a way of describing political modernity only grow in the late 1780s and 1790s. *Son of Ethelwolf* highlights problems with taxation and representation; *Edwy* and *Gaston* point to restrictions on trade and to the displaced rural population. In the face of these difficulties, a reversion to a standard of ancient liberty becomes increasingly implausible. Prince George appears an unlikely King Alfred; the author of *Edwy* finds the moment of ancient constitutionalism hard to locate; and in Radcliffe's *Gaston de Blondeville* the repetition that characterised *The Old English Baron* becomes a more baroque commentary on the use of history, ceremony and custom to underpin a political and social order. Tradition alone is not enough to legitimise rule, particularly given the (perceived) increase in mobility generated by the consumer economy. As Thomas Macaulay suggested in relation to the 1832 Reform Act: 'The great cause of revolutions is this, that while nations move onwards, constitutions stand still.'[132] Moving away from the static paradigm of ancient constitutionalism, increasingly historical novelists turned to stadial history to explore economic and political transition – and rupture.

## Notes

1. Bolingbroke, *Works*, 3: 201–2.
2. Bolingbroke, *Works*, 3: 201.
3. For other types see Kidd, *British Identities*.
4. Bolingbroke, *Works*, 3: 204.
5. Kramnick, *Bolingbroke*, p. 4.
6. Pocock, 'The Origins', p. 233.
7. Bolingbroke, *Works*, 3: 201.
8. See Kidd, *British Identities*, p. 80.
9. Lukács, *Historical Novel*, p. 19; Scott referred to *Otranto* in his 1829 General Preface; Scott, *Waverley*, p. 351. For *Otranto* as historical novel see Richard Maxwell, 'The Historical Novel', p. 67.
10. Lukács, *Historical Novel*, p. 19.
11. Pocock, *Virtue*, p. 255.
12. See Richard Maxwell, 'The Historical Novel', p. 67, p. 69; also Watt, *Contesting the Gothic*, p. 7, p. 12. For Reeve on *Otranto* see Reeve, *Old English Baron: A Gothic Story*, p. 5, subsequently *OEB*. For Walpole's response see Walpole, *Correspondence*, 41: 410. For the political meaning of 'gothic' see Emma Clery's introduction to Horace Walpole, *The Castle of Otranto*. Robert Miles, Cynthia Wall and Emma Clery are all interesting on the polysemy of the gothic.
13. [Thomas Leland], *Longsword, Earl of Salisbury: An Historical Romance*, 2 vols (Dublin: Faulkner, 1762); subsequent references are to this edition; Punter, *The Literature of Terror*, p. 47. For *Longsword* and its forerunners see Robert D. Hume, introduction to *Longsword* (1974), i–xxiii.
14. Wein, *British Identities*, pp. 49–69
15. Kelly, 'Clara Reeve, Provincial Bluestocking', pp. 113–24.
16. While the authorship of *Longsword* had been debated, in his 1974 edition of *Otranto* Robert D. Hume stated 'there now seems no real ground for doubt' (xxvi–xxvii).
17. Horace Walpole, enlarged by Thomas Park, *A Catalogue of the Royal and Noble Authors*, 5: 310, 309; the shorter first edition was published in 1758.
18. See John Robertson, 'Universal Monarchy', p. 352. David Hume, 'Of the Balance of Power', in *Essays*, p. 333.
19. Leland (trans.), *Orations*, 1: xiii.
20. Hibbert, *George III*, p. 35.
21. Pocock, *Virtue*, p. 254.
22. Colley, *Britons*, p. 90.
23. Leland, *Longsword*, 1: 18, 1: 24, 1: 26.
24. Leland, *Longsword*, 1: 79
25. Leland, *Longsword*, 2: 79; Shaftesbury, *Characteristics of Men*, p. 98.
26. Leland, *A Dissertation*, p. 3.
27. Leland, *A Dissertation*, p. 10, pp. 16–17.
28. Leland, *Longsword*, 1: 33.
29. Leland, *Longsword*, 2: 78.
30. Wein, *British Identities*, p. 5.

31. Leland, *Longsword*, 2: 33.
32. See Mowl, *Horace Walpole*, p. 187, and Mohr, 'The Picturesque', p. 264.
33. For exaggeration in *Otranto* see Morris, 'Gothic Sublimity', pp. 299–319.
34. Samson, 'Politics Gothicized', pp. 145–58; and Wein, *British Identities*, pp. 49–69; Mowl, *Horace Walpole*, pp. 170–89; Ketton-Cremer, *Horace Walpole*, pp. 198–203; Dole, 'Three Tyrants', pp. 26–35; also Walpole, *Memoirs of the Reign of King George the Third*, 1: 319–30; 2: 1–9.
35. Mowl, *Horace Walpole*, p. 171, p. 172.
36. See Watt, *Contesting the Gothic*, p. 14.
37. See Monod, *Jacobitism*, p. 27.
38. Walpole, *Correspondence*, 35: 146.
39. Walpole, *Otranto*, p. 21.
40. See Monod, *Jacobitism*, pp. 37–8.
41. Monod, *Jacobitism*, p. 54.
42. Bird, 'The Anxiety of Legitimacy', p. 188.
43. Samson, *Politics*, p. 150.
44. Walpole, *Otranto*, p. 21.
45. Walpole, *Otranto*, p. 114.
46. Walpole, *Otranto*, p. 112.
47. See Ruth Mack, 'Horace Walpole', pp. 367–87; Wein, 'Tangled Webs', pp. 12–22.
48. Walpole, *Otranto*, p. 5.
49. Walpole, *Otranto*, pp. 34–5.
50. Scott, *Lives of Eminent Novelists*, p. 545.
51. See Kendrick, 'Sir Robert Walpole', p. 421.
52. Reeve's father's reading includes Paul Rapin de Thoyras's *History of England*. See Bridget Hill, *The Republican Virago*, pp. 26–7, p. 29. For *Cato's Letters*, another of Reeve's father's choices, see Kidd, *British Identities*, p. 266.
53. Gary Kelly, *Varieties of Female Gothic*, 1: 24.
54. Leland, *Longsword*, 1: 24.
55. Reeve, *OEB*, p. 13.
56. Reeve, *OEB*, p. 38, p. 25.
57. Reeve, *OEB*, p. 21.
58. Reeve, *OEB*, p. 11.
59. Reeve, *OEB*, p. 22.
60. Coykendall, 'Gothic Genealogies', p. 477.
61. Reeve, *OEB*, p. 9.
62. Reeve, *OEB*, p. 3.
63. Reeve, *OEB*, p. 24, p. 25.
64. Reeve, *OEB*, p. 30.
65. Reeve, *OEB*, p. 32.
66. Reeve, *OEB*, p. 38.
67. Reeve, *OEB*, p. 34, p. 38.
68. Walpole, *Correspondence* 41: 410; see also Scott, *Lives*, pp. 545–50.
69. Reeve, *OEB*, p. 87, p. 94.
70. Paine, *Political Writings*, p. 87.
71. [Fuller, Anne], *Alan Fitz-Osborne, Roman Historique, Traduit de l'Anglois*, pp. 239–40.

72. 'The Magic Banner; Or, Two Wives in a House', *Monthly Mirror*, p. 119.
73. '*The Son of Ethelwolf*', *Allgemeine Literatur-Zeitung*, p. 650.
74. Fuller, *Son*, 1: v.
75. Fuller, *Son*, 1: 9.
76. Fuller, *Son*, 2: 2–3.
77. Fuller, *Son*, 2: 5.
78. Fuller, *Son*, 2: 5–6.
79. Fuller, *Son*, 1: vi.
80. Fuller, *Son*, 2: 208.
81. Fuller, *Son*, 2: 179.
82. Burke, *Reflections*, p. 111.
83. Burke, *Reflections*, p. 68. See also Gibbons, *Edmund Burke* and Tom Furniss, *Edmund Burke's Aesthetic Ideology*.
84. Burke, *Reflections*, p. 102, p. 103.
85. Burke, *Reflections*, p. 118.
86. Kamps, *Historiography*, p. 111.
87. Burke, *Reflections*, p. 111.
88. Burke, *Reflections*, p. 118.
89. Burke, *Reflections*, p. 86.
90. Scott, *Quentin Durward*, p. 51, p. 56.
91. King, *Essay*, pp. 362–3.
92. King, *Essay*, p. 363.
93. Wollstonecraft, *Vindication of the Rights of Men* in *Political Writings*, p. 8.
94. Anon, *Edwy*, 2: 130.
95. Anon, *Edwy*, 2: 58.
96. Anon, *Edwy*, 1: n.p.
97. For the politically subversive elements of *The Italian* see Chaplin, 'Romance', pp. 177–90. For Radcliffe, revolution and national identity, see Wein, *British Identities*, pp. 96–124.
98. Johnson, *Equivocal Beings*, p. 137.
99. See also Chiu in Ann Radcliffe, *Gaston*, x.
100. Radcliffe, *Gaston*, p. 3.
101. Radcliffe, *Gaston*, p. 11.
102. Burke, *Reflections*, p. 102.
103. Radcliffe, *Gaston*, p. 145.
104. Radcliffe, *Gaston*, p. 23.
105. For Radcliffe's earlier works and the pictorial and picturesque see Wheeler-Manwaring, *Italian Landscape*.
106. Radcliffe, *Gaston*, p. 28.
107. Wollstonecraft, *Works*, 6: 29.
108. Radcliffe, *Gaston*, p. 28.
109. Radcliffe, *Gaston*, p. 30, p. 32.
110. Radcliffe, *Gaston*, p. 31.
111. Radcliffe, *Gaston*, p. 33.
112. Radcliffe, *Gaston*, p. 70.
113. Radcliffe, *Gaston*, p. 72.
114. Radcliffe, *Gaston*, pp. 187–8.
115. See, for example, Hodson, *Language and Revolution*.

116. Radcliffe, *Gaston*, p. 188.
117. Radcliffe, *Gaston*, p. 75, p. 47; Adam Smith, *Theory of Moral Sentiments*, p. 23; I. i. 5. 1.
118. Radcliffe, *Gaston* p. 109, pp. 107–8.
119. Anon, *Edwy* 2: 126–8; Charlotte Smith, *Desmond*, pp. 147–8; Wollstonecraft, *Political Writings*, p. 16.
120. Radcliffe, *Gaston*, p. 69.
121. Radcliffe, *Gaston*, p. 34.
122. Radcliffe, *Gaston*, p. 37.
123. Radcliffe, *Gaston*, p. 38.
124. Radcliffe, *Gaston*, p. 99.
125. Radcliffe, *Gaston*, p. 69.
126. Radcliffe, *Gaston*, p. 86.
127. Radcliffe, *Gaston*, p. 153, p. 106.
128. Radcliffe, *Gaston*, p. 196.
129. Radcliffe, *Gaston*, p. 82.
130. Radcliffe, *Gaston*, pp. 81–2.
131. Radcliffe, *Gaston*, p. 73.
132. Cited in Burrow, *A History of Histories*, p. 330.

# Chapter 2

# The Labours of History

In the opening pages of Radcliffe's *Gaston de Blondeville* Willoughton's nostalgic 'vision' of the past glories of Kenilworth Castle contrasts with Simpson's harder-headed scepticism. While Willoughton declares that 'Antiquity is one of the favourite regions of poetry', Simpson replies: 'Who ever thought of looking for a muse in an old castle?' Having already seen the castle 'by sun-light, and almost by no light at all', Simpson has no desire to see it 'by moonlight' as well.[1] Willoughton's aesthetic sense and Simpson's practicality together contain a faint echo of the discussion between 'Arbuthnot' and 'Addison' in Richard Hurd's *Moral and Political Dialogues* (1759). In the third dialogue, the Tory, 'Arbuthnot' experiences pleasurable 'melancholy' on exploring the remains of Kenilworth, but 'Addison' contradicts him roundly. He feels 'sincere' pleasure in 'triumph[ing]' over the 'shattered ruins'. Kenilworth 'awakens an indignation against the prosperous tyranny of those wretched times, and creates a generous pleasure in reflecting on the happiness we enjoy under a juster and more equal government'.[2] Confronted with 'so uncommon' a vehemence, Arbuthnot argues crossly that Addison's position is 'not so much of the moral, as *political* kind'.[3]

Hurd's dialogue intervenes in a battle over the meaning of history. In his *Remarks on the History of England* Bolingbroke (who in his youth had supported the Jacobite cause) did not praise Stuart rule. Instead, he exploited the narrative of ancient liberties, arguing that such liberties were at their height under Queen Elizabeth. This allowed him to distance himself from his Jacobite past, to appeal to Protestant nationalism and to attack Sir Robert Walpole. Admiration for the past had strategic use. Hurd's account acknowledges this flexibility. The nostalgia sometimes associated with Jacobitism is collapsed together with both antiquarianism and the narrative of ancient liberties. Hurd's 'Addison' objects to this nostalgic (perhaps Jacobite) attitude. He implies that the liberties of the past are non-existent when weighed with those of the present.

Moreover, by setting the dialogue a year after the failed Jacobite uprising of 1715, Hurd implies that the victory of the Whiggish narrative of history as progress was swift.

Nonetheless, when Hurd wrote his dialogues, the battle between the narrative of ancient liberties and the discourse of history as progress was still ongoing. In addition, as the historical novel testifies, it was not only the discourse of ancient constitutionalism that contained internal tensions and contradictions. Although Hurd's 'Addison' avoids the language of sympathy, it became increasingly important in the history writing of the mid to late eighteenth century. As this chapter explores, both the use of sentiment in David Hume's (politically ambiguous) *History of England* (1754–61) and the role of sympathy in stadial history were potentially problematic. Broadly speaking, such histories emphasised progress yet their use of sympathy was potentially retrogressive: the danger was that sympathy itself worked to preserve feudal institutions. From the mid-1780s on, historical novelists began to query sympathy's role in historical narrative, interrogating whether the feelings and manners attached to chivalry deserved veneration and asking if sympathy in historical writing could be redirected, shifted from the aristocracy and monarch to the people. This interrogation of sympathy also led them to probe the meaning of progress and the purpose of government.

In 'Of Tragedy' David Hume remarks that for those of 'another age' the death of King Charles I would be one of the subjects 'regard[ed] as the most pathetic and most interesting, and, by consequence, the most agreeable', although he notes that Lord Clarendon hurries over it.[4] In his *History of England* he himself tries to elicit this sentimental interest for the king's death (although readers' responses suggest a varying degree of success). While Hume suggests that feeling and judgement will operate in tandem in his *History*, his 'sentimental vocabulary evokes interpretive possibilities often discontinuous with the larger political narrative of the *History*'.[5] Alongside Whiggish dislike for Hume's sympathy with King Charles, there was a broader and potentially more radical worry about the distorting effects of such sympathy. In Hume's account, the people mourned the fate of the king. Who mourned the fate of the people?

A related problem lurked in the narratives of stadial history. For stadial historians, whatever their particular differences on the subject, chivalry was 'the foundation of modern manners'.[6] In his *History of Charles V* (1769), for example, William Robertson links chivalry to modern sensibility and compassion. Rejecting the 'wild exploits' of 'romantic knights', he nonetheless speculates:

Perhaps, the humanity which accompanies all the operations of war, the refinements of gallantry, and the point of honour, the three chief circumstances which distinguish modern from ancient manners, may be ascribed in a great measure to this whimsical institution seemingly of little benefit to mankind.[7]

To Robertson the survival of the habits of chivalry into modernity seems desirable (although other stadial historians were less positive). Yet the notion of 'gallantry' was morally troubling, particularly for women writers, whilst the code of 'honour' was in tension with a modernity in which the government would gradually gain the monopoly on violence.[8] The connection between the feudal system and the 'operations of war' also had little appeal for writers like Charlotte Smith, Mary Wollstonecraft or William Godwin, who considered that such conflict served only vested interests.[9]

Veneration for the institution of chivalry and nostalgia for an idealised past could also, as Hurd's 'Addison' hints, obscure the financial suffering of the ordinary people. Once the site of Queen Elizabeth's pageant, the 'floating island' and all the other 'fantastic exhibitions surpassing even the whimsies of the wildest romance', Kenilworth Castle was built on 'the ruins of public freedom and private property'; now, in contrast, Addison boasts, the castle is destroyed and the 'property' of the 'meanest subject' is safe.[10] But the 'poor tenant' who now haunts the only serviceable part of the ruins deserves more attention than even Addison gives him. As historical novelists questioned the relationship between chivalry and sympathy, they began to examine the position of those 'meanest subject[s]' and to increase the numbers and types of people who could be seen as historical participants. This re-examination of sympathy also had an economic dimension, drawing attention to the material circumstances of both the nobility and the poor.

The sense that nostalgia obscures economic and political progress is extended in the 1780s' and 1790s' historical novel, becoming a broader exploration of the consequences of misplaced sympathy in history writing. The shift begins with Sophia Lee's *The Recess,* a historical novel which, like Hurd's dialogue, recalls the pageants of the reign of Queen Elizabeth. Lee's focus is on aristocratic suffering but the alternative narratives she provides draw attention to the economic hardships of the poor. The novel prepares the way for a question that is crucial in the 1790s' historical novel: what kind of history would emerge if the trappings of chivalry no longer inspired either nostalgia or sympathy? This query was closely related to another, made more ominous by the Terror of 1793 to 1794: what would be the attitude of the disadvantaged people to the customs and traditions that had kept them in dependent poverty?

In her *Vindication of the Rights of Men* Wollstonecraft remarks on Edmund Burke's 'pampered sensibility', which, displayed in his *Reflections on the Revolution in France*, leads him to become 'the adorer of the golden image which power has set up'. Were Burke's feelings to be redirected, Wollstonecraft hints, the *'inelegant* distress' of the poor might become more visible to him.[11] While Burke celebrates the hereditary basis of the constitution, Wollstonecraft points out that, even after Magna Carta, in the reign of Richard II, the 'poorer sort' were reduced to 'dreadful extremities', 'their property, the fruit of their industry, being entirely at the disposal of their lords, who were so many petty tyrants'.[12] Repurposing the stadial history that Burke draws upon his *Reflections*, Mary Wollstonecraft (in *An Historical and Moral View*), and Charlotte Smith try to imagine a form of historicised sympathy that could be applied to the people and to government. Godwin's *St Leon: A Tale of the Sixteenth Century* (1799) sensitively interrogates this project, though its date makes it a somewhat unusual work. After the Terror more moderate writers reshaped radical thought on the redistribution of sensibility. As the sense of the present or near past as history strengthens, works like *Charles Dacres, Lioncel,* Maria Edgeworth's 'Madame de Fleury' and Frances Burney's *The Wanderer* probe whether economic and sympathetic circulation can bind the classes together, and interrogate the nature of 'work'.

## Sophia Lee, Liberty and Progress

In his *Remarks on the History of England* Bolingbroke suggests that Queen Elizabeth laid the 'foundations' of 'the riches and power of this kingdom': 'these were some of the means she employed to gain the affections of her subjects. Can we be surprised if she succeeded?' Bolingbroke asks.[13] 'Commerce' allows the circulation of both money and affection and is implicitly linked to 'liberty'. In his contentious *History of England* Hume agrees with the connection between commerce and liberty but contradicts Bolingbroke's choice of reign.[14] Considering late sixteenth-century trade, Hume highlights the destructive effects of 'monopolies' granted by the queen to her servants and courtiers: this 'tended to extinguish all domestic industry'.[15] Moreover, Hume argues in relation to Elizabeth that:

> The prerogatives of this princess were scarcely ever disputed, and she therefore employed these without scruple; Her imperious temper, a circumstance in which she went far beyond her successors, rendered her exertions of power violent and frequent, and discovered the full extent of her authority.[16]

Elizabeth's particular character implicitly acts only as a magnifying device for the underlying nature of the ancient constitution: selfish emotion rather than shared sympathy constricts freedom, confining the benefits of rule to a particular group.

When Sophia Lee wrote *The Recess* she chose to comment on a contested moment in history. The struggle over Elizabeth's reign, particularly in relation to Mary Queen of Scots, was registered in William Sanderson's 1656 *A Complete History*.[17] In the eighteenth century Elizabeth's treatment of Mary became a point of tension between Hume and Robertson (with Robertson more sympathetic to Mary); and eventually infected the reputations of those two historians themselves with a similar controversy.[18] Such proliferating identities find an echo in the multiple narratives of *The Recess*, notably in the contradictory narratives of Matilda and Ellinor, the supposed illegitimate twin daughters of Mary Queen of Scots, but also in the tales of Mrs Marlow, Mary (Matilda's daughter), and Lord Leicester. These narratives compete in the text with Elizabethan attempts at image manipulation, through sentimental portraiture and history painting. Each narrative and image has its own emotional agenda. As narratives jostle, the selfishness and unreliability of Lee's aristocratic protagonists become evident, opening space for other, fainter voices, voices expressing economic hardship and inequality, murmurs of discontent usually considered unsympathetic, unworthy of inclusion in the historical narrative – even Catholic complaints of oppression and dispossession.

If Lee's interest in Enlightenment historiography is well documented, her treatment of sympathy has proved contentious. April Alliston and Jane Elizabeth Lewis suggest that Lee uses sentiment to construct a feminist historiography, but for Cynthia Wall the novel critiques any notion of female sympathy.[19] Such interpretative difficulties can be dispelled when Lee's use of a historically inflected concept of sentiment is placed in the wider context of the historical novel. Unlike previous historical novels, *The Recess* discards the narrative of ancient liberties. Nonetheless, the novel's focus on the reign of Elizabeth signals that this is after all not so much a departure from previous concerns, as a reflection of a debate between ancient constitutionalists and other historians. Rejecting Bolingbroke's portrait of Elizabeth's reign, Lee drew upon newer developments in eighteenth-century historiography, most notably sentimental and stadial history. The developments in sentimental history writing exploited by Lee allow the issues examined by the earlier historical novel to be more fully dramatised in relation to the individual. At the same time, for Lee, feeling itself becomes an awkward category in relation to historical progress. If Jacobite nostalgia is unacceptable, sympathy with the prosperous tyrannies of the past seems at odds with the Whiggish narrative of progress. Lee critiques both Hume's historical sensibility and William Robertson's views on chivalry. In doing so, she breaks with Clara Reeve's view of historical 'romance' as a form which promoted an idealised form of political morality (a 'high sense of virtue' as Barbauld put it).[20] Neither Elizabeth, with her wealth and iconographic displays, nor the twin daughters of Mary Queen of Scots, with their aristocratic connections, are satisfactory subjects for sympathy. Where, then, should it be bestowed? The moral and emotional economies of the past trouble Lee and, in creating this sense of anxiety, she foreshadows radical misgivings about the historically inflected nature of sensibility which emerge during the 1790s.

From the novel's opening pages, Bolingbroke's Elizabethan liberty proves elusive. When Lee's twin heroines, Matilda and Ellinor discover how their mother, Mary Queen of Scots, has been treated, they cease to 'desire' 'liberty'; conversely Mary herself desperately desires freedom only to see hope deferred.[21] Even when liberty is attained, it proves an uncertain good: forced by Elizabeth to marry the odious Lord Arlington, Ellinor celebrates his death with an apostrophe to 'the sweet idea of liberty'. Yet she asks herself: 'to what purpose is mine now restored? I beheld myself in the situation of a criminal, whose shackles are struck off only to launch him into the immense ocean in a little boat without a rudder'.[22] Even when released, the 'criminal' retains his identity as outsider, remaining without affective or financial credit. The emotional terms in which both freedom and isolation are discussed collapse into monetary ones. Alone, liberty is inadequate. In *Representing Elizabeth* (2002) John Watkins proposes that after the early eighteenth century the reign of Elizabeth is pictured as 'bourgeois fantasy' of 'magnificence and excess'.[23] It has no serious political lessons to offer. For Lee, though, the period of Elizabeth's rule still has significance: what is excessive is the queen's use of power. If this is the time when the ancient constitution finds its fullest expression (as Hume suggests), that constitution is inadequate. In addition, there is no suggestion that a recovery of past political practices from another period will aid in constraining monarchical absolutism. 'Deserted before the abolition of Convents', the ruins that become the recess prove a refuge first for monks during the Reformation and then for the sisters.[24] Yet, within, 'light proceeded from small casements of painted glass, so infinitely above our reach that we could never seek a world beyond'.[25] Even adjusted for the individuals they contain, the ruins of the Catholic past, for all Lee's sympathy, distort knowledge.[26] Such structures prove a temporary shelter – no real political solution, no real liberty, is generated by the attempt to escape present oppressions by a return to past practices.

Although Lee rejects ancient constitutionalism, she nonetheless remains wary about the notion of history as progress. While equivocal on the matter of Elizabethan liberties, David Hume also had rejected the Whiggish anti-Stuart position. Instead of seeing the Stuarts as an interruption to the continuity of ancient liberty, in the Stuart volumes of his *History* he wrote, as Karen O'Brien notes, 'a mock-epic reconstruction of the progress of religious and civil liberty', while adopting the 'feeling voice of the sentimental novelist'.[27] Contra Hume, in *The Recess* despite Matilda's hopes, the reign of James does not seem to lead to any further freedoms. Equally, Hume placed emphasis on 'the advancement of industry' and 'commerce': in *The Recess* the Jamaican governor is 'timid, mean, and avaricious', imprisoning Matilda without trial in order to seize her property.[28] Liberty is restricted not only in the centre, but also in the commercial and imperial fringe.

Lee's doubts about commerce stem from the peculiar mode of feeling connected with chivalry. For William Robertson, Adam Ferguson and later even (in his *Lectures on History* [1788]) the radical dissenter Joseph Priestley, chivalry, though irrational, still influenced modern manners. However, Hume was doubtful about its value. The 'pencil of the English poet [Spenser]', he writes, 'was employed in drawing the affectations, and conceits, and fopperies of chivalry, which appear ridiculous as soon as they lose the recommendation of the mode'; only fashion works to underwrite something so apparently effeminate.[29] And while Hume is rather ambiguous here about whether the mode was current even in Elizabeth's reign, Lee is condemnatory. Describing the festivities at Kenilworth, Matilda remarks: 'Elizabeth, in defiance of time and understanding, indulged a romantic taste inconsistent with either . . . the place resounded with panegyrics . . . labored and misapplied . . .'.[30] There is more at stake than Elizabeth's despotic image manipulation. As a source of modern feeling, chivalry is flawed.

The discourse of sympathy is constantly undermined by the language of competition and self-interest commonly found in political economy. When the Duke of Norfolk first sees Mary Queen of Scots, 'ambition' 'raised a flame in his heart, he mistook for love', whilst Mary:

> caught his frenzy, and realized the fictions of his brain with the same facility. His vast estates, numerous vassals, and still more, his extended and noble connections, flattered her with the hope of amply rewarding him, and she thought it but generous to let the recompence [sic] rather precede the service than follow it.[31]

The logic is torturous but still, fundamentally, that of commercial exchange: Mary imagines that Norfolk's possessions (and credit) will finance her speculative attempt to regain her crown. Part payment in advance cannot be in the currency of political power but is tendered through the flesh. As Mary's sexuality stands in for her later expectations, any distinction between the queen's two bodies collapses. Aristocratic and monarchical ownership of labour and the means of production generates an economy in which sensibility is fatally compromised. But although *The Recess* acknowledges that some adjustment of this economy is necessary, the novel's aristocratic focus suggests that change will be limited. Matilda wishes to be restored to her birthright. The chief aim pursued in the narrative is to redistribute sympathy and power to a group already allied to the monarchy.

Yet the text's fragmentary nature, its focus on alternate, competing agendas and its very suspicions about the interested nature of sympathy all suggest a resistant reading. What would the inclusion of different documentary evidence, different histories, reveal? The half-buried narratives of soldiers and slaves suggest the immorality and danger of excluding the worker from economic and sympathetic circulation. Imprisoned in Jamaica, Matilda is ultimately freed by Anana, the governor's mistress, but their textual relationship only lasts while Anana is useful. When Anana 'earnestly' asks Matilda to take her to England, Matilda recoils: 'The state in which she had lived with Don Pedro, supplied an objection at which my pride revolted.' Her objection 'almost instantaneously [gives] way to principle' but Anana conveniently dies.[32] The debt to the colonial other cannot be paid. Instead, death cancels it.

The story of Williams, which is not told by the man himself but emerges out of the narratives of Matilda and Ellinor, warns of the consequences of such aristocratic misconduct. Williams is 'a soldier', 'beyond the meridian of life, his person coarsely made, his complexion swarthy, and his face much scarred'. Nonetheless, Matilda narrates, although Williams is 'marked out thus by nature,' he 'ventured to raise his eyes to the royal, the beautiful Ellinor'. Signs of William's labour, a consequence of original accumulation, are naturalised by Matilda, read as tokens of innate sinfulness. Thus Williams is taxed with the 'insult[ing]' and 'daring boldness' of class transgression: 'Without any emotion or confusion, he pleaded guilty to the charge, but artfully endeavoured to exculpate himself from presumption, by alleging the rank in which we appeared.'[33] To camouflage the boldness of Leicester's speculation (the sisters will help him to greater power), he has disguised the sisters as lower-class musicians: they labour for him, but in a different sphere. Williams's defence is thus accurate (if disingenuous) and it points to a weakness in the contract – Lord Leicester can only ennoble Matilda, making Ellinor a target for further speculation. Williams, in attempting to exploit the situation, is only echoing his lord's conduct and yet Matilda's language criminalises him. Speculation on the part of those without property, or any attempt to gain access to the means of production, is unacceptable.

Williams's subsequent behaviour (he withholds letters from Leicester) in part justifies Matilda's accusations. Nonetheless, his unofficial trial sets off a series of narrative echoes that suggest a concern about inequality, at least in the text's unconscious. Having listened to Matilda's case, Leicester ships Williams off with Sir Francis Drake to fight against the Spaniards, "'send[ing] him," added he, with a gay air, "[off on] a long voyage, to teach him to keep a secret . . . the sailors are taught to consider him a madman, and have neither time"' nor inclination to listen to his tales: as a lower ranking worker, Williams can be labelled mad and hence silenced. Matilda is correct to be 'uneasy' on the subject of this private and arbitrary ruling.[34] It foreshadows her own fate, kidnapped after Leicester's death and carried on a long voyage to Jamaica.

The mistreated Williams also comes to occupy, rather threateningly, the sisters' original hiding place. When Matilda and Leicester fly from Elizabeth, they discover Williams and a troop of banditti in possession of the recess:

> 'You see at last,' cried the exulting villain, 'fortune's wheel has made its circle, and my turn is come, Lord Leicester. – How could you hope to conquer a man whose all was courage? Neither Sir Francis, nor even Elizabeth, could long confine one who dares precipitate himself into the ocean in search of freedom; not,' added he in an ironical tone, 'that I shall fail to requite my obligation to you.'[35]

Although Williams imagines history as cyclical (and thus as something which will facilitate his revenge), his occupation of the recess suggests a process of suppression and potential re-emergence. Like the persecuted monks and the sisters before them, Williams and his fellows adapt the ruins of history. Williams believes that his very lack of access to the means of production (his 'all was courage') renders him particularly difficult to erase – whereas Ellinor bemoans being cast adrift on the ocean like a criminal, Williams has had to overcome, not metaphor, but reality. Lower-ranking determination, born of hardship, leads to the return, not only of the repressed, but of the 'pressed' (those forced to join the navy, whose 'property' is in their 'nervous arms', as Wollstonecraft puts it in *A Vindication of the Rights of Men*).[36] By returning, Williams intends to repay his debt to Leicester through murder, and his debt to society through 'plunder and barbarity'; he will also gain a kind of ultimate control over the financial system by turning 'coiner'.[37] Ellinor suggests that she and her sister at the court of Elizabeth represent a kind of 'illusion', but the 'illusion' the lower-class Williams will construct is even more threatening to the existing social order.

Williams is also imagined as a threat to history writing itself. When Ellinor is taken to the robbers' haunt, she exclaims:

> – that room where once the portraits of our parents smiled peace and security on their now desolate offspring – how hideous was the change! – its bare walls, grimed with a thousand uncouth and frightful images, presented only a faint picture of the present possessors, on whose hardened faces I dare not fix my fearful eyes.[38]

Portraits of Mary Queen of Scots and of the Duke of Norfolk, images of sentimental and historical significance, have been erased, overwritten by the dirty scribbles of the largely anonymous masses. When these masses transform the sheltering spaces of the past, prior to issuing forth on their destructive course, they will not, Lee fears, write in the language of sentiment. The dissolution of historical discourse will accompany the removal of civilisation. What Lee briefly imagines here is change, not as progress, but as chaos.

*The Recess* is often likened both to Abbé Prevost's *Cleveland* (a novel translated into English in 1731) and to Baculard d'Arnaud's *Warbeck* (1774), which Lee had herself translated.[39] Yet its exploration and implicit criticism of the aristocratic politics of feeling distinguishes it from these works. In all three historical romances central figures have to hide in underground chambers or caves for shelter. However, whereas in *Cleveland* the hero has to retreat because of the threatening hypocrisy of lecherous Puritan Cromwell, Lee's focus on the concealment of the daughters of Mary Queen of Scots changes the emphasis from revolutionary to monarchical violence. Lee is moderate in her imaginings: if any power is to be redistributed, it will be from the monarchy to the nobility. Yet these aristocrats, alternative rulers, are also tainted by the corrupt sentimental economy.

*The Recess* was influential. John Whitehouse's *Poems* (1787) includes a sonnet 'To a Lady, with *The Recess, or a Tale of Other Times*', in which 'sensibility' and 'history' combine to produce pity for 'royal Mary's sorrow-faded form'.[40] In a 'postscript' to the Preface to *Plexippus* (1790) Richard Graves, 'saying a word on what are called historical romances' complains of a lady who insists that Mary Queen of Scots had twin daughters by the Duke of Norfolk (Graves's work responds to Lee's novel by having one of its characters hint that in contemporary Britain plebeian birth and a lack of fortune are likely to prove greater barriers to romantic happiness than 'religious bigotry').[41]

By 1797 some of the tropes associated with *The Recess* have become general: 'The Terrorist System of Novel Writing' stresses the importance of subterranean passages and a fearful heroine.[42]

It was not only that the novel's underground corridors and caverns (also foreshadowed by *Otranto*) became common tropes in the expanding form of the historical novel. It was also that such works began, often with far more unequivocal sympathy than *The Recess*, to examine the role of a persecuted aristocracy. Set in the sixteenth century, Rosetta Ballin's *The Statue Room: An Historical Tale* (1790) deals with the fictional daughter (Adelfrida) and granddaughter (Romelia) of Catherine of Aragon. While Ballin's work has little of Lee's critical approach to sentimental economics nor interest in historiographic transmission (even the briefly mentioned Statue Room itself is relatively uninteresting), it retains *The Recess*'s emphasis on Queen Elizabeth's (anti-Catholic) persecutions.[43] The anonymous *Lady Jane Grey: An Historical Tale* (1791) challenges the Catholic sympathies of *The Recess* but is even more effusive on the theme of persecuted aristocratic virtue. When Jane's cousin Anne departs for court, the future queen writes anxiously about how they have been inspired by 'a series of history' with 'a disgust of Courts and Royalty'. She has already learnt the lesson that Mrs Marlowe fails to teach *The Recess*'s Matilda. But whatever 'shiver[s]' of foreboding she feels, her fate is not Prince Edward's nor Princess Elizabeth's fault.[44] The Catholic monarch Queen Mary is treated harshly by the author, while at Jane's execution, the authorities 'dread' 'the compassion of the people'.[45]

Even narratives concerned with ancient liberties begin to take on features associated with Lee's novel. In the anonymous *Edwy* the hero spends a great deal of time in an underground cavern, suggesting his inability to reintegrate himself in the political order and highlighting the sufferings of a displaced aristocracy. Works dealing with the period of King Richard I follow *The Recess* in emphasising the nobility's pain but also suggest the potential for a moral and religious bond between the people and the king. The figure of Richard supposedly represents some at least temporary redemption for the ancient constitution after the Norman invasion and also carries the potential for Christian heroism.[46] Hence, whereas *The Recess* had suggested Elizabeth's tyranny over her Catholic subjects, in the anonymous *Montford Castle: Or the Knight of the White Rose. An Historical Romance* (1795), the author constructs a parallel between the hero's youthful struggle against corrupt priests, and the disputes of Henry II (Richard's father) with Thomas Becket. Tyranny is displaced onto the pre-Reformation church; the monarchy can survive by shifting (anachronistically) towards the reformed Protestant religion.

In the *Children of the Priory* (also set during the Crusades), an increasing number of aristocrats appear from underground. A virtuous nobility, true heirs to power, must re-emerge – only the plurality of candidates suggests the solution's inadequacy.

## Charlotte Smith and the Redistribution of Sensibility

In the historical novel *The Duke of Clarence* (1795), a work influenced by *The Recess*, E. M. Foster portrays a young boy and an elderly nobleman enthralled by 'the histories and atchievements [sic] of great warriors'.[47] But the attractions of militarism and chivalric splendour were less clear to poet and novelist Charlotte Smith. In Smith's early sentimental novel *Ethelinde* (1789), the hero's mother, Mrs Montgomery, describes her search for her husband's body on the battlefield of Minden (1759):

> livid bodies covered with ghastly wounds, from whom the wretches who follow camps, making war more hideous, were yet stripping their bloody garments. Heaps of human beings thus butchered by the hands of their fellow creatures . . . But Montgomery among them, left to be the food of wolves or dogs![48]

In this scene of dismemberment and human detritus (which foreshadows Walter Scott's Douglas larder in *Castle Dangerous* [1831]), exploitation is total. Before the 'wretches' take the soldiers' clothes and the wolves devour their bodies, the monarch steals their labour and their lives. War is clearly a commercial business far removed from dreams of personal honour. Destruction forms part of an ongoing cycle of historical misery. Mrs Montgomery's father dies fighting for Charles Edward Stuart at Culloden; her husband fights on the French side during the Seven Years War. Neither is rewarded. Smith suggests that the 'real miseries' of history remain implicit, unobserved, in favour of improbable fiction.[49] In *Ethelinde* the frivolous Clarinthia claims to read 'a great deal of history' but finds it 'fatiguing enough'. Instead she writes a novel in which her heroine disguises herself with walnut juice and 'a pair of black mustacios', journeying to France where she 'kills two or three men in defence of her lover'.[50] The fantasy of carefree violence overwrites suffering.

Discomfort with chivalric sympathy and its use in history writing were sharpened by the Revolution and more particularly by Edmund Burke's *Reflections on the Revolution in France*. For Burke, in the British context, at least, tradition forms a barrier against destructive revolutionary enthusiasm. However, when Burke considers events in France, he sharpens the narrative of stadial history. Whereas stadial historians had suggested that the chivalric code persisted in the present, Burke's use of chivalric language makes transition far more abrupt: 'the age of chivalry is gone. That of sophisters, economists, and calculators, has succeeded'.[51] Worse still, Marie Antoinette has implicitly been displaced by 'the unutterable abominations of the furies of hell, in the abused shape of the vilest of women' – those women, that is, who went to Versailles ostensibly to complain about the price of bread.[52] Burke's nostalgia for the chivalric past as instantiated in the beauty of Marie Antoinette, and his disregard for the suffering of the ordinary people was not allowed to go unchallenged. In his *Rights of Man* (1791), Thomas Paine argues that such writing has neither 'the sober style of history nor the intention of it'.[53] Burke, Paine argues, should remember he is writing 'History, and not *Plays!*'[54] Paine then rewrites Burke's account of 5 October, de-hyperbolising Burke's language: the 'furies of hell' become 'women, and men disguised as women'.[55] What is called the 'mob', Paine emphasises, exists as a consequence of 'old government' and the inequality it engenders.[56] A new way of interpreting past and present which facilitates a redistribution of sensibility is required.

In *Desmond* Smith attempts this project. The work is a historical novel of the recent past in which Smith tries to correct the way history is read by redirecting the use of sensibility in historical discourse away from the aristocracy towards the lower ranks. She does this in order to change the reader's interpretation of recent events in France, particularly in relation to the forces of counter-revolution. Set between June 1790 and February 1792 and divided between France and Britain, this is in many ways Smith's most uncompromisingly radical novel. Yet critics have been troubled by the work's seeming inconsistency: for all *Desmond*'s pro-revolutionary sympathy, its portrait of Geraldine Verney as dutiful (and perhaps ideal) wife has brought its radical credentials into question. Hence, for example, although Diana Bowstead and Chris Jones find the sentimentality of Smith's romance plot radical, Alison Conway doubts Geraldine's 'real power' and Katharine M. Rogers finds the book's 'central situation' 'drearily conventional, dripping with sentimental distress'.[57] The matter is put most clearly by Eleanor Wikborg, for whom the novel demonstrates that 'the political and the romantic are fundamentally incompatible'.[58] This unease is reproduced in the criticism that treats of *Desmond* as historical novel: hence Tarling concentrates on the political and Lokke on the personal.[59] This apparent tension between the political and the sentimental can be explained when *Desmond*'s historical analysis of chivalric sentiment is taken into account.

Smith underlines the weakness in British historical thinking through Desmond's conversations with the fashionable Miss Fairfax. When Desmond defends the National Assembly's decision to abolish titles by mentioning 'feudal' oppression, Miss Fairfax replies: 'I hope, Sir, I am not ungenerous, nor quite ignorant, neither, of the history of France'.[60] Miss Fairfax's use of the term 'ungenerous' associates her with chivalry but this, Smith suggests, is a distortive lens through which to read history. Miss Fairfax continues:

> I never expected to hear from a man of fashion a defence of an act so shamefully tyrannous and unjust, exercised over their betters by the scum of the people; an act that must destroy all the elegance of manners, all the high polish that used to render people, in a certain style, so delightful in France.[61]

The unexpected intrusion of the category of 'fashion' into the conversation works to expose Miss Fairfax's lack of judgment. The 'elegance' connected to such fashion is questionable. As Karen O'Brien notes, 'For Montesquieu, Hume, Mandeville and even to a limited extent for Burke, a people's manners, even if they are a little frivolous, must be evaluated in the light of their effect upon economic prosperity.'[62] Here the 'elegance of manners', the supposed symbol of affluence, appears rather skin-deep. The reality of chivalry is violent oppression – hence Miss Fairfax's vitriolic (and vulgar) reference to 'scum'.

Smith attempts to correct this reading of history, staging a series of debates between Montfleuri and the Abbé de Bremont, Montfleuri and Desmond, and Desmond and the Comte d'Hauteville. The Abbé suggests that tradition supports the wealth of the higher clergy and the close ties between church and state; Montfleuri, a progressive former aristocrat, maintains that 'Clovis', the first king of the Franks, was converted by the wealth of the church because, 'guilty of horrible enormities', he wished to gain 'the pardon of heaven'. 'In doing so', Montfleuri contends, '. . . [he] certainly did not make a bad bargain for himself; for it cost him only that of which he robbed his subjects.'[63] Rejecting polished manners with economic plain-speaking, Montfleuri also appeals to Protestant feeling. Here, and in conversation with Desmond, he implicitly contrasts Catholic and Protestant forms of religious and spiritual accounting.[64] Instead of the dissenting economy of individual spiritual profit and loss, the Catholic system of indulgences in which money is paid to an intermediate authority (a 'turnpike gate' between man and God as Paine put it in his *Rights of Man*) facilitates cruelty and viciousness in rulers.[65] The church, the monarchy and the nobility combine to commit spiritual and temporal fraud.

Smith then attempts to redirect sympathy away from the suffering aristocracy and senior clergy, to those people Miss Fairfax refers to as 'scum'. She does this by producing what she calls a 'sort of free translation of parts of a little pamphlet', entitled *Histoire d'un malheureux vassal de Bretagne, écrite par lui-même*.[66] In including this narrative, published in Paris in 1790, Smith is adapting Hume's advice in his *Enquiry Concerning Human Understanding* on historical sources – the advice that we trace one 'testimony to another, till we arrive at the eye-witnesses and spectators of these distant events'.[67] The opening section of the narrative (perhaps added by Smith) deals with the Breton's experiences of 'making a campaign or two against the English', whilst the second deals with his experiences as a landowner in the 'fief' of the Baron de Kermanfroi.[68] These, Smith hints, are two experiences of exploitation which stem from the same cause. At home on his estate but barred from fishing or hunting game, the frustrated Breton builds a pigeon-house:

> But alas! the comfortable and retired state of my pigeons attracted the aristocratic envy of those of the same species, who inhabited the spacious manorial dove-cote of Monseigneur; and they were so very unreasonable as to cover, in immense flocks, not only my fields of corn, where they committed infinite depredations, but to surround my farmyard, and monopolize the food . . .[69]

Rather bathetically, the pigeons' aggression suggests the grasping dislike that the upper ranks feel, confronted by bourgeois accumulation. Their depredations and monopolies are a barrier explicitly to self-reproduction but implicitly also to trade. The birds' siege and invasion also implicitly suggests that 'aristocratic envy' lies behind the destructive act of war. All this is allowed by legal '*precedent*' that also (Smith's inclusion of the 'oak' under which the Breton rests implies) threatens Britain; tradition is untrustworthy.[70]

Smith's rereading of the plight of the ordinary people in both the distant and more recent past prepares the reader for another act of decoding. In volumes two and three Smith's references to historical events, particularly the flight to Varennes (June 20/21 1791) are not merely, as Antje Blank and Janet Todd suggest, a 'ruse to lend greater historical realism to her narrative'.[71] Instead, Smith, like Paine, is encouraging a more active and suspicious reading of the events of 1791–2. In his *Rights of Man* Paine complains that: 'Mr Burke has spoken a great deal about plots' but not about 'plots *against* the revolution'.[72] Such plots form the background to Smith's own narrative and are interrogated through it. In a letter from Ross dated 11 June 1791, Desmond writes fearfully of Verney's attempt to force Geraldine to travel to France.

'Verney', he discovers, 'had no intention of meeting his wife at Paris, but was going to Metz with some other French noblemen deeply embarked in the cause, whatever it is, that now engages their intriguing spirit.'[73] Verney is involved in a counter-revolutionary conspiracy to extract the king from France. His politics mirror his own unforgivable domestic despotism. Meanwhile, even after the king's escape attempt fails and he is brought back to Paris a de facto prisoner of the National Assembly, Smith continues to focus on Geraldine's plight. Sympathy should be felt for the ordinary people rather than the monarch or his supporters.

Smith also warns against what she sees as the historical tendency to blame victims, not persecutors. Major Danby, for example, blames the 'troublesome, mutinous' dissenters for the 'riots that happened in July at Birmingham'. Bethel contradicts him: 'it was not the dissenters that rioted there!' – in fact it was a church and king mob that burned the houses of prominent dissenters in July 1791.[74] Similarly, when Geraldine travels across the tumultuous landscape of southern France, the banditti she encounters in her journey are not, after all, revolutionaries, as might be supposed, but aristocratic hirelings. In *The French Revolution* (2001) Georges Lefebvre suggests that the counter-revolution acted as provocation to the revolutionaries when he discusses the events of October and November 1791:

> aristocrats and refractory priests were more active than ever: in August they had provoked disturbances in the Vendee ... At Avignon on October 16, 1791, they killed the mayor, Lescuyer, and the Patriots avenged his death by a massacre at the Glacière.[75]

Although we hear reports of Verney's injury as early as 1 October, his location in Avignon indicates that he has acted as provocateur. When he dies as a result, justice has been done both personally and politically.

In tracing Geraldine's experiences during the Revolution, Smith is not merely intertwining the domestic and the political. Rather, in this stadially influenced account, she links the mode of government, the economic structures and the manners of a society. In Part II of *The Rights of Man* (1792) Paine comments on the features of hereditary government:

> Can we then be surprised at the abject state of the human kind in monarchical countries, when the government itself is formed on such an abject levelling system? It has no fixed character ... It changes with the temper of every succeeding individual ... It is government through the medium of passions and accidents.[76]

This 'variety' is the source of Verney's aristocratic volatility; it is exemplified by the suitably named Waverly. Even Desmond, with his radical political credentials, is implicated. His gothic dream at the chateau of the Comte; his decision to disguise himself as a monk; and his excitement regarding his ultimate ownership of Geraldine all indicate the pervasive corruption of chivalry. No wonder commentators have found Desmond's sentiment and Geraldine's obedience difficult to stomach: both are operating from within the system, even as they desire to change it.

Ironically, even Smith herself is infected. The novel contains an unconvincing vision of cooperation between the upper and lower ranks. On his estates, the model landlord Montfleuri ensures the circulation of sympathy between the classes. He:

> has therefore, whether he had resided here or no, made it the business of his life to make his vassal and dependents content, by giving them all the advantages their condition will allow ... the peasantry in this domain resemble both in their own appearance, and in the comfortable look of their habitations, those whose lot has fallen in those villages of England, where, the advantages of a good landlord ... enable the labourers to possess something more than the mere necessaries of life.[77]

A footnote inserted at this point by Smith undercuts this praise of England by lamenting the situation of those 'who ha[ve] only [their] own labour to depend on'; she is particularly concerned by an alienated labour further problematised by wages too low to allow self-reproduction. What we might further note about Montfleuri's ideal 'landlord[ism]' is that while feeling circulates freely, the benefits of property seem to flow in only one direction – from the landlord to the workers. There is no admission that upper-class wealth relies on the labour of those on their estates.

In Smith's *Desmond*, a kind of excess of imagination leads to a love for the 'baubles' of rank.[78] This veneration generates a misreading of history, which in turn causes inability to interpret the present accurately. Smith urges a rereading of both past and present, a rereading that hangs on the interrogation of custom, the analysis of cause and effect and, above all, the examination of experience. What this rereading generates is an acknowledgement of suffering. This in turn reveals the pernicious nature of the counter-revolution. The status quo is hard to escape but, in emphasising the possibility of reinterpretation, *Desmond* is still fundamentally optimistic.

Smith's next work, *The Old Manor House* (1793) is less so. For some time positioned as Smith's only historical novel, *The Old Manor House*'s structure foreshadows Scott's Waverley Novels. For the first two volumes of the novel, the hero, Orlando, waits at home, uncertain heir to ancestral estates. After experiencing the iniquities and injustice of the American War of Independence, he returns to an England filled with the lower ranks and, in Burke's words, with 'sophisters, oeconomists and calculators'; breakage has taken place.[79] It is not, though, the revolution that has generated this breakage. Instead, the old aristocratic order, represented by Mrs Rayland, owner of the estate, has retained power too long, failing to allow proper modernisation. The next generation of nobles either believe that the role involves heartless, egotistical luxury, or, like Orlando, have inappropriately chivalric notions of war. Neither attitude encourages progress. Despite this, like Harry Bertram in *Guy Mannering* (1815), Orlando ultimately regains the estate, combining ancient and modern. In *The Old Manor House* only the generic conventions of romance save the day. *Desmond* advised the interrogation of the past in order to understand the present yet in *The Old Manor House* the aristocracy remain as historically naïve as ever. Revolutionary rereading has not taken place.

## Rereading Radical History: Godwin's *St Leon*

Although as early as 1941 Florence Hilbish argued that Wollstonecraft's historical work 'may have gained some influences from Mrs Smith', the similar historiographical approach taken by the two writers has been little remarked.[80] Like Smith's *Desmond*, Wollstonecraft's *An Historical and Moral View* rereads history in order to redistribute sensibility, revealing that government should exist for the benefit of the people. Reclaiming stadial history from Burke, Wollstonecraft argues that after the conflict of the savage state, 'social systems' were formed by those wishing to 'fence round their wealth and power'.[81] The descendants of these conquerors maintain their authority by the 'fraud of partial laws', backed by factious concepts of virtue and duty, by religious and courtly shows and even by war itself. True progress, Wollstonecraft insists, reverses this fraud: government exists for the happiness of the many rather than the few. In spreading this understanding the political education of the 'mass[es]' is key – sympathy must be extended beyond the family to the human race.

In her 'Advertisement' Wollstonecraft notes how she has 'mark[ed] the political effects that naturally flow from the progress of knowledge'.[82] For Wollstonecraft, this 'progress' depends on the spread of 'science', which includes 'astronomy', 'mathematics' and 'printing' (crucial because it allows dissemination of knowledge) but also politics itself – a science linked to history since history allows 'demonstration'.[83] However, for

Wollstonecraft this is a difficult process, in which the frauds of chivalry and government are not the only obstacles. Wollstonecraft's work contains a critique of theatricality and even of fiction itself. While science allows the 'calm' development of understanding so that the 'heart imperceptibly becomes indulgent', 'artists have commonly irritable tempers', 'inflaming their passions as they warm their fancy'.[84]

Wollstonecraft's influence upon her husband, William Godwin, and in particular upon his 1799 work *St Leon: A Tale of the Sixteenth Century*, has been noted.[85] Not only does St Leon's reaction to his wife's demise rework Godwin's own feelings on the death of Mary Wollstonecraft, but Godwin also takes occasion to note that his marriage has modified his earlier stance on sensibility. Suspicious of sympathy in the first edition of *An Enquiry Concerning Political Justice* (1793), Godwin now, according to *St Leon*'s preface, celebrates the 'affections and charities' of private life, which may even, under certain circumstances, render a man 'more prompt in the service of strangers and the public'.[86] But the novel is ultimately less optimistic than this implies. As part of his process of constant self-revision, Godwin had in fact added to the 1798 edition of the *Enquiry* the suggestion that 'the voluntary actions of men are under the direction of their feelings'.[87] But if feeling, *not* reason, stimulates action, it remains an unreliable motivator. *St Leon* attempts to work through the awkward operations of sympathy as an historical force. Taking chivalric feeling as its starting point as Smith's *Desmond* had done, the novel responds to Wollstonecraft's suspicions of inflamed passions as much as to her positivity. If reason is, as the 1798 *Enquiry* suggests, 'a comparison and balancing of different feelings', *St Leon* encourages this comparative process against those 'pernicious' 'institutions calculated to give perpetuity to any particular mode of thinking'.[88]

Whilst *Things as They are; Or, the Adventures of Caleb Williams* is often positioned as the fictional counterpart of *Political Justice*, the dialogue between Godwin's *The Enquirer* (1797) and *St Leon* has been less remarked, possibly because the relationship is (as befits the essayistic musings of *The Enquirer*) somewhat more tangential. Nonetheless, the concerns with 'awakening the mind' in the first part of Godwin's series of essays, and with 'riches and poverty' in the second part, are echoed in the initial volume of *St Leon*. There is also a methodological similarity: the episodic nature of Godwin's 1799 novel corresponds to the model of 'experiment and actual observation' set out in the Preface to *The Enquirer*.[89] *St Leon* repeatedly foregrounds the idea of experiment.[90] Experiencing the roles of chivalric aristocrat, soldier and gambler, its hero descends to farmer and eventually to day labourer. These first-hand experiences prepare him to accept the stranger's secret and the philosopher's stone, gaining infinite resources, immortality and a distance from humanity which is unfortunate but in some ways rationally appropriate. As a first-person narrator St Leon is able to see the 'minute and near' in the way *The Enquirer* suggests is necessary but he also gains perspective.[91] Suffering under various economic and social systems, he shifts from scientific experiment to social observation and intervention: history itself becomes his laboratory.

*St Leon* also problematises the possibility of such experimental intervention. The difficulty is that St Leon is not neutral but has been shaped by historical forces. His flawed first-person narration allows Godwin sensitively to psychologise the difficulties involved in achieving genuine progress. At the same time it tries to remove the barriers to change that operate in the reader's mind, subverting the generic expectations of both romance and novel to do so. Freed from fictional convention, the reader is encouraged to turn experimenter and to re-evaluate the relationship between the individual and society himself. In this attempt to solve the structural problems of sympathy, historical fiction, it becomes evident, is key. Historical fiction allows the experimenter to enjoy 'the collision of mind with mind' without experiencing any of the dangerously persuasive effects of rhetoric or sympathetic contamination by the mob.[92]

Like *St Leon*, *The Enquirer* highlights the difficulty of bringing about beneficial change. Particularly in those essays concerned with common ideas of virtue and the uncertainty of personal reputation, Godwin explores the obstacles to constructing the better personal morality essential for social development. The problem is not only one of convincing others about the nature of virtue but also of altering our own selves. Historical writing suffers from this adhesive tendency: times change but, Godwin maintains, controversies remain the same. The struggle over the relative merits of Queen Elizabeth and Mary Queen of Scots (complete with ridiculous 'gallantry'), the 'eternal contention' over the character of King Charles I and the inaccurate, hostile perceptions of Bolingbroke's career all persist.[93] Along with religious and cultural discourses, history can be understood in terms of inertia as much as breakage. This point is reinforced in 'Of History and Romance', intended to be part of a sequel to *The Enquirer* but never published in Godwin's lifetime. There, Godwin suggests that an inquiry into man's 'progress from the savage to the civilised state' is best undertaken through the history of a (potentially fictional) individual.[94] However, he also emphasises that the 'march' of progress is 'slow' where modern history is concerned.[95]

In *St Leon* this sense of inertia is dramatised by the narrator himself. Like modern history, he is 'encumbered with . . . rank', with 'prejudices and precedents'.[96] Early on, for instance, St Leon indicates that: 'The immediate application of political liberty is, to render a man's patrimony or the fruits of his industry completely his own, and to preserve them from the invasion of others.'[97] This idea of political liberty (albeit reductive) corresponds with the novel's exploration of economic inequality and with St Leon's attempts in the last part of the book to alleviate Hungarian suffering. Yet despite the fact that St Leon, relating events retrospectively, has already made this benevolent attempt, he seems to have forgotten what he has learnt. Instead of championing such liberty, he insists that such 'petty detail of preservation or gradual acquisition' is less important than the 'great secret' of the philosopher's stone which 'endow[s] a man in a moment with everything that the human heart can wish'; he says this despite the torment and isolation that the stone has caused him.[98] Although Godwin's habit of sending the sheets of the manuscript to the printer as soon as each were completed might explain this inconsistency, an examination of the narrative yields two plausible causes for St Leon's stubborn desire for the alchemist's gifts: he continues to desire wealth both because of the hubris of his chivalric upbringing and because of a deep-seated fear of poverty, implanted when he sees his children starve.[99] Habit and suffering prevent the individual learning. Although Godwin comments on the mutability of character in *Political Justice*, St Leon's fixity here signals a process of historical accretion which impedes social development.[100] Titian's supposed portrait of the unchanging 'Signor Gualdi', introduced in a prefatory anecdote, underlines this historical difficulty. If the unchanging picture represents the detachment of the alchemist (or radical philosopher) who is outside systems of financial 'exchange', it also indicates the individual's resistance to alteration.[101]

The historical processes which retard St Leon's development are visible in society at large. Even at its height, chivalry is a dubious institution. When St Leon describes the Field of the Cloth of Gold, the 'costliness of dress' and the 'amphitheatre of spectators' are warning signs to a reader familiar with the *Historical and Moral View*: the emphasis is on the display of power.[102] Moreover, while Godwin's narrator follows stadial history in linking chivalry with refinement, like Wollstonecraft, Godwin doubts the efficacy of 'polish'. Chivalry worsens the suffering caused by inequalities of age and wealth and generates 'carnage'.[103] And although the novel foregrounds a stadial model of history, highlighting change, it also suggests such old, bad habits linger. After the Siege of Pavia, Godwin's narrator asserts the decline of the 'reign of chivalry' and its replacement by the reign of 'craft, dissimulation, corruption and commerce'.[104] Godwin is not, however, indulging in a moment of feudal nostalgia but complicating Burke's narrative of transition. It is King

Francis who 'bartered' his 'enterprising and audacious temper ... for the wary and phlegmatic system of his more fortunate competitor'.[105] Instead of the revolutionaries ushering in the new age of 'sophistry, economy and calculation', in *St Leon*, as in *Desmond*, the monarchy and aristocracy are responsible.

The chivalric desire for personal greatness survives, shaping aristo-cratic rule even in a more commercial age. This, I contend, is the true significance of St Leon's obsession with gambling. In *Enlightenment and the Shadows of Chance* (1993) Thomas Kavanagh argues that aristocratic gambling formed a way of coping with the change in status and role brought about by the new economy.[106] At the same time, it is worth noting that gambling represents a type of participation in that economy. In the first stage of St Leon's gambling career, his philosophic detachment underlines his participation in a form of pure speculation, an extreme form in which necessity does not play a part. The second phase (in which he plays even more intensely) highlights the social cost of entering into this cycle of boom and bust. As St Leon loses his estate on the throw of a dice, the fluctuations in Waverly's behaviour and the uncertainties faced by *Desmond*'s peasants under the *ancien régime* reverberate. Chivalric hubris generates economic instability.

In *The Enquirer* Godwin argues that 'one of the best [practical rules of morality] ... is that of putting ourselves in the place of another'.[107] This ability is worryingly absent in those, like St Leon, who have a chivalric fixation on personal greatness. However, in charting the two stages of St Leon's fall to poverty Godwin creates the necessary empathetic space, guiding the reader to sympathise not with the nobility but with the poor. When St Leon gambles away what he describes as his 'all' and is left with a 'miserable pittance', Marguerite can still (surprisingly) purchase 'a small, obscure but neat, cottage' with enough land to support all the family in the Swiss canton of 'Soleure'.[108] Here Godwin adapts the convention of the displaced aristocrat familiar from gothic and histori-cal novels. In narratives like *The Castle of Otranto* or *The Old English Baron*, displacement (often through usurpation) usually happens before the narrative begins; the (virtuous) aristocrat is rarely to blame; the story proceeds with little attention to economic minutiae; and the reader is trained to desire aristocratic restitution to power. Disturbing generic expectations, Godwin demands a far greater focus on the economic than is usually called for in romance. Since St Leon still owns the means of production, his portrait of his 'poverty', 'strip[ped]' of all his 'earthly fortune' by 'wretches' (debtors) appears overstrained.[109] In addition, through sickness and 'sullen' detachment, St Leon produces his former aristocratic status in miniature, continuing to exploit the labour of others even on the farm.[110] Although Godwin admits in his *Memoirs* that the 'change from one state to another' is more painful than poverty, here St Leon's emerging sense of self-disgust eventually alerts the reader that identification with aristocratic egotism is not the correct response.[111]

Marguerite's position, so attractive at first, is also problematised. The idea of retreat to a kind of rural Eden so important to Jean-Jacques Rousseau and repeatedly reworked by Charlotte Smith (in *Ethelinde*, for example, the Montgomerys withdraw to the Lake District), is here inflected in a particular Godwinian way.[112] When Marguerite suggests that 'the moderate man is the only free' individual and argues that whoever reduces others to 'a state of servitude' also imprisons himself, she echoes Godwin's arguments in *The Enquirer*.[113] While 'the pains [the spendthrift] suffers in himself are the obvious counterparts of the pain he inflicts on others', Godwin had suggested, the man who lives up to his fortune equally only manages to multiply the misery of labour.[114] In contrast, peasants, who farm their own land to subsist, Marguerite argues, are, 'comparatively more secure than any other large masses of men'.[115] She will add to their independence, 'a larger stock of ideas, and a wider field of activity': intellectual and aesthetic pleasures grafted onto self-sufficiency will, she proposes, lead to 'love of mankind' and behaviour for the 'public benefit'. As for Wollstonecraft, education is vital. Yet the economic independence on which this vision relies proves precarious. In the Marquis de Sade's *Misfortunes of Virtue* (1791) the virtuous heroine, Justine, is killed by lightening, underlining nature's moral indifference. Recalling that event, the hailstorm in *St Leon* devastates the crops, causing the absence of 'supply' and irksome inflation.[116] In this second stage of more absolute hardship, the audience's sympathy with the aristocrat is transformed into the reader's identification with the poor. From this understanding of precarity, it is harder to argue poverty is itself a form or indicator of immorality. It is notable that the satire *St Godwin* (1800) strips out the chivalric context that allows this sympathy to develop, emphasising only the debasement of poverty.

Having suggested the importance of moderation, Godwin is keen to prevent the reader repeating St Leon's mistake and avidly desiring wealth at all costs. After St Leon acquires the philosopher's stone, his isolation suggests that wealth alone is not sufficient, a point underlined by the episode of the honest jailor. Imprisoned, St Leon attempts the 'experiment' of bribery but Hector resists his importunities.[117] This poor man emphasises that 'justice' and his 'contract' with his superior are more important than money: both allow independence.[118] What he most desires, though, is a sympathetic bond with his employer – a bond that requires virtue. For Godwin, liberty is more than the negative of the removal of certain constraints. Rather, it involves being a fully actualised individual. For this it is necessary to be able to feel and exchange appropriate sympathy. Yet the rest of the book demonstrates that virtuous feeling is hard to sustain. Superstition, religious intolerance, nationalism (and the violence and war these generate in each social stage) are all caused by inappropriate affect.

The problem is that any 'little platoon' (to borrow Burke's phrase) has boundaries.[119] St Leon's indifference after the hailstorm to all but his own family foreshadows this point, which is also evident when the enlightened Swiss cantons refuse aid to outsiders. But the key trope for distorted sympathy is the crowd. When the Catholic 'populace' attack St Leon he attempts to reason with them, but this 'last experiment upon the power of firmness and innocence to control the madness of infuriated superstition' fails.[120] The 'noisy and clamorous mob' is hardly 'a proper subject upon which to make the experiment of the energy of truth', as the politically enlightened Marchese Filosanto points out.[121] Through his historical narrative, Godwin argues that extreme emotion, directed against those outside the community, prevents the more extensive use of individual feeling and 'reason' on the behalf of mankind. Larger imperial projects and greater religious differences only increase the problem, as the situation of war-torn Hungary, caught between Catholic West and Muslim East, and the hubris of Ferdinand and Solyman, exemplifies. Godwin has identified the kind of bootstrap problem familiar to Romantic reformist thinkers (including Wollstonecraft herself). A particular kind of sympathy – general benevolence without boundaries – is necessary for poverty and economic inequality to end, and yet that very inequality retards its emergence.

The extension of political and social knowledge throughout society may, as Wollstonecraft suggests, be desirable. However, the irrational mob or (as Godwin sees them) the equally dangerous sympathetic community of the nation or the church cannot facilitate this process. How is an improved political consciousness to spread? Here it should be remembered that the book itself is St Leon's final experiment. The novel's true importance lies in its attempt to draw the reader into the process of experiment and reflection. Marguerite's emphasis on the power of education corresponds with Godwin's radical educational vision at the beginning of *The Enquirer*. For Godwin the 'first lesson' is to 'Learn to think, to discriminate, to remember and to enquire.'[122] As the very existence of *The Enquirer* suggests, even though the mind gradually hardens, this educational process can be performed in adulthood. *St Leon* attempts to stimulate this process in a mature readership.

The importance of historical fiction as a vehicle for this endeavour is outlined in 'Of History and Romance'. There, Godwin contrasts the stadial enquiry into the development of the mass of mankind with the attempt to give the history of an individual. Godwin argues that studying the life of an individual is not only an extension of the 'solemn' dissenting duty of self-examination but that it also allows the examination of the 'machine of society'.[123] In other words, it performs the function of stadial history. It also improves upon it. Allowing the enquirer to 'scrutinise the nature of man' and to discover what 'social man is capable' of when confronted with large social and historical forces, this approach will 'add, to the knowledge of the past, a sagacity that can penetrate into the depths of futurity'.[124] As Godwin pursues his argument, it becomes evident that an even better vehicle for this project is historical 'romance', a form which adds greater psychological verisimilitude to the fictionality of history.[125] By examining the intersection of great social forces with great 'genius', historical fiction, even more than the individual history Godwin initially proposes, will enable the reader to 'judge truly of such conjectures and combinations . . . as, though they had never yet occurred, are within the capacities of our nature'.[126] What Godwin has done (even if the final paragraph of the essay represents a retraction) is to theorise a historical novel without any sense of inevitability. Such a work, concentrating on the rights of man, will allow the creation of a future that is more than the repetition of past events.[127]

With this combination of the stadial and the individual, *St Leon* is clearly the project that lays the groundwork for Godwin's suggestions in 'Of History and Romance'. However, it is also clear that the novel is a grander experiment than the casual reader of that essay might suspect. In 'Of History and Romance' it seems that 'the development of great genius' is one of the factors that introduces unpredictability into the operation of mass historical forces.[128] In *The Enquirer* Godwin suggests that 'genius' can be produced by 'learning to think, to discriminate and remember'; genius is not innate and can be produced anywhere.[129] The reflective processes of *St Leon* are an attempt to cultivate this 'genius' in its readers. Providing an education in political liberty, Godwin guides the emotional and intellectual responses of his audience to sympathise with poverty without seeing wealth as its corrective and to understand the terror and isolation generated by the hoarding of sympathy. In Godwin's account, although persecution persists, the progress from self-examination to social rationality that began in the Reformation (the background to *St Leon*) and that was promoted by the religious and political dissent of the 1790s, will now be driven forward by the reader's reflection.[130] Unlike members of the mob or nation, the individual reader is isolated, capable of both feeling and reason. Yet he is also part of the wider community of the reading public. Even if *St Leon* is, as Collings suggests, 'a book of the impossible', Godwin's anarchist vision of fiction as vehicle for social change is a powerful one.[131] Addressing each member of the mass individually, (historical) fiction becomes a key mechanism in the construction of social rationality.

## History at Work

In *The Enquirer* Godwin notes that the 'children of peasants' have the 'promise of understanding' and 'quickness of observation' that can lead to the socially transformative quality of genius.[132] These qualities are trained out of them when they 'are enlisted at the crimping-house of oppression' and 'brutified by immoderate and unintermitted labour'.[133] Although Godwin's attention to work as an obstacle to sympathy and social progress is unusual, his focus on the pains and poverty of labour is part of a larger trend. During the eighteenth century bread riots had been a common occurrence in France.[134] But the events of 1789–94, particularly the Terror (5 September 1793 to 28 July 1794), suggested such outbursts of popular resentment could have far-reaching consequences when combined with a growing national debt, unequal taxation and a growing and radicalised political class.[135] Wariness concerning the prospect of mass political activity led historical novelists concerned with social stability to examine the lot of the ordinary worker – and the potentially brutal nature of work itself.

The link between hardship, labour and revolution was, for instance, felt by Ellis Cornelia Knight – her very determination to separate the issue of suffering and that of unrest in her 1792 *Marcus Flaminius* suggests as much. In the first volume, after the Battle of Teutoburg Forest (CE 9), Germania strangely becomes the scene of the French Revolution. The Cheruscans are driven by idleness and effeminacy to drive away 'the few chiefs who would not consent to their determination in favour of universal equality'.[136] It is only when Knight deals with Rome in the second volume that she touches upon the hardship experienced by Roman slaves. Even then, involved in aristocratic political plots, these unfortunate individuals remain largely unsympathetic. Knight refuses to suggest that hunger and poor working conditions might generate popular political activity. The anonymous writer of *Montford Castle*, on the other hand, supplies a reminder (missing even in Smith's *Desmond*) about the dependence of the upper ranks upon the lower. As the subversively named and remorselessly prosaic servant Launcelot exclaims to his aristocratic master: 'directly you refused poor Sir Walter's honest lad's assistance, a judgement overtook you. D'ye think if he had been with you, you would have had to wander in the woods two days without a bit to eat?'[137] Rescued repeatedly by the lower ranks, Edmund should know that, without a squire his 'prowess, [his] abilities, [his] this and t'other' are 'as of as little use . . . as a boot without a sole'.[138] Loyal workers like Launcelot sustain the system and are entitled to their minor insolences.

Influenced by *The Recess* but also, and more directly, by *Caleb Williams*, the author of *Montford Castle* also raises the possibility of an alternative social space outside such conventional class tensions. Escaping the castle through a tunnel, the novel's hero joins a woodland community of banditti, which consists of Normans, Saxons, 'ancient Britons, whom even the Welch mountains have not been able to shelter from persecution', Irish, Scots, Germans, Frenchmen: 'in short most of the countries of Europe have contributed by the chance of war, or by ecclesiastical or civil persecutions, to increase our community'.[139] No 'distinctions' are preserved, the regulations are 'few, equitable, and easily observed'. Significantly, when factions occur within the group, instead of general warfare and bloodshed, the rival leaders themselves fight it out. These 'freebooters' are, the narrator unconvincingly claims, symptomatic of '*the Age of Chivalry*', temporarily governing themselves by their own notions quite successfully.[140] As Godwin had done when he praised 'historical romance' in his essay 'Of History', the writer of *Montford Castle* reclaims romance, making it something more radical than it was for Clara Reeve.

Interclass cooperation also preoccupies Ann Yearsley in *The Royal Captives*. A labouring poet (styled 'Lactilla') with a troubled relationship to her own patron, Hannnah More, Yearsley had already written a radical drama focusing on ancient liberties, *Earl Goodwin* (1791).[141] In her novel Yearsley evokes the Shandyian sentimental tradition to suggest the need for cross-rank solidarity. When, for instance, the mistreated brother of King Louis IV of France is succoured by a fearful fisherman, he reflects: 'man is only amiable when impressed by the influence of social love. I banished his dismay, and he procured me food'.[142] After the nobility acknowledges its reliance upon such prosaic help, sympathy between the ranks becomes possible. Henry, the protagonist, suggests that man makes 'a progress towards perfection' only when he feels, 'Harmony within, arising from the gentler passions of his Nature': such sympathy is vital for social and individual advancement.[143] Yearsley also supports workers' education, with the figure of Anna, who labours in the day and studies, 'meditate[s]'and 'mourn[s]' at night. No wonder

Horace Walpole disapproved of Yearsley's suggestion that she had been inspired by *Otranto*.[144]

Some of the most significant explorations of work and the worker emerge through historical novels of the recent past. As I have discussed elsewhere, these works were themselves generated by the acute sense of the present as history that came out of the French Revolution.[145] This sense is felt, for instance, in *Charles Dacre: Or, the Voluntary Exile. An Historical Novel, Founded on Facts* (1797), where the anonymous author dwells at considerable length on the historical nature of his novel, suggesting that the idea of the present as history emerges from the Revolution's impact upon citizens from merchants to 'poetasters'.[146] Similarly, the author of *Lioncel; Or, the Emigrant: An Historical Novel. Trans. By Louis de Bruno, a Native of the Banks of the Ganges* (1803) depicts the Revolution as a block on social sympathy performed by corrupt aristocrats in collusion with envious workers. These Jacobinical individuals, who disrupt and pervert labour and government, are opposed by the aristocratic hero and those workers (surgeons, ironmongers, soldiers) willing to aid benign members of the ruling orders. As the workers labour, circulation of sentiment substitutes for the circulation of wealth (a problem which is never addressed).

One of the most thoroughgoing reimaginings of work and the worker is Maria Edgeworth's 'Madame de Fleury', an apparently simplistically didactic story that was part of the first series of *Tales of Fashionable Life*. Like Louis de Bruno, Edgeworth opposes the corrupt relation between aristocracy and envious worker with the beneficial social ties that she believes possible when gratitude is felt between the ranks. Madame de Fleury establishes a school for the working poor, including the virtuous Victoire, and is eventually rewarded when the children hide her from revolutionary soldiers. However, *The Critical Review* described 'Madame de Fleury' as 'of inferior merit' to *Ennui* (1809). While the *Quarterly Review* suggested in 1809 that the narrative was based on a rare and comparatively unlikely circumstance, in 1812 *The London Quarterly Review* argued that many of Edgeworth's works were marked by a similar fault.[147]

For all the unlikely moralism of the tale, Edgeworth's lesson extends beyond supplying 'several minute practical lessons to charitable females of rank, who undertake to superintend the education of the children of the poor'.[148] With her stadial emphasis on the need for economic progress, Edgeworth proposes work as a corrective to the dangers of a class relation based on luxurious display. However, it must be the right kind of work. When, before the Revolution, Madame de Fleury, helps the children of a 'workwoman' who has been forced to leave them alone in order to make a living wage, she rescues them from both idleness and danger.[149] Persuaded of the benefits of a habit of labour, Madame de Fleury ensures the children will learn 'knitting and plain work, reading, writing and arithmetic', as well as other domestic skills.[150] And when her protégée, Victoire, writes a poem to her benefactress, Madame de Fleury thinks that to encourage her 'to become a mere rhyming scribbler, without any chance of obtaining celebrity or securing subsistence, would be folly and cruelty'.[151] In this society poetry is a dubious product. With little direct utility, it is subject to the fluctuations of a high-end market. As this is an area in which the whims of fashion may count for more than talent, the poet may come to require a negative form of patronage based on personality rather than skill. However, Madame de Fleury's pupils avoid such perils: Victoire becomes apprentice to a lace-maker, Rose to a mantua-maker and Susanne to a confectioner. Whilst the society Edgeworth imagines will, it seems, still have its minor indulgences, such treats have a solidity that poetry lacks: Victoire's labour is productive and its success is dependent on the market rather than on individual favour. There is no acknowledgement here that such markets can fluctuate. Instead, properly managed, they allow financial and sympathetic exchange.

The emotional extremes of admiration and disgust, of the sublime of kingship and the sublime of the mob, presented by Burke in the *Reflections*, are, Edgeworth suggests, unnecessary, only generated by inappropriate relations between the classes. Her point is underlined by the story of Manon, who is taken in by a 'rich lady' to live in the family house as a 'sort of humble playfellow for her children'.[152] 'Humble' rather than independent, taught only 'accomplishments', she is associated with the superficiality and vanity of fashion. She does not produce physical goods; she merely crafts appearance.[153] Eventually she steals her employer's 'snuff box' and later, at Victoire's school, lies about the amount of cotton she has wound. Yet Edgeworth is not making the familiar point that luxury generates dishonesty; rather, Manon's training is at fault. Edgeworth constructs a parallel between Manon's behaviour and that of her lover, a former hairdresser. The profession is also singled out for obloquy in Elizabeth Hamilton's *Memoirs of Modern Philosophers* (1800) where Vallaton, a hairdresser is a revolutionary who claims (bogus) aristocratic origins. Closely associated (like the wig-makers who had in fact found their trade crippled by the Revolution) with the culture of courtly extravagance, after the Revolution such personal servants became a symbol of revolutionary discontent, used by counter-revolutionaries to taint the new regime with the corruption of the old. Edgeworth adds to this by making her hairdresser a dealer in the *assignat*, the French Revolutionary currency. As Rudé notes, October 1791 to June 1793 was 'a period of rising prices and depreciating paper money'; the 'inflationary movement is reflecting in the heavy depreciation of the *assignat*; from a level of 82 per cent of its normal value . . . in November 1791 it declined to 36 per cent in June 1793'.[154] The shaper of appearances speculates financially and politically. Thus, in this account, the selfishness, the fascination with appearance, and the unreality which were associated with the *ancien régime* become features of the Revolution.

Edgeworth's 'Madame de Fleury' comes close to suggesting how economic forces can shape the individual's fate. Yet its moral dimension is in tension with this. When Edgeworth effectively punishes Manon for her habits of non-production, she comes close to suggesting that the worker can, as a result of poor choice of occupation, be held responsible for revolution. Frances Burney's last novel, *The Wanderer*, may be read as a response to such a critique. Begun in the 1790s but only published in 1814, *The Wanderer* is sometimes referred to as an 'historical novel of the recent past'.[155] Setting her novel during the Revolution's most violent phase, Burney is certainly aware of the sense of disjunction or 'metamorphosis' it caused – as her revolutionary convert Elinor Joddrel expresses it, society, it seemed, was to be 'new modelled'.[156] This crisis, Burney suggests, needs to be tackled by restoring a particular sense of history: historical progress is not a matter of abrupt breakage between past and present but should be of gradual growth. Yet Burney's arguments, informed by stadial history, are complicated by her analysis of work. Burney critiques the notion that there are economically good and bad forms of work, querying the notions of independence, choice and moral agency as they apply to workers. As Burney analyses labour, she also evokes and undercuts the notion of historical progress through social stages that Elinor invokes with confidence earlier in the novel. For Burney, whose depression and anxiety in relation to her own employment at the court between 1786 and 1791 is recorded in her journal, it is not the choice of occupation but the nature of labour itself – in all its forms – that causes suffering, difficulty, and discontent.[157] Notably, it was during this period that she turned to writing historical drama: *Edwy and Elgiva*, for instance, suggests that she viewed exploitation, at least in part, as a political matter.[158] Whatever remnants of other social stages litter the landscape of England in *The Wanderer*, the horror of labour is inescapable.

On a boat, escaping from France, the radically inclined Elinor Joddrel suggests that 'We want nothing, now, but a white foaming billow . . . to . . . surprise out our histories'.[159] But, Burney makes evident, such individual histories must be understood in a wider context. For Elinor (mistakenly, it seems), this context is Rousseauian. She outlines her 'happiness' 'in going forth into the world at this sublime juncture, of turning men into infants, in order to teach them better to grow up'.[160] In this somewhat perverse education, the chains of social convention (mentioned by Rousseau at the beginning of his *Social Contract* [1762]) are removed by returning to a kind of social infancy. In *Emile; or On Education* (1762) Rousseau had imagined an education for his pupil outside artificial and wrong-headed social influence; Elinor suggests that this kind of radical experiment can be carried out not only 'individually' but 'collectively': 'when all the minor articles are progressive, in rising to perfection, must the world in a mass stand still . . .?'[161] And whilst the mention of 'progress' might recall stadial history, the reference to 'perfection' suggests the Godwinian stress on mankind's perfectability. Moderating this, Harleigh, Burney's hero, in an unconscious echo both of Wollstonecraft and the more conservative Knight, argues that 'Unbridled liberty . . . cannot rush upon a state, without letting it loose to barbarism'.[162] Developing Elinor's parallel between the development of the 'mass' and the tuition of the individual, he imagines the stages of social progress in educational terms – for Harleigh, education:

> works its way by the gentlest graduations, one part almost imperceptibly preparing for another, throughout all the stages of childhood to adolescence, and of adolescence to manhood? If you give Homer before the Primer, do you think you shall make a man of learning?[163]

In language, science or combat, Harleigh suggests, progress must be gradual. Burney's plot confirms that this view of social progress as gradualist rather than spontaneous is necessary. After exchanging religion for revolutionary philosophy, Elinor repeatedly attempts to commit suicide. Rapid change is destablising.

Having established an anti-revolutionary framing (a framing which Burney intermittently reinforces by having Elinor make renewed attempts on her own life), Burney quickly moves on to the economic issues that occupy much of the book.[164] Having lost her purse, travelled with Mrs Ireton as a kind of maid, and made herself domestically 'useful in any way' that was proposed, Burney's Juliet attempts to gain 'self-dependence' through work.[165] Her experiences are carefully organised by Burney who initially focuses on the issues of luxury and worker's responsibility. At first working as a music teacher (forced to accept patronage but in some sense self-employed and working within private spaces), she is soon being propelled by the fine ladies that employ her into public performance. Although one of the fragments of paper in the

Berg Collection (perhaps, Barbara Darby proposes, an early sketch for a dramatic version of *The Wanderer*) reads:

Labour – sweetened by rest
Privation – recompensed by ease
Temperance – enjoyed by Health –
& Spirit in every exertion, & every
sacrifice, rewarded by Independence

Juliet's independence is limited.[166] Her control over how she labours is shown to be virtually non-existent while the hardship of the role, Burney underlines, is considerable.

Burney particularly emphasises, however, that this kind of service – although part of the culture of luxury – requires payment just as other forms of labour do. While Lady Arramede ironically asserts 'to play and sing are vast hardships', Giles Arbe, who in some sense is Burney's equivalent of the Shakespearian fool, emphasises that if a performer is 'an artist of luxury', ''tis of your luxury, not his'.[167] The argument that it is not 'as essential to the morals of a state, to encourage luxuries, as to provide for necessaries', made by Mr Scope, is similarly dismissed.[168] Although he makes his case in the general ('putting this young lady always out of the way'), his words are accompanied by 'sneers' and 'cordial applause' from Juliet's debtors.[169] For Burney the argument that performing for the aristocracy is an unpatriotic or even an immoral choice on the part of the worker is merely a self-interested mode of avoiding payment. Moreover, Juliet faces the same hostility even when she begins to produce the physical objects of luxury. Like Victoire, she tries to earn a living by needlework but, initially self-employed, she finds she needs 'capital'; similarly, to train in the milliner's a 'premium' is necessary and although this is paid for Juliet by Sir Jaspar, the publicity of the work is distressing.[170] Mantua-making, although perhaps rather less luxurious than the 'light work' of the milliner's also presents various difficulties, not least because Juliet, in attempt to retain 'self-dependence', is 'engaged but by the day'.[171] Unlike Edgeworth, Burney confronts the fluctuations of the market and their effects on the worker.

Having seen the energy of 'commerce' at Romsey, where the 'workmen and manufacturers' are joined by market women carrying 'butter, eggs, and poultry', Juliet journeys to the New Forest, where she experiences the life of a prosperous farmer, the existence of a shepherd and the hunting activities of the poacher, before eventually arriving at Stonehenge.[172] In this movement from luxury, to commerce, to agriculture to primitivism her journey ironises the imagined social stages of conjectural history. Removing herself from the 'busy hum of man', on her entry into the forest Juliet imagines how her pursuers 'will go on ... from stage to stage, from mile-stone to mile-stone'; seemingly devoid of the divisions of space that characterise capitalist modernity, the solitude of the forest seems to be a 'paradise'.[173]Yet staying in a hut deep within the forest (with people whom she believes murderers) Juliet is shocked to find that 'so mercenary a spirit could have found entrance in a spot which seemed suited to the virtuous innocence of our yet untainted first parents'.[174] And while material conditions are better in the farming community on the edge of the forest where she stays (since 'plenty was not bribed away to sale'), the farmer is still 'interested' and ill-tempered, mastered by the weather.[175] Even the 'shepherd, or husbandman', although he has less risk, has no 'hope', 'no view of amelioration'; the 'imagery of poesy' proves inaccurate.[176] Returning to the depths of the forest, Juliet discovers that the hut of her previous adventure contains not murderers, but poachers. Hunting has been criminalised in the feudal and commercial stages that displace 'barbarism', a perversion underlined when Juliet herself is (at several points) hunted through the forest.

Juliet cannot escape modernity either in the agricultural fringes or in the primitive centre of the forest. No return to origin is possible, a point underlined when Juliet, trying to escape from her husband, finds herself at Stonehenge with Sir Jaspar's faeries. In England, whatever initial appearances or literary fantasy might suggest, there is little in way of combined and uneven development. The commercial age is everywhere and to imagine anything else is to believe a fiction. Both Juliet's false husband, 'an agent of the inhuman Robespierre', and the British aristocrat Lord Denmeath, pursue Juliet out of interest, the one to gain money, the other to preserve what he already has.[177] Neither the monarchy nor the Republic is advantageous to the worker: both systems co-exist with commerce and in both systems those with authority are 'interested'.

Even while Burney herself gives no direct political programme, in *The Wanderer*, the drawn-out nature of Juliet's plight indicates the need for reform – not only in relation to 'female difficulties' but in relation to work more generally. While Burney displays the sensitivity to gradations of rank and wealth that she displays in her earlier novels, particularly *Camilla* (1797), here her analysis deepens as she, like Godwin, takes into account the way character is inevitably shaped by economic forces. When Juliet asks 'must we be creditors, and poor creditors ourselves, to teach us justice to debtors?', she suggests that the most persistent social categories are economic.[178] What underlies the distribution of power is credit, capital and money itself: the satire of individuals as representative of social groups for which Burney is known, becomes the satire of a system. Thus mockery of those who labour is undercut – as

Juliet exclaims, 'Alas . . . how little do we know either of the labours, or the privations of those whose business it is to administer pleasure to the public.'[179] Suggesting that both historical discourse and poetry have obscured the suffering involved in all forms of employment, *The Wanderer* calls for a better, more sensitive understanding of the worker's lot.

In 1824 the Utilitarian philosopher John Stuart Mill attacked 'Hume's romance of the Stuarts'.[180] He blames this kind of focus on the 'pleasures and pains of an individual' for engendering a 'habit' of considering the individual's pleasure as 'of more importance the great interests of mankind'. Some of the historical novelists of the 1780s and 90s share his suspicion of the misdirections of history. To correct the tendency to concentrate on the sufferings of the few, Wollstonecraft, Smith and Godwin find it necessary to take a new perspective on the past. *Desmond* and *St Leon* attempt to engage the reader in this historiographic project. The endeavour is particularly important because, as *An Historical and Moral View* makes clear, knowledge of the past can generate 'progress'. History, then, for these writers, is a, if not *the*, crucial site of political re-education. But as both Smith and Godwin are well aware, such attempts to guide, or even imagine, transition are fraught with difficulty: chivalric sympathies linger to sabotage the endeavour. For Godwin, in particular, the problem is not only the survival of aristocratic influence in the commercial present, but the structure of sympathy itself. To counter the exclusive tendencies of feeling, Godwin tries to imagine an anarchist sympathy, felt not by the group, but by the individual towards mankind. Godwin's structural examination is unusually far-reaching. By the time he wrote *St Leon* the recuperation of radical sympathy was well under way.

After the September Massacres and the Terror, moderate novelists had been stimulated by fears of a violent popular politics to picture the possibility of a non-violent 'transition'. Their fascination with the painful French journey from absolutism to modernity provided a kind of cover under which they could explore the unstable and changing nature of commercial society itself. Longstanding anxieties about the supposed increased social mobility allowed by commerce and luxury took a new direction. The authors of *Marcus Flaminius*, *Charles Dacres*, *Lioncel* and 'Madame de Fleury' all had knowledge of precarity, of the pains of labour and of the mob action that such circumstances could generate. These works code popular unrest as a type of 'envy' stemming from the wrong type of production or the wrong mode of aristocratic behaviour. At the same time, they try to find an alternative social relation that will not stimulate mob violence or aristocratic self-indulgence and yet will facilitate economic 'progress'. Instead of redirecting sympathy towards the lower ranks, as Smith had advised in *Desmond*, these novels emphasise that the circulation of sympathy and capital *between* the lower and upper ranks should be the focus of attention. Distinguishing between supposedly good and bad modes of labour and government, these novels insist that the modern commercial order need not necessarily lead to the radical social mobility of revolution. Instead, by an emphasis on sensibility as a circulating commodity, the aristocratic order can be maintained by productive forms of trade and work. The revolution that these works prepare for is not of the social but of the industrial kind. Only Burney remains to testify to the hardship of labour.

## Notes

1. Radcliffe, *Gaston*, p. 17.
2. Hurd, *Moral and Political Dialogues*, p. 96.
3. Hurd, *Moral and Political Dialogues*, pp. 99–100.
4. David Hume, *Essays*, p. 224.
5. O'Brien, *Narratives of Enlightenment*, p. 62.
6. O'Brien, *Women and Enlightenment*, p. 111.
7. William Robertson, *History of Charles V*, 1: 72.
8. See Fiona Price, '"A Great Deal of History"', pp. 264–6.
9. Hurd, *Letters*, p. 8.
10. Hurd, *Moral and Political Dialogues*, p. 97, pp. 99–101.
11. Wollstonecraft, *Political Writings*, p. 6, p. 12, p. 9.
12. Wollstonecraft, *Political Writings*, p. 10.
13. Bolingbroke, *Remarks on the History of England*, p. 161.
14. For a brief account of the troubled reception of Hume's *History* see, for example, Schmidt, *David Hume*, p. 294.
15. David Hume, *History*, 4: 241.
16. David Hume, *History*, 4: 229. As Russell Harding notes, Hume suggests that James I reversed these abuses, returning to the system operating under Henry VI; Harding, *David Hume*, p. 114.
17. Sanderson, *A Compleat History of the Lives and Reigns of Mary Queen of Scotland*.
18. See David Hume, *History of England* (1754–62), William Robertson's *History of Scotland* (1759), and for the interrogation of the characters of the rival historians, W. Tytler, *An Inquiry, Historical and Critical, into the Evidence against Mary Queen of Scots* (1772).
19. Alliston, 'The Value of a Literary Legacy', pp. 109–27, Lewis, '"Ev'ry Lost Relation"', pp. 165–84. Wall, '"Chasms in the Story"', pp. 21–40.
20. Barbauld, *The British Novelists*, 22: ii–iii. The remark is made in her preface to Reeve's *The Old English Baron*.
21. Sophia Lee, *Recess*, p. 12.
22. Sophia Lee, *Recess*, p. 210.
23. Watkins, *Representing Elizabeth*, p. 13.

24. Sophia Lee, *Recess*, p. 22.
25. Sophia Lee, *Recess*, p. 8.
26. See also Gores, *Psychosocial Spaces*, p. 122.
27. O'Brien, *Narratives of the Enlightenment*, p. 60.
28. Schmidt, *David Hume*, p. 257; Sophia Lee, *Recess*, p. 144.
29. David Hume, *History*, 5: 509.
30. Sophia Lee, *Recess*, p. 80.
31. Sophia Lee, *Recess*, p. 27, p. 28.
32. Sophia Lee, *Recess*, p. 150.
33. Sophia Lee, *Recess*, p. 71, p. 72.
34. Sophia Lee, *Recess*, p. 74.
35. Sophia Lee, *Recess*, p. 99.
36. Wollstonecraft, *Works*, 5: 15.
37. Sophia Lee, *Recess*, p. 100.
38. Sophia Lee, *Recess*, p. 173.
39. [Antoine François Prévost d'Exiles], *The Life and Entertaining Adventures of Mr. Cleveland, Natural Son of Oliver Cromwell*. Sophia Lee (trans.), *Warbeck*.
40. Whitehouse, *Poems*, p. 88.
41. Graves, *Plexippus; Or, the Aspiring Plebeian*, pp. viii–ix, p. xi.
42. Anon, 'The Terrorist System of Novel Writing', p. 104. See also Maxwell, 'Phantom States', p. 177.
43. For a brief discussion of *The Recess*'s links to sectarian struggles in the1780s and to religion in *The Statue Room*, see Angela Wright, *Britain*, pp. 43–7.
44. Anon, *Lady Jane Grey*, 1: 9.
45. Anon, *Lady Jane Grey*, 2: 108.
46. As Johns-Putra notes, Richard's massacre of 2,000 Muslim prisoners at Acre rendered him 'a troublesome epic hero'. Johns-Putra, 'Eleanor Anne Porden's *Coeur de Lion* (1822)', p. 360.
47. E. M. Foster, *The Duke of Clarence*, 1: 13.
48. Charlotte Smith, *Ethelinde or the Recluse of the Lake*, 1: 60.
49. Charlotte Smith, *Desmond*, p. 380.
50. Charlotte Smith, *Ethelinde*, 2: 167.
51. Burke, *Reflections*, p. 170. Rendall, '"The Grand Causes"', p. 2.
52. Burke, *Reflections*, p. 165.
53. Paine, *Political Writings*, p. 72.
54. Paine, *Political Writings*, p. 73.
55. Paine, *Political Writings*, p. 73.
56. Paine, *Political Writings*, pp. 70–1.
57. Bowstead, 'Charlotte Smith's *Desmond*', p. 237; Jones, *Radical Sensibility*, pp. 160–84; Conway, 'Nationalism, Revolution and the Female Body', p. 406; Rogers, 'Inhibitions', p. 75.
58. Wikborg, 'Political Discourse versus Sentimental Romance', p. 531. For a different emphasis, see Nicola J. Watson, *Revolution and the Form of the British* Novel, p. 36.
59. Tarling, '"The Slight Skirmishing of a Novel Writer"', p. 71; Lokke, 'Charlotte Smith's *Desmond*', p. 60.
60. Charlotte Smith, *Desmond*, p. 73.

61. Charlotte Smith, *Desmond*, p. 74.
62. O'Brien, *Women and Enlightenment*, p. 182.
63. Charlotte Smith, *Desmond*, p. 94.
64. Cf. Mackenzie, *Swedish Mysteries*, 3:10.
65. Paine, *Political Writings*, p. 78.
66. Charlotte Smith, *Desmond*, p. 151.
67. David Hume, *Enquiries*, p. 46.
68. Charlotte Smith, *Desmond*, p. 144, p. 148.
69. Charlotte Smith, *Desmond*, pp. 148–9.
70. Charlotte Smith, *Desmond*, pp. 150–1.
71. Charlotte Smith, *Desmond*, p. 28.
72. Paine, *Political Writings*, p. 71.
73. Charlotte Smith, *Desmond*, p. 267.
74. Charlotte Smith, *Desmond*, p. 347.
75. Lefebvre, *The French Revolution*, p. 208.
76. Paine, *Political Writings*, p. 163.
77. Charlotte Smith, *Desmond*, p. 115.
78. Charlotte Smith, *Desmond*, p. 141.
79. Burke, *Reflections*, p. 170.
80. Hilbish, *Charlotte Smith*, p. 509.
81. Wollstonecraft, *Works*, 6: 18.
82. Wollstonecraft, *Works*, 6: 5.
83. Wollstonecraft, *Works*, 6: 18.
84. Wollstonecraft, *Works*, 6: 112.
85. See Clemit's introduction to the 1994 edition of Godwin's *St Leon*, xv–xvi.
86. Godwin, *St Leon*, ed. Pamela Clemit, xxxiii–iv (all references are to this edition). See, though, Daniel E. White, *Early Romanticism and Religious Dissent*, p. 111.
87. Godwin, *Political Justice* (1798), xxvi.
88. Godwin, *Political Justice* (1798), xxvi.
89. Godwin, *Enquirer*, p. 1, p. 161, vi. See Klancher on 'conversational stops and starts' of *The Enquirer* ('Godwin and the Genre Reformers', p. 22).
90. For discussion, see, for example, Batsaki, 'From Alchemy to Experiment', pp. 174–92.
91. Godwin, *Enquirer*, vi.
92. Godwin, *Political Justice*, ed. Philp, 3: 15. For conversation and rhetoric, see Myers, 'William Godwin', pp. 415–44; and Mee, '"The Uses of Conversation"', pp. 567–90.
93. Godwin, *Enquirer*, p. 297.
94. Godwin, 'Of History', p. 359.
95. Godwin, 'Of History', p. 365.
96. Godwin, 'Of History', p. 365.
97. Godwin, *St Leon*, p. 2.
98. Godwin, *St Leon*, p. 2.
99. For composition, see Cameron and Reiman, *Shelley*, 1: 343.
100. For the 'protean self' see McGeough, 'Unlimited Questioning', pp. 3–10.
101. Godwin, *St Leon*, xxxii. See also Collings, who in 'The Romance' equates immutable life with 'immutable reason', linking it to Godwin's appendix

'Of Health and the Prolongation of Human life' in *Political Justice* (p. 864).

102. Godwin, *St Leon*, pp. 5–6.
103. Godwin, *St Leon*, p. 19.
104. Godwin, *St Leon*, p. 26.
105. Godwin, *St Leon*, pp. 25–6
106. Kavanagh, *Enlightenment and the Shadows of Chance*, p. 241
107. Godwin, *Enquirer*, p. 298.
108. Godwin, *St Leon*, p. 71, p. 73.
109. Godwin, *St Leon*, pp. 71–2.
110. Godwin, *St Leon*, p. 88.
111. Godwin, *Collected Novels*, 1: 65.
112. For a later reworking of this situation see the removal of the Percys to a smaller estate in Maria Edgeworth's 1814 novel *Patronage*.
113. Godwin, *St Leon*, p. 85.
114. Godwin, *Enquirer*, p. 172.
115. Godwin, *St Leon*, p. 85.
116. Godwin, *St Leon*, p. 95.
117. Godwin, *St Leon*, p. 230.
118. Godwin, *St Leon*, p. 236.
119. Burke, *Reflections*, p. 135.
120. Godwin, *St Leon*, p. 278, p. 285.
121. Godwin, *St Leon*, p. 285.
122. Godwin, *Enquirer*, p. 10.
123. Godwin, 'Of History', pp. 361–2.
124. Godwin, 'Of History', p. 363.
125. Godwin, 'Of History', p. 368.
126. Godwin, 'Of History', p. 363.
127. For 'romance' in the 'Essay' see Klancher, 'Godwin and the Republican Romance', pp. 68–86.
128. Godwin, 'Of History', p. 364.
129. Godwin, *Enquirer*, p. 16, p. 6.
130. See Godwin, *St Leon*, p. 338 for a parallel between the Inquisition and the Irish Rebellion of 1798.
131. Collings, 'The Romance', p. 870.
132. Godwin, *Enquirer*, p. 16.
133. Godwin, *Enquirer*, p. 16, p. 17.
134. See Rudé, *The Crowd*, pp. 139–79 and 'La Taxation populaire', pp. 305–29.
135. I am not, of course, arguing that the fiction of the 1790s was the first to draw upon working life for its material, but that, given the influence of stadial history, there was a sense of and curiosity about the place of labour and labourers within the system that was new. As Marx notes in the *Grundrisse*, Adam Smith made an 'immense step forward' in his analysis of 'labour in general'; the works under consideration here begin to make and explore such an analysis in the realm of historical fiction (p. 104).
136. Knight, *Marcus Flaminius*, 1: 103.
137. Anon, *Montford Castle*, 1: 88–9.
138. Anon, *Montford Castle*, 1: 88.

139. Anon, *Montford Castle*, 1: 192.
140. Anon, *Montford Castle*, 1: 199–200.
141. For *Earl Goodwin* see Kasmer, *Novel Histories*, pp. 60–6. For Yearsley's status and relationship with her patron, Hannah More, see Kahn, 'Hannah More and Ann Yearsley', pp. 203–23.
142. Yearsley, *Captives*, 1: 127.
143. Yearsley, *Captives*, 1: 181.
144. Yearsley, *Captives*, 1: 185; Walpole, *Correspondence*, 31: 219.
145. Lukács, *Historical Novel*, p. 25; Fiona Price, 'Making History', p. 147.
146. Anon, *Charles Dacres*, 1: 125–6. The writer also insists he will '*shew men as they are*' (1: xi).
147. 'Art. VIII. *Tales of Fashionable Life*', *Critical Review*, p. 191; 'Art. VII, *Tales of Fashionable Life*', *Quarterly Review* (August 1809), p. 143; 'Art. VIII. *Tales of Fashionable Life*', *London Quarterly Review* (June 1812), p. 330.
148. 'Art. VII, *Tales of Fashionable Life*', *Quarterly Review* 1809, p. 143.
149. Maria Edgeworth, *Tales*, p. 55.
150. Maria Edgeworth, *Tales*, p. 67.
151. Maria Edgeworth, *Tales*, p. 85.
152. Maria Edgeworth, *Tales*, pp. 88–9.
153. Maria Edgeworth, *Tales*, p. 89.
154. Rudé, 'Prices', p. 253.
155. Burney, *Wanderer*, xiii.
156. Burney, *Wanderer*, p. 7.
157. Frances Burney, *Journals and Letters*, pp. 236–332.
158. See Darby, *Frances Burney*, pp. 51–64.
159. Burney, *Wanderer*, p. 15.
160. Burney, *Wanderer*, p. 18.
161. Rousseau, *Emile*, p. 19; Burney, *Wanderer*, pp. 18–19.
162. Burney, *Wanderer*, p. 19.
163. Burney, *Wanderer*, p. 20.
164. See Crump, '"Turning the World Upside down"', pp. 325–40. For the use of such 'diversionary ploy[s]' see Johnson, *Jane Austen*, pp. 19–21, p. 21. See also Wallace, 'Rewriting Radicalism' for Wollstonecraft and Elinor's and Juliet's experiences.
165. Burney, *Wanderer*, p. 82, p. 296.
166. Cited in Darby, *Frances Burney*, p. 2. I am indebted to Christina Davidson for drawing this to my attention.
167. Burney, *Wanderer*, pp. 322–3.
168. Burney, *Wanderer*, p. 323.
169. Burney, *Wanderer*, p. 324.
170. Burney, *Wanderer*, p. 403, p. 289.
171. Burney, *Wanderer*, p. 451, p. 455.
172. Burney, *Wanderer*, p. 666.
173. Burney, *Wanderer*, pp. 675–6.
174. Burney, *Wanderer*, p. 678.
175. Burney, *Wanderer*, p. 692, p. 691.
176. Burney, *Wanderer*, p. 698.
177. Burney, *Wanderer*, p. 739.

178. Burney, *Wanderer*, p. 369.
179. Burney, *Wanderer*, p. 321. See, though, Burgess, 'Courting Ruin', p. 142, for *The Wanderer* as a 'thorough retreat into the bosom of the genteel family'.
180. Fieser, ed. *Early Responses to Hume's* History of England, p. 293.

# Chapter 3

# Uneasy Alliances:
# Liberty and the Nation

Cannon smoke bisects Robert Ker Porter's *Buonaparte Massacreing Fifteen Hundred Persons at Toulon* [sic] (c. 1803), severing the bewildered revolutionary soldiers above from the grieving people below. In its emphasis on distress and division Porter's picture amounts to a visual argument that the gap in French society is not, as might be supposed, between the people and the forces of the *ancien régime*, but between the people and the Revolution itself. As the dead lover and unfortunate mother at the bottom of the picture suggest, the mode of government fractures romance and prevents the reproduction of family and polis. Yet the missing term here is nation. Toulon had been delivered to the British navy by Baron d'Imbert on 1 October 1793. The omission of the Anglo-Spanish and counter-revolutionary forces allows Porter to imply that radicalism causes the people's distress. Porter's painting reflects the way that the rhetoric of revolution brought the political importance of the people to the fore. It also suggests how, during the French Revolutionary and Napoleonic Wars, this idea would be tested and exploited in the service of nation and empire. In the historical novel, in particular, the focus on the 'masses' and their legal and electoral rights was complicated by a narrative of nationhood in which romance and history jostled uneasily.

In the 'General Preface to the *Waverley* Novels' Scott states that, along with the editorship of *QueenHoo Hall* (1808), it was 'the extended and well-merited fame of Miss Edgeworth' that led him to recollect the unfinished manuscript that became *Waverley*.[1] Scott's remarks inadvertently support the assumption that the national tale precedes the historical novel. This assumption, albeit carefully nuanced, can, for example, be traced in Katie Trumpener's *Bardic Nationalism*. Although she acknowledges that 'in eighteenth-century Ireland, Scotland, and Wales nationalist antiquarians edited, explicated, and promoted their respective bardic traditions', her examination of the role of the historical novel

Figure 3.1    Sir R. K. Porter, *Buonaparte Massacring Fifteen Hundred Persons at Toulon*, Anne S. K. Brown Military Collection, Brown University Library.

in the development of the tale effectively begins with Scott.[2] In such accounts, tales by Edgeworth and Owenson make use of stadial history, a use that Scott is then seen to transform and develop.[3] However, in the 1790s, historical novelists had adopted a probing approach to nascent national identity, in part by manipulating mainstream historiographical tropes. Of course, anxieties over the internal and international balance of power, as well as doubts over the ethics of colonialism, had preoccupied earlier historical novelists, as Janina Nordius explores in relation to Sophia Lee's *The Recess*, for example.[4] Nonetheless, in the 1790s the fear of mass political activity caused by the French Revolution, alongside the use of the methods of stadial history to interpret events in France, shaped this interest in nation and empire in a particular way.

In his *Discourse on the Love of our Country* (1789) Richard Price had argued that, as the Glorious Revolution demonstrated, the people had the right to 'cashier' their 'governors', including kings.[5] But Burke's *Reflections* attacked this contention. 'So far is it from being true,' Burke insisted, 'that we acquired a right by the Revolution [of 1688] to elect our kings, that if we had possessed it before, the English nation did at that time most solemnly renounce and abdicate it, for themselves and for all their posterity for ever.'[6] While Burke's idea of an eternal contract was rejected by radicals including Wollstonecraft, his phrase 'English nation' points to an even greater potential difficulty in relation to other parts of Britain and Ireland. In the 1790s historical novels began to examine the relationship between the people and the monarch and to query the nature of liberty. In the British context, this examination was complicated by the composite nature of the Union and by the troubled stories of succession which underpinned it.

The early 1790s had seen a spate of historical novels that examined the political significance of the ancient constitution. But, although versatile, this narrative was Anglo-centric. In search of an alternative, in the early 1790s historical novelists tackled the history of the relationship between England and the 'sister' kingdoms of Scotland and Ireland. *Monmouth: A Tale, Founded on Historic Facts* (1790) by Anna Maria Johnson (later Mackenzie) and Henry Siddons's *William Wallace* (1791) are attempts to assess, in historical terms, the nature of liberty. Both ask what constitutes rebellion. Is it rebellion to reject a king that does not share a nation's religion or views of liberty? Should the people be condemned as treacherous if oaths have been taken on mistaken premises or under duress? Such issues are inevitably played out against a background of dynastic and military struggle: the questions of liberty and the issue of Union are linked. A similar phenomenon (differently nuanced) can be traced in historical novels which deal with Ireland. In

James White's *Earl Strongbow* (1789) and Anna Millikin's *Eva, an Old Irish Story* (1795) the emphasis is not on cashiering rulers (although there is a sense of irresponsible rule in Ireland past and present) but on a cautious renegotiation of the symbolic relation between Ireland and England.

These works figure the preoccupation with liberty in terms of sexual choice. In *Sentimental Literature and Anglo-Scottish Identity* (2015) Juliet Shields suggests that from the mid eighteenth to early nineteenth century Scottish writers 'responded to Scotland's lack of independent sovereignty by seeking in sentiment, or virtuous feeling, a compensation for political dispossession'.[7] However, in the historical novel, as dynastic succession becomes modern romance, sentiment seems under strain. The composite nature of Britain and Ireland is uneasily exposed. As the 1790s continue, the French Revolutionary and Napoleonic Wars impact upon such concerns, driving demand for narratives of patriotism and allegiance. In Ellis Cornelia Knight's *Marcus Flaminius* and the anonymous *Arville Castle* (1795) Britain becomes the vehicle for defending liberty or, paradoxically, for exporting it to its subjugated colonies. The standard heterosexual pairing of romance is insufficient and must be supported by wider reproduction, of either an ideological or a literal type. Yet even those works which promote a Roman and imperial heritage still, in their fervency, highlight the plight of the smaller nation. As such, the historical novel, a cautious and sometimes imperial form, foreshadows the national tale.

## Romancing the Nation?

In *Contesting the Gothic* James Watt remarks that 'from around the time of the British defeat in America' 'numerous [. . .] "historical" romances, served an unambiguous moral and patriotic agenda'.[8] Watt's words echo the eighteenth-century association of romance with feminised overproduction. Connected with nostalgia for feudalism, and underpinning the nation, the 'romance' is – strangely – at once dully conservative and stubbornly improbable. A glance at the writing of Clara Reeve complicates this account. In her *Progress of Romance*, Reeve suggests that romance had formerly been read by 'young persons as true Histories'; this encouraged them 'to copy exploits universally rewarded by praise and imitation' but generated inaccurate ideas.[9] In *Memoirs of Sir Roger de Clarendon* Reeve tries to improve the model. Denouncing what she sees as the contemporary radical tendency to 'falsify historical facts', Reeve has 'framed a story that does not in any respect contradict the annals of history; which may entertain [young and ingenuous minds] without corrupting their hearts'.[10] Although Reeve wishes to 'show princes and heroes as men, not as angels', her project displays an idealising tendency reminiscent of the *Progress*.[11] Despite the title's insistence on the pseudo-factual 'memoirs', this is the conservative '"historical" romance' which Watt described.

Yet even in this text, there is a drift towards a modern narrative of nation. Implicitly acknowledging the erosion of aristocratic inheritance, and fearing the instability of popular rule (the 'succession' of constitutions and of governments seen in France), Reeve proposes an alternative.[12] Greatness itself has a national character: 'We respect the climate, the air, the soil, and every thing that contributed to produce and foster such [great] men; we believe that they must of necessity produce a succession' of them.[13] With this horticultural metaphor, Reeve extends the family bonds and sexual unions that ensure succession. By identifying the 'glorious ancestors' of 'Britain' with the 'soil', she fuses the aristocracy and the nation.[14] But she also proposes a general propagation: values will be spread amongst readers, 'tender', 'flexible' and young, like plants capable of adapting and multiplying.[15] Exposure to history – and historical novels – encourages the reproduction of national greatness in the readership. The idea of a 'succession' of governments, representing the changing will of the people, has been replaced by a 'succession' of great men, both aristocrats and readers, who selflessly identify with the nation.[16]

Although *Memoirs* is an attempt to create this determinedly patriotic historical novel, Reeve's vision of the genre is conservative fantasy. Nonetheless, her emphasis on the moral duty to nation that 'every son of Britain' should feel is indicative of a national reinvention at work more broadly in the historical novel: a reinvention that draws upon the changing form of the romance.[17] In *Imagined Communities* (1983) Benedict Anderson argues that 'nationalism has to be understood by aligning it ... with the large cultural systems that preceded it, out of which – as well as against which – it came into being'.[18] Alongside religion, 'dynastic' succession is key: 'Antique monarchical states expanded not only by warfare but by sexual politics.'[19] He adds that these sexual politics are 'of a kind very different from those practiced today'.[20] However, as Reeve's words suggest, the historical novel is a site where greatness, often implicitly of a dynastic kind, is expanded to meet with the idea of the nation. The sexual politics of dynastic succession become relevant to the whole population. Romance, a courtly form, now has a broader ideological role.

In eighteenth-century commentary on the historical novel, the entry of this modern sexual politics into romance is viewed in stadial terms.

William Robertson had positioned chivalry as the source of modern sensibility and in the preface to her 1795 historical novel *Mysteries Elucidated* Anna Maria Mackenzie attempts to reconstruct this process in a history of fiction. Comparing ancient and modern romance, she suggests that the former needed to be 'reduced to a reasonable standard' but had 'dignity' – it was chivalric.[21] In contrast, modern romance had been improved by Richardson and Fielding but damaged by their followers. In their work, the knight becomes 'a libertine lover, an insignificant beau, or modern enamorato'.[22] Mackenzie hints that in the right hands, the historical novel will fuse the dignity of the older chivalric form with modern 'good sense' found in the proper use of 'historical facts'.[23] This involves the rejection of modern works in which the heroine finds '*cross guardians*' substituted '*for cruel dragons – travelling chaises* for *flying chariots* – and vulgar *post boys* for *rosy cupids*'.[24] Enflamed passions should be removed: the sexual choice that inheres in modern romance is dangerous. The danger proves acute in the historical novel when the dynastic marriages that underpin the nation are under discussion.

Katie Trumpener, J. Th. Leerssen, and Mary Corbett, among others, have all examined the 'allegories of union' that occur in the national tale: one form such allegories take is that of a romance between representatives of centre and periphery (England and Ireland, for example), which ends in marriage symbolic of the union between two countries.[25] How is the shape of the historical novel different? In the historical novel, tensions around romance as a trope of union and as a generic form are exposed by past events – and by the various frameworks used to read such events.[26] Writers as diverse as Reeve and Godwin suggested that history might have a moral role and when Burke compared 'the republic of Paris' and 'the republic of Rome' in *Reflections*, he suggested how this might function: through analogy rather than allegory.[27] Thus, in the historical novel Alfred and Wallace are not allegorical figures: broadly speaking, the idea is that their just behaviour should find its analogy in the present. Yet, as the works of Godwin and Charlotte Smith suggest, it can be difficult to extract a moral example from descriptions of past behaviours – and this is perhaps never more true than when imperial conquest is under consideration. Narratives of dynastic succession also have the potential to undermine narratives of national integration. While, for example, Mary Queen of Scots and Queen Elizabeth I have a range of symbolic functions, the threat of union or disunion that their relationships represent is, in the first place, actual rather than ideal.[28] Although, as the twin daughters of Mary Queen of Scots in *The Recess* indicate, there is space for romance and its allegories, this space is often at the edge of historical record – in speculations on feeling and motivation, and in the realm of rumour (hence the importance of illegitimacy in such narratives).[29] In contrast, actual historical events cannot always bear the allegorical weight that is required of them. Certainly, in the case of the marriage between Strongbow and Eva at the time of the Norman invasion of Ireland, the weight of history makes it difficult to present a convincing love story or to imagine a sexual choice that facilitates a healthy relation between the two countries. In such works, the movement between history and romance complicates allegory: the idea of choice inherent in modern romance leads to the reassessment of nation.

## Scotland

Anna Maria Mackenzie's *Monmouth* demonstrates how the discussion of liberty in the historical novel is intimately entangled with issues of Union, engendering a hesitant form of national romance. The novel is an attempt to transfer the debate about liberty from the English context of Alfred's reign, to a Scottish one.[30] As the full title suggests, *Monmouth: A Tale, Founded on Historic Facts* is a fictionalisation – and to some extent an extenuation – of the Monmouth Rebellion of 1685, when James Scott, Duke of Monmouth and natural son of Charles II, attempted, on his father's death, to seize the throne from King James II. The novel is curiously placed politically. Monmouth is participating in a rebellion yet the events of 1688–9, when James was displaced by William of Orange, lend the sanction of history to the hero's attempt. Hence while Mackenzie cannot fully endorse her hero's actions, she still positions him on the side of Protestant liberty against what she styles as the Catholic 'tyranny' of King James and his followers.[31] In this narrative, the Scottish nobility has a key role to play in constructing the 1707 Act of Union between England and Scotland.[32] Yet the politics of dynastic succession by which the Stuarts are eventually replaced by the Hanoverians complicate this argument for Scottish centrality – and Mackenzie's uneasy use of romance suggests this difficulty.

The novel begins by suggesting the role of the Scottish nobility in protecting liberty. This role, figured by the fortress described in the opening pages, is, we are to assume, nearly at an end: the castle is in a state of decay. The structure of the castle is, the author indicates, a defensive one. In the distant past it preserved the liberty of the inhabitants against 'besiegers' who 'sought the extirpation of every clan'.[33] Its 'wide destructive fosse' recalls the supposed 'fossa' later discovered by the titular character of Scott's *Antiquary*. It is not, like the ditch in Scott's novel, without actual military significance, but it is defunct, 'filled with rubbish'. Equally, the 'portcullis' is no longer threatening, having 'long remained in a situation utterly inimical to the possibility of doing any service or even of removal' – as frozen as the still life description of Tully-Veolan, village and fortifications, in *Waverley*. The period of invasion is over and liberty is safe.

This narrative of historical distance is quickly destabilised. This is not the eighteenth but the seventeenth century; moreover, that troubled period of civil war is seen as implicitly analogous to the present. The moderate Donald Bruce watches with dismay both 'the distress and misery CHARLES the First was bringing upon himself – his family and country – by his arbitrary' rule and 'equally condemned those rigid Covenanters, who aimed to explain away and reduce the rights of Majesty'. Wishing to avoid such extremes, Donald spends his days in a retirement:

> where the calm enjoyment of a well-ordered life was not empoisoned by a slavish dependence upon the will of despotism, or an unbounded and licentious gratification of indulged passions . . .[34]

The choice between despotism and (as the syntax of the full sentence implies) the passions of radicalism recalls the events of the French Revolution (even if the religious orientations are different). Both alternatives are aestheticised and rejected. Donald refuses to hear 'the soft and enervating melody of the flute' (redolent of courtly luxury but also of the degraded form of the 'amiable virtues' Adam Smith associates with an advanced social stage).[35] But he similarly repudiates the 'martial drum and trumpet': mass conflict is not, at least initially, seen as a corrective for monarchical luxury. Instead, 'this primitive Scotsman was gratified by that kind of harmony which, to ears tuned to its rough and sonorous notes, gave the most ample satisfaction'. 'The national and customary amusement of the bagpipe' now represents, not Scottish aggression, but moderation – and simplicity: Donald listens to it while eating 'his morning repast of eggs, milk, and honey'.[36]

In stadial terms, the memory of the 'awful virtues' of primitivism here forms a potential corrective to luxurious aristocratic corruption.[37] But for this improved form of liberty to be protected, Scottish values need to be exported. Arthur, the son of Donald, tries to rein in the tendencies of 'the martyred King' when Charles I decides to contend:

> for that despotic form of government, which, in the estimation of a proud and freed people, took the appearance of tyranny, and seemed to indicate an intention of acquiring an unbounded sway over the subjects, who had not long been emancipated from Papal authority – an arbitrary Queen – and a submission even to the stake, rather than forfeit their steady adherence to the Protestant faith.[38]

The challenge Arthur faces is the preservation of liberty for a 'proud and free people' – but the national contours of this quality are peculiarly arranged. In insisting on continuity between the despotism of Charles's reign and the behaviour of Queen Mary, the narrator challenges the Tudor association with liberty. Instead of despotism being a Stuart and hence a Scottish import to England, it now becomes a common problem. Together the Scots and English must move beyond dynastic politics to assure the 'freedom of a Briton'.[39] Arthur is not initially a rebel – he fights for the Royalists in the Civil War. But the luxurious excesses of the Restoration jar with the Scottish taste for simplicity engendered by the environment of Skye. This, along with the Catholicism and the apparently arbitrary rule of James Duke of York (later James II), eventually determines Arthur to support the Monmouth rebellion.

This tale of rebellion also has its allegory of failed sexual union. Arthur leaves Margaret, his daughter, behind on Skye where she encounters Monmouth and falls in love. Brought up in a court, Margaret nonetheless 'cheerfully adopted the modes and habits congenial to the island: – but there was taste in the make, disposition, and colour of her simple attire'.[40] Since she combines an adherence to tradition with the 'elegance' of modernity, her marriage and its offspring would offer a bridge between cultures and countries, rather like the marriages in the national tale. Yet Margaret cannot find a suitable mate. Although the 'ferocious' Argyle falls in love with her, Margaret refuses this sexual bond: Argyle's brutality (which figures the brutality of rebellion) is unacceptable.[41] Margaret's attachment to Monmouth is similarly ill-fated. Reflecting historical fact, Monmouth is already married to Anne Scott, the first Duchess of Buccleuch, but the logic of romance has made it evident that the real reason that hero and heroine cannot unite is because Monmouth is a rebel.[42]

This allegory of failed romance is complicated by the hero's own family background. In the novel Mackenzie capitalises on questions regarding Monmouth's illegitimacy. Monmouth is convinced that his mother, Lucy Walter, married Charles but that Charles chose dynastic politics over affect in his marriage to Catherine of Braganza. Although there is some correspondence between Monmouth's tale and the historical record (he *was* educated, for instance, by Henrietta Maria, the widow of Charles I), Mackenzie fully exploits the space of rumour and affect. In one fictional episode Lucy decides to see the monarch for one last time and plead for her son, leading to Catherine feeling 'the indignity [Charles] had offered in espousing her as a free agent'.[43] According to the logic of the narrative, King Charles II's sin has distorted the romance of the next generation. Although Monmouth avoids his father's error, his connubial affections for Anne Scott prove dangerous to his cause. The novel repeatedly depicts attempts to rescue imprisoned wives and daughters which lead to the heroes' capture; as in *The Recess*, escape is followed by confinement. King James even uses Monmouth's wife to try to make the rebel renounce his claim to the throne. But if rebellion cannot bear immediate fruit, after Monmouth's execution in 1685, his wife, we are told, has a son. In reality, the last of Anne's children was born in 1683 (she had seven). In *Monmouth* this late birth symbolises the untainted continuity of the Buccleuch line. Significantly, the novel is dedicated to 'His Grace the Duke of Buccleugh [sic]' (the great-great grandson of Monmouth and Anne Scott, friend both of Walter Scott and Adam Smith).[44] The family survives to influence the Union.

Although Skye represents simplicity where the court of Charles II is overly refined, *Monmouth* does not contain the sense of stadial inequality which the Irish national tale later contests. Instead, in this book, Scottish simplicity will correct luxurious modernity, eventually promoting the common cause of British Protestant liberty and underpinning the Union. The narrative also does not contain that sense felt so strongly in the Waverley Novels and in historical fictions of the 1790s, of alteration from the feudal to the commercial. There is, though, some suggestion of where these narratives emerge from: while the Stuart monarchy, like the Bourbons, is given a set of associations, most notably with luxury, a Protestant reformist resistance is linked with simplicity. When Scott writes his own historical novels, the commercial stage that represents progress will also in part be shaped by this dynamic. Of course, in stadial terms, it is difficult to position commerce as primitive. Scott eventually manages to do so by distinguishing earlier and later stages within commerce itself (in *St Ronan's Well*, for example) and by, as Ian Duncan remarks, creating a 'primitive' like Rob Roy who is also 'expert . . . in the modern arts of commerce and negotiation'.[45] Here, however, by presenting commerce as somehow simplified, linked with production and industry rather than excess, the author of *Monmouth* begins to historicise the market.

While *Monmouth* tries to balance some of the elements within the Union to ensure a unified future in which the interests of monarch and people are balanced, *William Wallace: Or, The Highland Hero. A Tale founded on Historical Facts* is potentially more provocative. Written by Henry Siddons, son of the actress Sarah Siddons, at the outset the narrative evokes both the sentimental novel and the sexual mores of modern romance, detailing the struggles of Wallace's father, the romance of Wallace's formative years, and the 'history' of Montieth. In fact, although the word 'history' is repeated several times in this context, the actual narrative is only faintly coloured either by the broader sense of national history or by the historical memoir that, following the Civil War, had become so important to British historical writing.[46] Instead, in this interpolated story, Montieth tells Wallace how his father was tricked into believing his wife and friend unfaithful. Montieth is disinherited and only reinstated after the death of the usurper. Montieth's romance narrative suggests that succession will be restored. Yet the departure of Wallace's father and Wallace's own narrative of painful separation from his mother and his wife suggest that the fight for liberty will have a profound personal cost.

The nature of this 'liberty' is explored when the book deals with Wallace's martial endeavours against the English: in these episodes the novel becomes both slightly more historical and, interestingly, more radical in tone. In one sense, *Wallace* is an early example of the phenomenon considered in the last chapter: in the scenes where the Scottish followers of Wallace combat King Edward I a new focus emerges on the importance of the people. Wallace's 'countrymen' have sworn allegiance to the king. Nonetheless, Wallace insists he is not a 'rebel' and the narrative is quite explicit in suggesting that the people can reject this feudal bond.[47] Additionally, Wallace's militarism is tempered by the urge to justice – he functions as a quondam Alfred. In an incident very similar to that found in *Son of Ethelwolf*, Wallace is approached by the angry officer Alexander who has been challenged by a subordinate. On enquiry, it emerges that the challenger, a humble soldier, Douglas, is protecting his wife (who, in a manner entirely familiar to readers of this kind of historical fiction, has disguised herself as a young Highlander in order to accompany her husband). Alexander bridles under the investigation: 'What, then, will you encourage reptiles like these in mutiny?':

> 'By no means,' was the answer of our hero; 'but, at the same time, these *reptiles*, as you are pleased to term them, have an equal right to justice with yourself.'[48]

In the face of aristocratic excess, the individual has a right to justice – and to unsullied heterosexual romance. Moreover, these rights correspond with the people's right to justice on a national level: Douglas's actions are not mutiny just as Wallace is not a rebel. Although these parallels between individual, familial and national struggles are dangerously radical, the writer insists that such a Lockean language of rights has both military and moral benefits for those in power. Wallace is saved on the battlefield by 'a common Highland soldier, whose countenance was horribly disfigured by blood': the apparently lower ranking figure appears brutal and terrible, but behaves ethically.[49] When the principles of justice are followed, the masses are no longer threatening. Instead, they become knowable: the soldier is none other than Douglas himself.

These works suggest that, in examining the nation, the historical novel records patterns of allegiance and patriotism that are not necessarily straightforward.[50] Neither *Monmouth* nor *William Wallace* condemn the Union. On the contrary, *Monmouth* supports it, while *William Wallace* at least remains silent on the issue. Both books are also cautious as far as any nationalist agenda is concerned: Monmouth's rebellion is in part justified by subsequent events and Wallace is said to have never desired the throne but to have fought on behalf of king and nobility. Nonetheless, *William Wallace*'s emphasis on liberty was clear enough to earn the disapproval of the *Critical Review*: 'Were even Mrs Siddons to plead with all her former pathos and persuasive powers, she could not alter the decrees of criticism, which condemn this novel as trifling, improbable, and absurd.'[51] The schoolboy should 'have been better employed' and was 'to be severely reprehended for such idle engagements'. While *Wallace* discusses the issue of irresponsible or unjustified kingship, for the reviewer the real problem is a national one: 'The Highland chief, contending with Edward, is said to be fighting in the "cause of liberty!"' Both novels are in fact complicated by the composite but uneasy nature of Britain. In *Modern Romance* Ian Duncan suggests that in nineteenth-century Britain, instead of 'Constitution, we have Romance'; here romance is troubled, suggesting a difficulty with the Union itself.[52]

## Ireland

The difficulty of constructing a romance of Union is even more evident in the Irish context. In *O'Donnel* (1814) Owenson remarks that she was originally tempted to write 'the romantic adventures and unsubdued valour of O'DONNEL *the Red*, Chief of Tirconnel, in the reign of Elizabeth' but that such 'historic facts' would only promote 'discord'.[53] The violence of the colonial period is one painful reason that Ireland at first receives relatively little direct attention within the historical novel but Owenson's words also suggest the contested nature of 'historic facts' themselves. Such 'facts' were particularly hard to come by in the Irish context as a result of attempts by England and Protestant settlers from Edmund Spenser on to overwrite, distort, or destroy the evidence of Irish history. The continuing controversy and its impact on the historical novel can be clearly seen in relation to Leland himself. Leland, a Church of Ireland clergyman, was the author of a *History of Ireland from the*

*Invasion of Henry II, with a Preliminary Discourse on the Ancient State of that Kingdom* (1773) (the *DNB* comments the work 'was never highly regarded').[54] Yet his earlier historical novel *Longsword*, published in Dublin and set in the reign of King Henry III, evokes the ancient constitution of the Anglo-Saxons.

Ireland's lack of centrality in *Longsword* is in part explained by the preliminary discourse to Leland's history. Initially, Leland remarks on the neglect of Irish history after the Norman Invasion of Ireland: the 'circumstances of Ireland' had led to 'prejudices and animosities' that rendered history difficult to write.[55] But while Leland attempts to position himself as a figure of integrity, his next comments on ancient Irish history reflect an ongoing antiquarian debate. The work of seventeenth-century antiquaries Geoffrey Keating and Roderic O'Flaherty, who wished to give the Irish a Milesian origin and to position them as an ancient society rich with learning, had been followed in the eighteenth century by Catholic antiquarians Charles O'Conor and Sylvester O'Halloran. However, there were those who, like Leland himself, insisted on 'the opposing Scytho-Celtic model, in use for generations to promote and confirm the barbarity of the Celts'.[56] Leland remarks a supposed Irish tendency to indulge a 'vanity' of ancient origins but suggests that the evidence of any 'transactions' before the introduction of Christianity into Ireland is scanty.[57] Attacking Keating and Roderic O'Flaherty, he writes that from 'domestic evidence of Irish antiquity' the antiquarian 'forms a regular history, (mixed indeed with childish and absurd fables) of a long succession of kings from the earlier ages of the world'.[58] His own viewpoint is evident when he writes that this preliminary section deals with the period before 'the crown of England' established its authority 'in a country, now, a respectable member of the British empire'.[59] From this Anglo-Irish perspective, after Henry II's invasion, the issues of ancient constitutionalism, played out in England and discussed in *Longsword*, apply to both countries. No separate novelistic treatment is necessary. Published in Cork, Anne Fuller's *Son of Ethelwolf* shares the same emphasis.[60]

The stadial and sentimental histories drawn upon by Sophia Lee in *The Recess* allowed the issue of Ireland to at least be broached: the novel contains episode set in the Ireland of the Nine Years War (1594–1603) but the subject seems, as Owenson later suspects, unlikely to further the cause of 'CONCILIATION'.[61] Lord Essex invites Ellinor, one of the novel's twin daughters of Mary Queen of Scots, to fly with him to Ireland, 'the only place on earth where [she] can be entirely safe' from Elizabeth's tyranny.[62] Travelling alone, she is kidnapped in her 'way towards Ulster' and imprisoned by the amorous 'Tyrone' 'or, as some called him, O'Neal'.[63] Ellinor is, like her sister Matilda, rather too self-absorbed to be rated an entirely reliable narrator but she finds herself 'environed by a set of beings who in complexion alone bore any resemblance to myself, their language, manners, and lives, seeming no more analogous, than those of the inhabitants of the Torrid Zone'. Despite Ellinor's desires to escape Elizabeth, the Irish are presented as an unsettling other. Any romance between Tyrone and Ellinor appears infeasible to the heroine once she finds out that Tyrone has been undermining Essex's position with Elizabeth. Tyrone continues 'to expatiate on his hopes of wholly expelling the English, and ascending the throne of Ireland', but Ellinor asks, 'but what after this unwary and black discovery could his views be to me?'[64] His struggles against Elizabeth, although not precisely condemned, cannot be said to be endorsed. Although *The Recess* draws attention to the gap between official and private accounts, there is little suggestion that the struggle over history is particularly acute in the Irish context.

Neither sentimental and stadial history nor ancient constitutionalism seems to have offered an appropriate tool for examining the Irish situation. Their unsuitability is highlighted by James White in his satirical novel *Earl Strongbow*, which, in its second volume, deals with the twelfth-century Norman invasion of Ireland, a particularly critical point in such antiquarian debates given that Sylvester O'Halloran writes, from this time, the English pursued the 'most savage policy' of abusing Ireland and destroying its 'domestic records'; only rejecting this 'brutal policy' in the 'century past'.[65] Nonetheless, for James Watt, 'while [*Strongbow*] is overtly critical of rapacious imperialism', the novel ultimately supports a 'nation myth': here the 'conquest' of Ireland is represented as 'a particularly beneficial one for the "undisciplined barbarians"'.[66] While Watt acknowledges White's use of humour in the novel, he underestimates its power to challenge such national myths. Alongside the twelfth-century setting, White's amused scepticism regarding antiquarian and historical researches enables him both to counter the genre's usual fascination with Anglo-Saxon England and to interrogate chivalry. Such scepticism reflects White's radical sympathies – also present in his work on abolition and his translations of Mirabeau's speeches and Rabaut de Saint-Étienne's *The History of the Revolution of France* (1792).[67] For White, the myth-making of the imperial centre invites ridicule.

In White's novel an antiquarian finds a manuscript from the reign of Charles II. But departing from the polite fiction of authenticity in Walpole's *Castle of Otranto*, White's manuscript is a record of conversations between the king's prisoner and the ghost of Richard de

Clare – with the ghost effectively becoming the main narrator.[68] When, in the preface to *Mysteries Elucidated*, Mackenzie attacks the tendency to combine the gothic and the historical, she might have had White's novel in mind. In Mackenzie's view, the 'wild, vast and terrific' ideas of the kind produced by Radcliffe become even more suspect when they are combined with 'historical traits'.[69] Nonetheless, the novel does not promote the 'superstition' Mackenzie ostensibly fears. To an even greater extent than Walpole, White (who afterwards writes the similarly deflationary *The Adventures of John of Gaunt* [1790] and *The Adventures of King Richard Coeur-de-Lion* [1791]) uses the gothic to generate a comic unease with history. When the prisoner asks Strongbow why he does not speak in a conventional 'hollow tone', Strongbow replies that, when ghosts do so, it is from 'mere affectation'.[70] The spirit also reveals that, far from having perfect knowledge, spectres are only aware of what happened in their own lifetime and are otherwise reliant on vulgar gossip. Remembering the ponderous antiquary of the frame narrative and his conversations with his elderly female host, it becomes easy to connect such behaviours with the dubious practices of modern scholars. The physical traces that antiquarians prize prove equally unreliable: in this narrative monuments are erected, only to vanish. The spectral Strongbow even pleads with the prisoner to erect a new monument to his corrupt squire Otho.[71] The past can be manufactured at a later date. Whereas Mackenzie, writing in the more cautious climate of 1795, thinks that the function of history in the novel is 'the elucidation of mysteries', White suggests that history itself obfuscates, particularly where patriotism is concerned.[72]

National pride is also belittled. The chivalry that informs Strongbow's narrative is presented as a kind of transnational code, but one in which country determines allegiance. Nonetheless, when an English knight tricks a Welsh soldier at a tournament, the national tension sketched seems to remain on the rather petty level of sporting rivalry. In the second volume, Mac Murragh, King of Leinster (Diarmait Mac Murchada) undermines the chivalric further when he asks for foreign aid in order to regain his position (the event that led to the Norman Invasion of Ireland, in 1169). Mac Murragh's speech ends with a mock epic 'he said', inserted baldly at the beginning of a paragraph, and the evocation of chivalry in the speech is similarly tinged by bathos. He insists that 'Glory' is the 'only object to a knightly mind' and yet he also offers a 'portion' of Leinster's (sexualised) 'fair and fertile plains . . . well-built cities' and 'extensive shores' along with his daughter Eva's hand.[73] Even more dangerously for the chivalric code, he enjoins the knights not to be concerned by the difficulty of the undertaking:

> Recollect, ye that owe allegiance to king Henry, that England, brave, opulent, and united beneath the sway of one magnanimous and martial sovereign, submitted to the swords of your ancestors; and that William, victorious by a single battle, annexed the crown of the Anglo Saxons to the coronet of Normandy.[74]

England, Mac Murragh reminds us, succumbed to invasion before Ireland. At the same time the model of centre (England) and periphery (Ireland) is also disturbed by the presence in the narrative of the independent Welsh prince 'Lewellyn', by the Danes of Dublin and by the evocation of a shared Norman heritage. The strong sense of division, of fractured and shifting territories and peoples, makes it hard to map contemporary national pride (particularly English pride) onto the twelfth-century political landscape.

Having established this point, White addresses the English patriotic myth more directly. Following Edmund Spenser's disrespect for the Irish bards, Leland had linked the Irish 'filea or bards' with 'abuses' and 'oppression'.[75] White responds by including a sketch of a minstrel employed by Strongbow:

> Oppression, discord, rapine, cease:
> Erin, fair England shall to thee
> Impart the principles of peace
> And teach to love true liberty[76]

Although this verse celebrates the benefits of English colonialism, Claribert's message has already been doubly undermined. Not only has his function as a propagandist been discussed at length in the text, but even here he only begins to sing after Strongbow has asked him 'to make a further impression on this illustrious audience'.[77] Strongbow employs minstrelsy to strengthen his chance of leading the troops into Ireland.

Once in Ireland, the knights' performance is scarcely more heroic. White gives pages of debate concerning military strategy to be pursued and, according to Tompkins, 'we begin to detect beneath the helmets of Strongbow's barons the features of the faithful commons of George III': Fox (Fitzstephens), Pitt (William Fitz-Aldhelm), Burke (Sir Theodore Fitzhenry) and Sheridan (Redmond Cantimere).[78] Yet the prolixity of the discussion ensures it reflects well on no one, whilst the identification of Strongbow with the vice-royal 'Lord Temple' (George Nugent-Temple-Grenville, 1st Marquess of Buckingham), which Tompkins also argues for, is potentially unflattering.[79] In July 1782 Temple became Lord Lieutenant of Ireland. At this time, the Constitution of 1782 gave Ireland greater legislative independence, independence which was supplemented by the Renunciation Act of 1783, in which Temple was credited with playing an important role.[80] Temple had also 'instituted enquiries into petty fraud among the minor officials State'. Yet, while Strongbow, like Lord Temple, fights against corruption, in White's narrative, he has also introduced it by appointing his avaricious and 'jobbing' squire to a position of responsibility.[81] In this context, Strongbow's '*perhapsing*' about the improvement of Ireland (in a speech that is reminiscent of Gulliver's political fantasies in Jonathan Swift's *Travels* [1726]), seems unconvincing.[82] Even if 'the time may come, when the senate of Britain shall owe its brightest ornaments, her theatre its wittiest pieces, her armies their wisest generals, to the nation she now despises', the supposed 'imperfection[s]' of 'the natives of Hibernia' appear unlikely to be improved by English rule.[83]

James White's novel challenges ancient constitutionalism by offering a broader perspective on the shifting dynastic politics of the eleventh and twelfth centuries – and it also destabilises the connection between chivalry and eighteenth-century sensibility. The romance of chivalry itself seems under threat in Strongbow's narrative, particularly where Ireland is concerned. Although Strongbow desires 'the beautiful Geralda', immediately after her death he marries Eva.[84] Eva was 'fair' but 'I loved her not', he narrates.[85] The countries are joined not by mutual affection but by 'the seeds of young ambition'.[86] In *Eva, an Old Irish Story* Anna Millikin rewrites this account, suggesting that the dynastic relationship between Eva and Strongbow had at least some kind of sanction in affection.

Like *Longsword* and *Son of Ethelwolf*, Millikin's earlier work *Corfe Castle; Or, Historic Tracts. A Novel* (1793) is set in the period of 'Aethelred (surnamed the Unready)' and suggests a decline in the justice associated with Anglo-Saxon kingship.[87] Significantly for Millikin's later novel on Ireland, the real barriers to justice seem to lie with the sexual politics of dynastic succession. The heroine Algitha cannot marry her lover Sigefert because she is pre-contracted to another lord (who luckily, in a drunken haze, marries someone else); a similar difficulty is encountered by the minor character Maud in an inset story (her choice, Edwin, is already betrothed although shortly after marriage his wife conveniently dies). Most significantly of all, Queen Emma, wife of Aethelred, reveals that she is in love with Canute. She had, she explains, met him in her youth in Normandy before she was forcibly married off to aid cross-channel relations. The novel ends with the celebration of their marriage, implying an acceptance of the Danes. Genuine harmony and justice between peoples can only occur, Millikin suggests, if the sexual politics of dynastic succession are replaced with a more modern narrative of mutual affection.

The point is even more strongly made in *Eva, an Old Irish Story*. Although the Norman Invasion of Ireland was sanctioned by the Pope (in an attempt to bring the Irish church more fully under Papal control), Millikin bypasses this issue. Instead the narrative focuses on the sexual behaviour of 'Dermot the Duke of Leinster'. Dermot is dispossessed of his kingship by 'Roderic' (High King of Ireland, Ruaidri Ua Conchobair) because of his abduction of Dervorghal (wife of the King of Breifne, Tiernan O'Rouke). Historically speaking, the actual age of Dervorghal when abducted is uncertain. However, in this tale, the youthful Dermot first falls in love with her while at the court of Murchard. When, later, during a war with her husband, he meets her again he indulges 'that passion which was now become criminal'.[88] Not only Dermot but also Regan (the young hero, Eva's Irish suitor) and Donogh, the old retainer, condemn such behaviour: 'the hand of Heaven itself was armed against the guilty Dermot, while Roderic's cause was good, who fought against an adulterer'.[89]

Dermot disrupts both familial and dynastic ties yet, despite his self-blame, he learns nothing. As well as inviting in foreigners to reclaim his territories, against his daughter's wishes he promises her hand in marriage to Strongbow, Richard de Clare. Although Dermot temporises over this pledge, delaying in an attempt to gain the support of Eva's lover, Regan, his territorial ambitions ultimately lead him to insist that the ceremony take place. 'Thou art my child and I have used a parent's right in disposing of thee, for thy benefit and mine', he storms when Eva expostulates with him.[90] The lesson Leinster fails to grasp but which Millikin underlines is that while individual desire should not break existing contracts, such agreements must involve some kind of mutual affection. Equally, contra Burke, one generation should not make agreements that bind the next.

In Millikin's account, Leinster's failure to curb his lusts leads to the invasion of Ireland. Perhaps reflecting Millikin's Anglo-Irish background, while the author's condemnation of Dermot amounts to an implicit rejection of the invasion, her position regarding the Normans (and English) themselves is more equivocal. Strongbow is shown to have similarly suffered as a result of dynastic pre-contracts and his worthiness (as a husband if not as a ruler of Ireland) is made quite plain when Regan, Eva's lover, urges from his deathbed: 'take [Eva] as my dying gift, I bequeath her to thee'.[91] Yet while this masculine contract seems to have authorial sanction, Eva's silence is telling, signalling an equivocation allowed by romance. In sentimental terms, the 'history' of Strongbow may have left the Irish princess somewhat reconciled to her fate but feminine modesty forbids utterance. In national terms she cannot agree to the marriage since, as the final sentence has it, Strongbow's invasion 'led the way for King Henry, who not long after landed, and assumed the sovereignty of Ireland'.[92]

Eva's ambiguous feminine silence seems suitably cautious given the difficult political conditions both at home and internationally. Millikin's novel was published against the menacing backdrop of war with France (the French had declared war against Britain on 1 February 1793) and in an Ireland where a far more radical strain of rhetoric was gaining ground. The Society of United Irishmen, formed in 1791, was, Jim Smyth writes, 'to a contemporary foreign eye ... readily identifiable as an Irish Paineite ... or Jacobin-style movement'.[93] Their struggle for parliamentary reform became a struggle for independence, leading to the rebellion of 1798. Besides this, the kind of cautious national conscious-ness evident in White's and Millikin's works appears relatively unthreat-ening. Neither novel rejects the imperial connection between Ireland and England, whilst the 'milliners', 'Countesses', and 'Lads of Westminster and Eton', whom White mockingly identifies as his readership in his *Adventures of Richard Coeur de Lion*, seem unlikely revolutionaries.[94]

Yet White criticises Ireland's government and Millikin is silent on Ireland's consent to a closer relation with its invaders. Equally, like the Scottish historical novels, both works connect nation with the allegori-cal potential of romance and hence raise the issue of choice in relation to national identity. Given this, White's apparently playful decision to arrange his readers into camps is perhaps more significant than it might initially seem. While the milliners reject the novels, the lads of Eton, he writes, 'are determined to stand by me. *Victoria! Huzza! Huzza!*'.[95] This sense of contest, even if bathetic, references the ferocity of the war of ideas. In *Adventures of John of Gaunt* (1790) White suggested he expected a hostile response to his work and Reeve's *Memoirs of Sir Roger de Clarendon*, set, like White's novel, in the reign of Edward III, provided it.[96] Whereas White mocks the exaggeration of past chivalry, Reeve describes a period of 'splendour' and 'glorious patronage and protection'.[97] Ultimately it was far easier to articulate an uncomplicated national romance from the centre.

## Rome

Even as writers expressed their unease regarding both the Union and the rights of the people, the patriotic demands of the French Revolutionary Wars generated the need to imagine greater solidarity at home. If narra-tives of romance that envisaged union between England, Scotland and

Ireland depicted only an uneasy alliance at best, an alternative narrative that promised to combine the rhetoric of liberty with colonialism was available. In *William Wallace* the hero addresses his troops: 'history's page shall rank us with those Roman heroes who fought, who bled, who *died* for liberty'.[98] Like Burke's comparison between Rome and Paris, Siddons's wording was influenced by the narrative of Roman liberty which the revolutionaries employed. As Lynn Hunt notes, while English radicals referred to the 'purity of their Saxon pasts' and American radicals to the 'new world', the French 'hearkened to . . . a 'mythic present', 'leap[ing] over the French national past and turn[ing] to Roman and Greek models for inspiration'.[99] Defiantly co-opted, a similar narrative could be useful to those writers who wished to ensure British solidarity in the face of the French threat.

Ellis Cornelia Knight wrote *Marcus Flaminius* as an armchair guide to Rome and the second volume has lengthy descriptions of monuments and their Republican meaning. But Knight has made the Republican dream represented by these fragments of antiquity more attractive by exploring the alternatives of revolution and despotism earlier in the novel. The work opens with the Roman defeat at the Battle of Teutoburg Forest (AD 9). Imprisoned by the Cheruscans, stranded in alien Germania, Marcus writes (largely unanswered) letters to Septimius in which he describes the primitive tribe's decline. As I have discussed elsewhere, these letters are on one level an analysis of the causes of the French Revolution: not only the problems of labour, but also philosophy, false notions of liberty and a corrupt priesthood generate unjustified unrest amongst the Cheruscans.[100] Aware of contemporary parallels between Germania and the British constitution, Knight draws on Tacitus to produce a picture of decay. Tactitus's account of the Germanic tribes had been used by Adam Ferguson to provide evidence of the primitive social stage in his *Essay on the History of Civil Society* (1767).[101] In contrast, Knight's stadial adaptation of Tacitus concentrates on the Cheruscans, a tribe he had suggested was in decline. Their insolent behaviour suggests the possibility of revolution in Britain. Worse still, her account of Marcus's adventures in Rome emphasises the potential for luxurious decline amongst the upper classes. The Roman Republican constitution was sometimes seen as reflecting the British system of checks and balances. Alluding to Gibbon's *The Decline and Fall of the Roman Empire* (1776–88) and choosing to discuss a period when this constitution was in decline, Knight suggests that Britain, like France, is in danger from corrupt rule.[102]

If Knight's novel suggests that the British lower and upper ranks are both vulnerable to decay and revolution, her book is also a study of centre and periphery, an examination of the correct mode of imperialism. In this account, whether considered as a small political unit, like the tribes of Germania, or as an imperial force, like Rome, the kingdom can and should defend itself. But the ability to do this is dependent on the right values, those of the Roman Republic. In *Marcus Flaminius* the imperial centre and small nation face decline for a similar reason – the predominance of luxurious self-interest. While other historical novels like *Monmouth* had begun to suggest that the luxury of the centre might be cured by the hardiness of the periphery, and to envisage romance or, more particularly, marriage as a kind of vehicle for this, Knight's fear of the persuasive negativity of luxury leads her to argue against this position. Instead of a marriage between centre and periphery, she proposes a union based on Republican virtue. The scenario that allows the exploration of such combined and uneven development seems familiar from the later national tale.

A reluctant wanderer, finding himself enduring an enforced stay in an apparently barbarous country, begins a process of cultural exploration and comparison. Although Marcus, Knight's hero, is a first-century Roman, his depth of feeling marks him as a sentimental hero of the late eighteenth and early nineteenth century. Marcus, for instance, comments upon the 'vivacity of [his] imagination', a quality he shares with Owenson's hero, Horatio, in *The Wild Irish Girl*, a 'genius' whose mind has 'the bright colouring of romantic eccentricity'.[103] Further, after the Battle of Teutoburg Marcus's distress at his survival of his regiment and sense of isolation from Rome combine a sense of historical verisimilitude (some of Valerius's generals are said to have committed suicide) with the emotion of a man of feeling. With his suicidal urges, Marcus shares a national characteristic with the modern English (supposedly inclined to melancholia). But his drive to self-destruction is civically rather than personally motivated. In this significant way, Marcus is unlike the cosmopolitan wanderer typical of the national tale. In contrast to Owenson's Horatio, at the beginning of the novel Marcus already has a purpose and a strong sense of duty, following the advice of Valerius to 'prove [himself] a descendant of those Romans who had saved their country from domestic slavery and foreign invasion'.[104] Although Marcus's society may be in decline, he himself is a representative of what for Knight is a better model of power.

Marcus's position in relation to the Cheruscan women reads as an approximate if less optimistic template for the later cross-cultural sexual adventures of the early national tale.[105] Knight suggests that Marcus's growing intimacy with the daughter of a Cheruscan chieftain is dangerous. Initially, the Cheruscan women possess the simplicity and genius of Owenson's Glorvina.[106] Praising the early purity of the German tribes, Tacitus wrote that they lived 'uncorrupted by the temptations of public shows or the excitements of banquets. Clandestine love letters are unknown to men and women alike'.[107] But such simplicity proves vulnerable when Philocles, the revolutionary 'philosopher', decides to hold a banquet at which 'A beautiful young woman about eighteen years of age' sings 'an ode in praise of Apollo'.[108] The performer, Bertha, becomes sexually aware, carving Marcus's name in 'Roman characters' on 'a large oak'.[109] The step from performance to corruption is short.

The Republican Marcus should not marry the representative of 'rude' Germania but neither must he select a bride tainted by the luxurious imperial centre. Marcus's Roman fiancée, Aurelia, not only espouses another man but is complicit in a plot to overthrow the Roman emperor. In this stadial account, neither primitivism nor sophistication form a suitable basis for the strong nation or empire. Instead, Marcus marries the virtuous daughter of the Republican Valerius and they have, not children, but guests – British princes who are instructed in the true Republican history. After going to the Portian hill (perhaps a reference to the home of Marcus Porcius, Cato the Elder, known for his strict adherence to the virtues of ancient Rome and his thrift), the princes say that they had been 'pleased with the situation, but had not perceived anything remarkable in the house'.[110] Valerius, the good Republican friend of Marcus, corrects them:

> You have seen . . . the most interesting spot in this neighbourhood, the spot that deserves to be viewed with the most exalted reverence. Art and luxury are at this time in great perfection . . . But remember, princes, that the greatness of Rome does not consist in sumptuous buildings.[111]

Here 'Art and luxury' have an insidious influence, skewing the taste of even the most politically virtuous and ensuring that written 'history' itself becomes unreliable. Under these circumstances, it becomes crucial, Knight implies, to be able accurately to read the landscape. 'Colossal figures . . . and porticos of immeasurable length' are not, one must realise, symbolic of strength: they distort the judgment so that even if the 'magnificent pyramid of Caius Cestius' is a record of 'disinterested generosity', its grandeur connects it with social decline, while the Rostral Column, celebrating the naval battle of Mylae, in its starkness represents Roman virtue.[112] Knight is making a kind of disambiguation of the Burkean sublime: significance must be distinguished from mere magnificence. Through such reading, the princes and Marcus are interpolated in a narrative of national glory. In *Marcus Flaminius* the romance that will finally unify 'tribes' of Britain is an ideological one reliant on a certain

– antiquarian – reading of history in the landscape. Like the Roman Empire, the British Empire will eventually export such values, allowing union between the conquerors and their subjects.

Some of the same preoccupations (without the stadial influence) are present in the much slighter work, *Arville Castle: An Historical Romance* (1795). This anonymous work is far less historiographically self-conscious than *Marcus Flaminius*; it invokes 'fancy', 'fiction' and 'sensibility' in the verses on its title page and commences with a string of family and love relationships.[113] Although both Clara Reeve and Jane West wish to claim a more weighty meaning for historical romance as a form which presents what is ideal as well as patriotically aspirational, at first *Arville Castle* seems to be a 'historical romance' in the lightest sense – a story in which the laws of probability are only lightly observed. *The Critical Review* describes it as 'a wild, romantic story, violating without scruple, all the laws of nature and probability, – about forests and banditti, – murders and apparitions, – wandering damsels, and faithful lovers' – in short, 'a delectable and perfectly harmless entertainment' for those with nothing better to do.[114] Nonetheless, set in the first century against the backdrop of Boadicea's defence of 'Britain' against the Romans, and her subsequent suicide, this work examines resistance against imperialism: all the family relationships so carefully detailed are compromised by the apparent patriotic duty of struggling against the Romans. More startlingly, after portraying the brutality of the invasion, the author then unexpectedly makes a case for integration and adaption to a new ruling class. Romance becomes re-envisaged as a kind of cross-national breeding programme. This is surprising if read as a reflection on the French Revolutionary Wars but makes rather more sense if viewed as a commentary on the need for solidarity within the Union in a time of conflict.

*Arville Castle* owes a significant debt to *The Recess*. Both books register the suppression of part of the ruling class, recording their exile from the structures of power. However, *Arville Castle* also envisages their return to authority. When Boadicea heads 'a considerable army against' Suetonius, the Baron Arville, a former 'prodigy in the field of battle' and his two sons, Edwin and Eldred fight for their 'country'.[115] All are presumed dead. Nonetheless, on the arrival of the Romans at the castle, some of the family's women escape – with the help of a domestic – to the recess-like cave. Typically for the sentimental novel, and in what becomes an increasingly important motif in historical fiction, what is imagined is an aristocracy that survives because of the support of the peasantry. In a curious reversal of the scene in *Ethelinde* describing the aftermath of battle, Ellen goes in search of the corpses of the male part of her family and her lover, Raymond. 'Thousands of slain were yet above the surface of the earth, many in part devoured by the birds and animals of prey.'[116] At first reluctant to become a 'plunderer' of the dead, Ellen determines, after a dream, that she will rob their corpses.[117] In a move apparently sanctioned by the narrator, the very bodies of those who fought for 'Britain' become the means of the defunct aristocracy supporting themselves. Gradually, too, the family in the recess take supplies from their castle, despite the Romans, ultimately even managing to abstract beds and tables. Living off the surplus of former days, and aided by Leonard, the domestic, the aristocracy wait to recover their rights.

The route to this recovery in the face of invasion is not straightforward. At first the Romans display all the villainous characteristics expected of invaders – Suetonius is 'sanguinary'; 'the whole race of [Druids]' are 'extirpated by the cruel Romans'; and 'their men either killed or made prisoners, left not hope for the wretched females of those days'.[118] Rape or death seem the only alternatives for the remaining British women. But this female-orientated society (mirroring that found in *The Recess*) gains a kind of symbolic fertility: as Ellen, one of the novel's heroines, discovers after she dons male clothes, neither the Druids nor all the British men are dead. Not only can marriage still (implicitly) be celebrated, but the reader discovers that Raymond, Ellen's lover, is still alive. Raymond is protected by the virtuous Roman Julius and travels to Rome, on his return 'conciliating the differences betwixt the Romans and the Britains, intermarrying the women with those under his command, and by that means endearing the families to each other'.[119] The family structures severed by war are put back together but on a national scale. Moreover, during this process, the Romans, with their 'prolific' 'wives', become 'naturalized to Britain', displaying a fertility echoed by the landscape itself. In this narrative, the colonised areas become superior to those that still resist Roman rule ('no part of Britain was better cultivated or more populous').[120]

Against this background of fertility and generation, the aristocratic family still remains resistant. Their continuing opposition to Roman rule (an opposition largely carried out by non-cooperation through hiding) suggests some narrative difficulty. Even while promoting integration, the author finds it difficult to imagine a ruling class surrendering power over the nation. Hence, in Rome Raymond himself refuses to marry Constantia daughter of Claudius, remaining loyal to Ellen and thus to the older national bloodline. A greater difficulty still is faced by Alice, wife of Edwin, who, separated from the rest of the women in the castle, becomes trapped during the Roman occupation. Alice spends much of the narrative insane, indifferent to Julius's besotted attempts to ensure her recovery. Alice represents a failure to accept regime change or historical breakage: she is imprisoned in the past, talking to those presumed dead, or subject to uncontrollable fits of grief. The logic of the narrative dictates that only some serious experimentation with gender can aid her. Disguised as the male harper, Leod, Ellen gains Julius's trust and plays outside Alice's room. Asked 'the subject of the song', she replies, 'One made, my Lord, at the beginning of the battle, which ended so fatally for Britain.'[121] Played on the harp, here presumably a national symbol for the whole of Britain, this song elicits some signs of memory from Alice. History must be acknowledged and accepted before the family can be regenerated. After this performance, the cure is eventually completed when Ellen/Leod 'disguises' herself as a woman and when Alice is reintroduced to her child, a 'diminutive' version of his father.[122] The living family (albeit strangely distorted) restores national consciousness.

Although Julius eventually marries the Saxon Elfrida, this dislike of miscegenation amongst the ruling classes continues (underlined by an unpleasant passage later in the book when Edwin and Elfred record how they were 'rather too agreeable' to the 'black virgins' of Barbary).[123] The larger the potential empire, the greater the problems of union. The issue, in Britain at least, is solved in relation to the rule of law. Here the narrative reinterprets the episode in *Caleb Williams*, where Caleb experiences first the brutality, and then the philosophy, of a gang of thieves. In Godwin's novel, inequality and injustice linked with the legal system and with society more generally is the target. As Mr Raymond, the leader, puts it: 'We, who are thieves without a licence, are at open war with another set of men, who are thieves according to law.'[124] In *Arville Castle* the situation is given not just a social, but an explicitly national context. Raymond and another young man, Leodine, are 'traversing a large forest near the close of night when the most dismal shrieks' draw their attention.[125] Hijacked by the banditti responsible, they are taken to community in forest where the leader remarks:

> 'I spent my youth,' continued he, 'in the service of my country, but found it unable either to reward my courage, or give me a stability in it; I therefore left the world in disgust, and retired here with my wife, my family, and several others of my neighbours . . .'[126]

Here patriotism is invoked only to evaporate: it is the lack of reward that has caused Dunstan's retreat. Equally, Dunstan's remarks suggest that domesticity is a key feature of the enclave, only for the friends to discover forced prostitution is the custom of the gang. The promises of the extra-national community gradually all prove false. When the 'lawless ravishers with which Britain now abounded' turn out not to be Romans but treacherous Britons, the Arvilles and the Romans unite in common cause against the threat.[127] Class privilege is more important than national affiliation. To preserve such privilege, previous and present rulers may join in matrimony.

Both *Marcus Flaminius* and *Arville Castle* connect liberty and the nation, albeit in sometimes surprising, even distasteful ways. Indeed, ironically, because these works are pro-Union they can encourage greater national fervour than works that are equivocal on the subject. From a position of hegemonic confidence, both novels picture an extended national family (whether ideological or actual) in order to encourage widespread identification with the nation. Through a blend of symbolism, historiography and romance, they subsume the struggle for rights and representation into the idea of national liberty. However, the form of national liberty they construct is curiously empty. *Marcus Flaminius* and *Arville Castle* foreshadow the 1800 Act of Union, which would remove political power from Dublin to London, and implicitly justify colonialism.

## National Liberties, National Tales?

Using the Second Partition of Poland (1793) and the Kościuszko Uprising of 1794 Jane Porter's *Thaddeus of Warsaw* (1803) offers a lesson to the English on the subject of political freedom. After the First Partition of Poland in 1772, King Stanislaus Augustus had executed a series of modernising military, political and economic reforms. Despite this, in 1792 the Russians invaded, leading to the Second Partition and the loss of substantial territories. Following popular protest, in March 1794 the patriot Tadeusz Kościuszko led an uprising which was quickly crushed, the event with which the novel opens. In one battle for Polish independence against the Russians, Porter's hero, Thaddeus, fights with and saves a young man, Pembroke Somerset. Informed that Pembroke is not Russian but English, Thaddeus exclaims 'An Englishman! And raise his arm against a country struggling for liberty!'[128] Somerset has been persuaded to fight for the Russians against the Polish by his tutor, Loftus. Re-educated by Thaddeus, Somerset protests against Loftus's *'ardour in the cause of insulted Russia, and [his] hatred of that levelling power which pervades all Europe'*.[129] The tutor has been deceived by claims (made by Catherine the Great extra-textually and Baroness Surowkoff within the novel) that Poland's attempts at independent political reform are influenced by French Jacobinism. The danger, Porter argues, to the English as well as Loftus and Pembroke, is that, while they combat France, their appreciation for other forms of liberty becomes eroded. Whereas Knight occasionally bemoans the unreliability of Britain's allies, Porter sees them as a corrupting influence.

For Porter sympathy for the freedom of the small country is essential to British liberty. This sympathy is particularly important because of, this stadially influenced narrative argues, the dangers of selfish commerciality in England.[130] The corruption of this late stage means that Somerset can only learn 'real disinterested *amor patriæ*' by studying the Polish past and present.[131] Staying with the Sobieskis at Villanow, former residence of John Sobieski, Pembroke acknowledges that his own ancestry had only provided him with a 'lesson which [he] conned over in drowsy carelessness at home'.[132] In Poland, in contrast, 'the noble dead seem to address me from their graves; and I blush at the inglorious life I might have pursued'. It is not only that the novelty of other examples is necessary to 'awaken' proper 'associations' but that in Poland past examples find their echo in the present. The dead voices which 'address' Pembroke do so through Thaddeus himself. In an example of what Colley describes as the construction of an aristocracy of service, Thaddeus allows Porter to modify British rhetoric against Napoleonic and Russian imperialism.[133] Thaddeus teaches Somerset to distinguish between 'the patriot and the assassin; between the defender of his country and the ravager of other states'.[134] Patriotism should be defensive rather than expansionist.

As *Thaddeus of Warsaw* indicates, the historical novel represents both possibilities and limitations when it comes to inscribing nationalism. Porter distinguishes between reform and rebellion. She displays a wariness concerning empire and encourages sympathy for the nationalist project. But this sympathy is only to a point: Thaddeus's patriotism is cautious and, like the impoverished O'Donnel in Owenson's 1814 novel, he is restricted in his opportunities to use his military skills. The potential for national independence is raised only to be foreclosed: Poland awaits 'with firmness the approach of the earthquake which was to ingulph it in the neighbouring nations'.[135] Whilst Porter particularly excels in creating an atmosphere of inevitability, it is true that in the historical novel more generally what has already happened tends to restrict what can be: hence in the context of the home nations, the form tends to accept union (even if it tries to advantage the smaller nation within the larger geopolitical entity). In line with this, instead of providing an antiquarian history 'under the sign of the bard', the historical novel tends to be more cautious.[136] Antiquarianism is mocked (White), displaced (Knight) and interrogated. The bardic (seen here most clearly in *Arville Castle*) is used to support the union – the novel's anonymous author kills the 'druids' off except for one who (in contrast to Gray's bard) aids colonial integration. Even supposedly indigenous instruments (the harp, the bagpipe) perform similar functions.

Nonetheless, by amassing nationalist tropes, the historical novel opens a space for the novelistic consideration of nationalism and the independence of the small nation. In particular, through its use of stadial history, its interest in romance (and therefore in choice) and its inter-rogation of colonialism, the historical novel of the 1790s foreshadows the national tale. The complex history of the latter genre falls outside the scope of this enquiry.[137] However, it is worth noting that in Maria Edgeworth's *Castle Rackrent* (1800), the post-French Revolution sense of the recent past as history is fused with the dynastic romances found in the historical novel of union. But romance fails and domestic dishar-mony underlines the failure of progress in Ireland. On the other hand, in what is often acknowledged as the first national tale, *The Wild Irish Girl* (1806), Sydney Owenson uses romance to frame antiquarian debate and to transform the stadial reading of the Irish as barbarous. In doing so, she reverses the structure of the historical novel.

Whereas in *Castle Rackrent* the stadial development from feudal to commercial runs alongside a series of failed marriages, Owenson's prac-tice overhauls Ellis Cornelia Knight's. In *Marcus Flaminius* Knight had imagined an encounter between social stages in terms of a failed romance: in her account the primitive Bertha is an unsuitable match for Republican Marcus. Owenson, on the other hand, has a project of conciliation that must at least allow for a future marriage. Like Bertha and Marcus, who represent 'barbarism' and 'civilisation', Glorvina and Horatio seem to embody the different stages, primitive and commercial, of stadial history. But Owenson wishes to challenge the idea of the barbarity of the Irish and this means that stadial history, with its evocation of a 'rude' earlier stage, must itself be challenged. Here Owenson's choice of a contempo-rary rather than historical setting is decisive. Operating in the present, Glorvina and Horatio are freed from the constrictions of the historical novel, allowing Glorvina to become one of the primary means by which Owenson's version of Irish history is promoted. Glorvina, and, alongside her, the priest shape the way the stages are conceived by emphasising the antiquarian narrative of 'a glorious ancient Gaelic past' and drawing on the 'native Gaelic myth of Milesian origins'.[138]

Glorvina's account of the Milesian origins of the Irish and of Gaelic pre-Christian greatness, is supplemented by Owenson's extensive use, in the footnotes, of the work of Irish Protestant and Catholic antiquar-ians who supported this version of history. Whereas James White attempted to dismiss English and Anglo-Irish constructions of Irish history by mocking Norman minstrels and interrogating antiquarianism, Owenson's textual apparatus reverses this strategy. She draws upon Joseph Cooper Walker's *Historical Memoirs of the Irish Bards* (1786), and on Charlotte Brooke's *Reliques of Irish Poetry* (1789) to refute Macpherson's claims in *Ossian* of Scottish bardic superiority, and she uses the works of Sylvester O'Halloran and Charles O'Conor to reclaim the Irish antiquarian traditions upon which such accounts of Irish cultural richness were based. As Ina Ferris notes, Owenson 'make[s] palpable' the 'struggle' to maintain literary and historical memory.[139] But she also picks a side: the interaction of romance in the text and history in the notes ensures that this is a battle that Leland has essentially lost. The references co-opt even those historians with doubts about Irish pre-Christian greatness wherever possible.[140] Additionally, in the face of Glorvina's erotic performance of Irishness, the determination to insist, as Leland does, on the fabulous status of Irish history seems churlish. The urge is to succumb, like Horatio, to Glorvina's pedagogy.[141] The suspect desires of the dynastic matches found in the historical novel are replaced with modern romance. This modern romance contains and transforms the materials of the national past.

Owenson's rearrangement of the materials makes *The Wild Irish Girl* somewhat of a historiographic tour de force and this in turn influences Edgeworth. Except in the editor's pro-Union framing, *Castle Rackrent* seems to offer little hope for improvement. However, Edgeworth's later Irish fictions, *Ennui* (1809), *The Absentee* (1812) and *Ormond* (1817), introduce the possibility of re-education and regeneration by modifying the modern romance employed by Owenson. The writers remain distinct in their approaches and their doubts. While Edgeworth pushes towards utopian transparency of exchange in which the Irish absentees self-exiled by Union will return home educated in proper progressive fashion, Owenson continues to modify her arguments concerning the often fantastic performance of history. But both register concern regarding the malleable nature of the past. As the forged seals and forged letters of *Patronage* (1814) and *Helen* prove, Edgeworth is well aware that even outside colonial space the signs of Enlightenment authenticity are easily hijacked. The progress that depends on such accuracy is fragile. Correspondingly Owenson realises that the very performance of history that is supposed to allow escape from the position of colonialism easily comes to reinforce it. Like Tiberius's subjects in *Marcus Flaminius* who are forced to perform in the way the emperor wishes, the hero of her novel *O'Donnel* must act – and the colonisers decide what part he should play. It takes the considerable ingenuity of the Duchess of Belmont or, later, of the heroine of *Florence Macarthy: An Irish Tale* (1818) to avoid the trap.[142]

Miranda Burgess divides criticism of the national tale into two opposing categories. The first, headed by Nicola Watson and Gary Kelly,
suggests the genre 'propos[es] "formal and thematic resolutions"'; the
second sees the form as less concerned with 'stability' and more with
'dialogue and critical assessment'.[143] This division signals an anxiety
concerning the tales' relationship to nationalism and national independence, an anxiety that reflects an ambiguity in the nascent national tale
itself. Although Owenson's and Edgeworth's tales are post-Union and
contain conciliatory elements, their presence also signals that the union
has not yet been (and perhaps never truly will be) completed. As such,
they build on the ambivalence of the 1790s historical novel of nation.
That genre ostensibly supports the composite nature of Britain and
Ireland and supports Hanoverian rule but, in the act of reimagining,
points to sites of anxiety concerning the nation's origins. This is not least
because 'liberty' is a key term in such works. In the British historical
novel, the examination of the construction of the political liberty and
prerogatives of the individual subject leads almost inevitably to the consideration of the freedom of the nation, sometimes with peculiar results.

The Anglo-Saxon novel of ancient liberties had proved an efficient
vehicle for examining judicial fairness and the balance of power.
However, by expanding the territory of the historical novel beyond
England, authors were able to introduce other, more radical topics.
When Siddons considered Scotland, he could broach not only the issue
of equality before the law, but also the problem of legitimate rule. But
if Wallace is a sign under which political liberty and national independence are connected, when the historical novel deals with more recent
Scottish history the relationship between the freedoms enjoyed by the
individual subject and the liberty of the nation becomes more baroque.
Mackenzie's justification of the Monmouth Rebellion also signals a
need to justify the Glorious Revolution and the 1707 Act of Union.
With the removal of the Stuarts, there is no dynastic underpinning to
union: instead, Mackenzie proposes a romance between individual (if
aristocratic) Scottish subjects – such relations will allow the courtly
luxury of the centre to be tempered by peripheral simplicity. But even
as the Union subsumes the idea of individual political liberty, containing radicalism, the strange logic of the historical novel reveals that to
accept Hanoverian Britain is to accept ongoing political change – even,
perhaps, to countenance revolution itself.

In Mackenzie's work, stadial history, common beliefs and modern-
ised romance join the English and the Scots. But in the Irish context all
these were unavailable. Not only was there no common belief between
the Irish Catholic majority and the English, and no royal marriage to

overwrite, but also the issue of Irish progress at any particular period was a matter of contention, connected with the meaning of English rule. Thus, whereas the historical novel suggested it was possible to imagine political expression for Scotland within the Union, the genre underlines that this was scarcely possible for Ireland. When the historical novel seeks to strengthen the ties between England and Ireland, its uneasy romantic fictions expose historical contingency and reveal the legitimacy of choice. Even the appeal to a Roman heritage made by Knight and the anonymous author of *Arville Castle* has a similar effect. Although such a heritage could not be easily mapped onto Ireland, Scotland or parts of Wales, these novels attempt to underpin alliances at home and imperialism abroad. Such works (sometimes distastefully) expand romance, but in doing so open a space not only of imperial but also of nationalist desire. Ultimately, the elements of stadial history and romance found in the historical novel would be recombined in the national tale, persuasively redirecting and containing the troubled elements of Irish history.

When considering the 1790s historical novel of nation, as when considering the national tale, it is worth remembering that 'conciliation' is an ambiguous term. Mentioned by Owenson in her dedication *to O'Donnel*, the word brings to mind a moment of genial understanding that replaces hostility – it recalls King George III's reaction to *Castle Rackrent* – he 'rubbed his hands & said "what what – I know something now of my Irish subjects"'.[144] Yet to Lord Clare in the year of the Irish Rebellion it meant something much more unpleasantly radical. After the Earl of Morin urged both the English and Irish House of Lords to 'conciliatory measures' on 19 February 1798, Lord Clare insisted at extreme length that 'Concession and conciliation have produced only a fresh stock of grievances'.[145] Referring to the Constitution of 1782, which had removed legal restrictions from the Irish parliament and introduced a time of relative legislative freedom, Clare suggests such conciliation becomes a kind of fruitless appeasement. It functions as an admission of the unfairness of Westminster's political dominance that only generates further anger. To conciliate is to come close to recognising the legitimacy of independence. The arrangement of history and romance in the historical novel exposes a similar ambiguity. If dynastic succession gives legitimacy and modern romance suggests a positive selection of national partner, within the historical novel the erotics of desire for union do not quite work. Dynastic arguments appear thin, choice seems compromised. The potential for harmonious, mutually beneficial union is raised only to be immediately haunted by its opposite.

The historical novel of this period also offers a warning concerning the danger of fusing the concepts of liberty and nation. Its uneasy romances demonstrate that while the nation can certainly function as a vehicle for promoting the political liberties and representation of the people, it can also be a way of channelling the radical desire for individual liberty into a narrative of self-sacrifice for the larger unit. As allegory and history struggle, the historical novel of the 1790s raises the possibility of constitutional reform and of national independence. It does so cautiously, intermittently, sometimes, seemingly, even despite itself. In the next decade historical novelists would build on the idea of history as romance and the idea of history as science to promote loyalty to the nation as the major form of political self-expression.

## Notes

1. Scott, *Waverley*, p. 352.
2. Trumpener, *Bardic Nationalism*, p. 4.
3. For Scottish Enlightenment influence on Scott see, for example, Garside, 'Scott and the Philosophical Historians', in relation to Scott's *Quentin Durward* (1823), pp. 503–4.
4. See Nordius, 'A Tale of Other Places', pp. 162–76.
5. Richard Price, *A Discourse on the Love of Our Country*, p. 34.
6. Burke, *Reflections*, p. 104.
7. Shields, *Sentimental Literature*, p. 1.
8. Watt, *Contesting the Gothic*, p. 7.
9. Reeve, *Progress*, 1: 57.
10. Reeve, *Memoirs*, 1: xx, xxi.
11. Reeve, *Memoirs*, 1: xx.
12. Reeve, *Memoirs*, 1: xix, 1: xviii.
13. Reeve, *Memoirs*, 1: x
14. Reeve, *Memoirs*, 1: xx.
15. Reeve, *Memoirs*, 1: x.
16. For the ways in which 'romance' and the novel might be said to make the country, see, for instance, Burgess, *British Fiction* and Duncan, *Modern Romance*.
17. Reeve, *Memoirs*, 1: xiii.
18. Anderson, *Imagined Communities*, p. 12.
19. Anderson, *Imagined Communities*, p. 12, p. 20.
20. Anderson, *Imagined Communities*, p. 20.
21. [Mackenzie], *Mysteries Elucidated: A Novel*, 1: i–ii.
22. Mackenzie, *Mysteries*, 1: vi.
23. Mackenzie, *Mysteries*, 1: iv, 1: ix.
24. Mackenzie, *Mysteries*, 1: vii.
25. Corbett, *Allegories of Union*; Leerssen, 'Fiction, Poetics and Cultural Stereotype'.
26. In her *Progress* Clara Reeve distinguishes between the 'elevated' romance and the 'familiar' novel (1: 111). However, in the period the terms were sometimes used interchangeably. See Williams, ed. *Novel and Romance*;

Burgess, *British Fiction*, Ian Duncan, *Modern Romance*, Labbe, *The Romantic Paradox* and Johnston, *Enchanted Ground*.

27. Burke, *Reflections*, p. 88.
28. In his *History of England* Hume, for example, comments on the fear in 1553 that the Queen of Scots would 'by her succession, render England, as she had already done Scotland, a province to France' (3: 395).
29. See Richard Maxwell, 'Pretenders in Sanctuary'.
30. Anna Maria[Mackenzie], *Monmouth* 3: 10. Although the title page lists 'Anna Maria Johnson', the author later wrote under the name 'Mackenzie' and for this reason I have adhered to that surname throughout. Mackenzie wrote numerous other novels, including *Feudal Events, or Days of Yore. An Ancient Story* (1800), *Swedish Mysteries* (1801) and *Slavery: Or, the Times* (1793).
31. Mackenzie, *Monmouth*, 3: 10.
32. During the rebellion the Duke of Argyle had landed in Scotland and raised troops there, but Monmouth's largest base of support was the West Country.
33. Mackenzie, *Monmouth*, 1: 2.
34. Mackenzie, *Monmouth*, 1: 3.
35. Mackenzie, *Monmouth*, 1: 3. Adam Smith, *Theory of Moral Sentiments*, p. 23; I. i. 5. 1.
36. Mackenzie, *Monmouth*, 1: 3.
37. Adam Smith, *Theory*, p. 23; I. i. 5. 1.
38. Mackenzie, *Monmouth*, 1: 4–5.
39. Mackenzie, *Monmouth*, 1: 3.
40. Mackenzie, *Monmouth*, 1: 5.
41. Mackenzie, *Monmouth*, 1: 15.
42. For Mackenzie's treatment of history and romance in *Swedish Mysteries* see Nordius, '*Gustavas Vasus* in a Gothic Mirror: Anna Maria Mackenzie's *Swedish Mysteries*', p. 13.
43. Mackenzie, *Monmouth*, 1: 34.
44. Mackenzie, *Monmouth*, 1: np.
45. Duncan, *Scott's Shadow*, p. 113.
46. See Gallagher, *Historical Literatures*.
47. Siddons, *William Wallace*, 1: 90.
48. Siddons, *William Wallace*, 2: 7.
49. Siddons, *William Wallace*, 2: 70.
50. Henry Siddons was born in Wolverhampton (and his mother, Sarah Siddons, in Brecon). Loeber, Loeber, with Burham (eds), *A Guide to Irish Fiction, 1650–1900* describes MacKenzie as an English author (np).
51. *William Wallace*, *Critical Review* 3 (1791), p. 235.
52. Duncan, *Modern Romance*, p. 4.
53. [Sydney Owenson], Lady Morgan, *O'Donnel*, 1: ix–xi.
54. Dibdin, rev. Nilanjana Banerji, 'Henry Siddons', *DNB*.
55. Leland, *History*, 1: iii.
56. Mhunghaile, 'Anglo-Irish Antiquarianism', p. 186.
57. Leland, *History*, 1: vi; 1: vii.
58. Leland, *History*, 1: vii; Clare O'Halloran, 'Irish Re-Creations of the Gaelic Past', p. 72. See also O'Halloran, *Golden Ages*.

59. Leland, *History*, 1: ii.
60. See 'Anne Fuller' in Loeber, Loeber, with Burham, (eds), *An Electronic Version of A Guide to Irish Fiction, 1650–1900*. See also Fuller in 'Obituary of Eminent Persons', *Gentleman's Magazine*, p. 669.
61. Owenson, *O'Donnel*, 1: np.
62. Sophia Lee, *Recess*, p. 215.
63. Sophia Lee, *Recess*, p. 224.
64. Sophia Lee, *Recess*, p. 229.
65. Sylvester O'Halloran, *An Introduction to and a History of Ireland*, xi–xii.
66. Watt, *Contesting the Gothic*, p. 43.
67. James White, *Hints for a Specific Plan for an Abolition of the Slave Trade* (1788); *Speeches of M. de Mirabeau* (1792). See 'Art. XIX. *The History of the Revolution of France*', *Monthly Review*, pp. 565–7. See also Gause, 'White, James (1759–1799),' *DNB*.
68. Percy, *Reliques of Ancient English Poetry*, p. 3. See also Macpherson, *The Poems of Ossian and Related Works*.
69. Mackenzie, *Mysteries* 1: xi–xiii.
70. [White], *Strongbow*, 1: 13.
71. [White], *Strongbow*, 2: 130.
72. [White], *Strongbow*, 1: xiii.
73. [White], *Strongbow*, 2: 9–10.
74. [White], *Strongbow*, 2: 10.
75. Leland, *History*, ix–x; xv.
76. [White], *Strongbow*, 2:26.
77. [White], *Strongbow*, 2: 25.
78. Tompkins, 'James White, Esq', pp. 150–1.
79. Tompkins, 'James White, Esq', p. 151.
80. Lord Clare, 'Lord Clare's Speech', pp. 215–16. Compare with the remarks of Temple's brother, William Grenville, '5th March 1783', pp. 395–7.
81. [White], *Strongbow*, 2: 94.
82. [White], *Strongbow*, 2:66.
83. [White], *Strongbow*, 2: 65.
84. [White], *Strongbow*, 2: 127.
85. [White], *Strongbow*, 2: 128.
86. [White], *Strongbow*, 2: 127.
87. Millikin, *Corfe Castle*, 1:10.
88. Millikin, *Eva*, 1: 24.
89. Millikin, *Eva*, 1: 10.
90. Millikin, *Eva*, 2: 61.
91. Millikin, *Eva*, 4: 225.
92. Millikin, *Eva*, 4: 235.
93. Smyth, 'Wolfe Tone's Library', p. 423.
94. James White, *The Adventures of Richard Coeur de Lion*, 1: xv–xvi. Stevens notes that *Eva* appears in 25.7 per cent of the circulating library catalogues she examined and *Strongbow* in 23.1 per cent (*British Historical Fiction* p. 70). For a full list see Stevens, *British Historical Fiction*, pp. 69–71.
95. James White, *Adventures of Richard Coeur de Lion*, 1: xvi.

96. James White, *The Adventures of John of Gaunt, Duke of Lancaster*, 1: v.

97. James White, *John of Gaunt* 1: 78–9; Reeve, *Memoirs*, 1: 2.

98. Siddons, *William Wallace*, 2: 57.

99. Hunt, 'The Rhetoric of Revolution in France', pp. 81–2. See also Baxter, 'Two Brutuses', pp. 51–77.

100. Fiona Price, 'Making History', pp. 147–52.

101. Ferguson, *An Essay on the History of Civil Society*, 2.3.73.

102. Knight, *Marcus Flaminius*, 1: vii–viii.

103. Knight, *Marcus Flaminius*, 1: 32; Sydney Owenson, [Lady Morgan], *The Wild Irish Girl*, p. 3.

104. Knight, *Marcus Flaminius*, 1: 10.

105. See Leerssen, 'Fiction, Poetics and Cultural Stereotype', p. 273.

106. For original simplicity in Irish society see, for example, Owenson, *Wild Irish Girl*, p. 79, p. 65, p. 14. See also the preface to Maria Edgeworth, *Castle Rackrent*, p. 62. For the dangers of this tactic see Kelly, *Women, Writing, and Revolution*, pp. 184–6.

107. Tacitus, *Germania*, Ch. 19.

108. Knight, *Marcus Flaminius*, 1: 40–1.

109. Knight, *Marcus Flaminius*, 1: 66, 2:11.

110. Knight, *Marcus Flaminius*, 2: 261.

111. Knight, *Marcus Flaminius* 2: 261–2.

112. Knight, *Marcus Flaminius*, 2: 262, 2: 261.

113. Anon, *Arville Castle*, 1: np.

114. '*Arville Castle*', *Critical Review*, p. 115.

115. Anon, *Arville Castle*, 1: 2, 4

116. Anon, *Arville Castle*, 1: 51.

117. Anon, *Arville Castle*, 1: 52.

118. Anon, *Arville Castle*, 1: 8–9, 1: 23.

119. Anon, *Arville Castle*, 1: 93–4.

120. Anon, *Arville Castle*, 1: 94.

121. Anon, *Arville Castle*, 1: 79.

122. Anon, *Arville Castle*, 1: 183.

123. Anon, *Arville Castle*, 2: 163.

124. Godwin, *Caleb Williams*, p. 216.

125. Anon, *Arville Castle*, 1: 144.

126. Anon, *Arville Castle*, 1: 149–50.

127. Anon, *Arville Castle*, 1: 5.

128. Jane Porter, *Thaddeus of Warsaw* (1803), intro. Jane Porter, Standard Novels 4, p. 37.

129. Jane Porter, *Thaddeus*, p. 57.

130. See McLean, 'Nobody's Argument'.

131. Jane Porter, *Thaddeus*, p. 52. For the Polish models for Porter's patriotism, see Francis Zaptka, 'Jane Porter's Kościuszko'.

132. Jane Porter, *Thaddeus*, p. 47.

133. Colley, *Britons*, pp. 177–8.

134. Jane Porter, *Thaddeus*, p. 52, p. 51.

135. Jane Porter, *Thaddeus*, p. 59.

136. Trumpener, *Bardic Nationalism*, xii. See also Larrissy, *The Blind and Blindness*, pp. 36–63 for the 'Celtic bard'.

137. It has been ably handled by Trumpener, Leerssen, Corbett, Butler, Burgess and Ferris, amongst others.
138. For an account of the rival myths and the relation between Protestant and Catholic antiquarians, see Mhunghaile, 'Anglo-Irish Antiquarianism', p. 184.
139. Ferris, 'The Irish Novel 1800–1829', p. 239.
140. For instance, while Thomas Campbell argues against Sylvester O'Halloran regarding the pre-Christian antiquity of Irish learning, he is prepared to suggest the priority of Irish music – and that is what Owenson chooses to cite (*Wild Irish Girl*, p. 73). The argument about music is (as Owenson records) in Campbell's *A Philosophical Survey of the South of Ireland*, p. 453. For his argument in favour of the 'barbarous' Irish before Christianity see Campbell, *Strictures on the ecclesiastical and Literary History of Ireland*, pp. 8–13. For Campbell's ambiguous politics, see Clare O'Halloran, *Golden Ages*, p. 14.
141. See Kirkpatrick's introduction to Owenson's *The Wild Irish Girl*, xvii.
142. Owenson, *Florence Macarthy*. See Tessone, 'Displaying Ireland', p. 171. By the time of *The O'Briens and the O'Flahertys* (1827) Owenson's doubts about performing history have grown. See Thuente, 'Lady Morgan's Beavoin O'Flaherty', p. 34. For Thuente, Owenson shifts from antiquarianism to a kind of universal history. See also Julia M. Wright, '"The Nation Begins to Form"', pp. 939–63.
143. Burgess, 'The National Tale', p. 42.
144. Richard Lovell Edgeworth to Daniel Beaufort, 26 April 1800, cited by Marilyn Butler, *Maria Edgeworth*, p. 359.
145. Lord Clare, 'Lord Clare's Speech', p. 210.

# Chapter 4

# Conserving Histories:
# Chivalry, Science and Liberty

'HAIL! Noble ages of ancient chivalry!', wrote C. Butler: 'It is in your glorious annals, in the historic page, that we must seek for examples of pure and constant affection, for models of perfect virtue, since the age in which we live cannot, alas! supply them.'[1] The opening to *The Age of Chivalry* (1799) suggests a breakage or fall, the nature of which is indicated by the title page: the book is an adaption of *Knights of the Swan* by 'Madame Genlis'.[2] Genlis's book had contained what some regarded as a rather cruel portrait of Queen Marie Antoinette, a queen encouraged by 'favourites' 'to hold the people in disdain'.[3] Even when the queen's subjects act towards her with 'generosity and sincerity,' the 'English' Eadburga continues in folly and political intrigue, surrounding 'herself with a crowd of people whose aversion to the revolution was notorious'.[4] Although this queen is inevitably displaced from the throne, Genlis suggests that it would be a mistake to execute her: 'were she to fall the victim of popular fury . . . the enemies of the revolution would make her a heroine'.[5] Throughout this chivalric work, the rights of the people are canvassed. In contrast, *The Age of Chivalry* is, Butler assures readers, shorn of 'exceptionable' 'political subjects'.[6] Even if the present is corrupt, it is still possible to provide an education in the (un-revolutionary) spirit of chivalry.

For twenty years after Edmund Burke's *Reflections* the death of chivalry was a matter of constant remark. Yet its demise proved greatly exaggerated. The code had been injured by radical attempts to debunk it, maimed by depictions of economic suffering and damaged by critiques of union. Nonetheless, somehow readjusted, it could still serve a purpose. Cleansed of subject matter dangerous to the status quo, the idea of chivalry might allow 'liberty' to be recast in terms of the nation rather than considered in relation to the rights of the individual. But 'chivalry' was essentially aristocratic, fantastic and hard to pin down chronologically, always apparently past its zenith. Violent but heroic, it was hard to apply to a commercial nation or to the British nobility. Above all, it was connected with (Catholic) superstition. In the decade before *Waverley* historical novelists traced two main solutions to these difficulties. Chivalry could be redefined, purged of its warlike excess and expanded to apply to the people rather than merely to the aristocracy, an endeavour perhaps most notably undertaken by Jane and Anna Maria Porter. Alternately, elements of radical and dissenting discourse, particularly the association with science, could be co-opted. In his *Lectures on History* (1788) Joseph Priestley comments that 'all the extravagancies of books of chivalry' might be taken as 'undoubted truth' without 'philosophical knowledge', that is, an acquaintance with 'the powers of nature and art': to read history, a systematic knowledge of physical and human nature was necessary.[7] Distancing themselves from certain aspects of radical thought, Elizabeth Hamilton and Jane Porter would, in different ways, exploit this paradigm. Replacing the chivalric or pagan associations of history, an emphasis on the past as data could, they suggested, create a new kind of scientific history, christianising the contemporary status quo.

If Butler had suggested a division between chivalric past and fallen present, Anna Maria Porter, sister of Jane Porter, wished to suggest both its historical authority and its modernity. In the preface to the second and third editions of *The Hungarian Brothers* (1807) 'a friend' (probably Jane Porter) notes that 'this Romance was begun, and had proceeded as far as the middle of the third volume, long before the disastrous events took place which overturned the Germanic empire'.[8] The novel is therefore, in some sense, like *Thaddeus of Warsaw*, a history of the recent past – but one still more dramatically overtaken by current events. Anna Maria Porter carefully plots her novel against the background of European conflict, providing 'the summary', as she puts it, 'of more than five campaigns'.[9] The hero, Charles, has his first significant military experiences during Austria's campaigns against France as part of the First Coalition. Like the Archduke Charles of Austria, Duke of Teschen (one of Napoleon's greatest opponents), Porter's hero fights under Marshal Wurmser – and attracts his 'favour' during his 'first campaign in 1793'.[10] He is involved in the Battle of Montenotte (styled 'Montelezoni' in the novel) on 12 April 1796 and, under Giovanni Marchese di Provera, holds a ruined castle while Count Argenteau's ('the flying A-g-u') troops retreat.[11] With the peace of 1797, the respected soldier returns home to mentor his impetuous brother. The aristocracy are due to be schooled in the ways of chivalry.

Porter's next chosen 'scene', 'Vienna, in honour' proves challenging for the brothers to negotiate.[12] It is only when Demetrius and Charles fight in the War of the Second Coalition (1798–1802) that the heroic lessons learned come fully into play. Demetrius takes part in the Battle of Magnano in northern Italy on 5 April 1799 ('Magnan') and participates in the sieges of Peschiera del Garda and Mantua as well as the Battle of Novi, while Charles fights in Switzerland.[13] Then, in the last volume the brothers' adventures occur against the background of War of Third Coalition (1803–6). Finally, Porter records the Austrian truce with France that followed the battle of Austerlitz.[14] But, despite this pattern of war and peace, *The Hungarian Brothers* is not, like Jane Porter's *Thaddeus*, a novel in which the hero leaves a defeated, chivalric nation and struggles to retain his honour in modern commerciality. Despite the preface's mournful suggestion that 'all is now changed', this is not an elegy but a guide.[15] Each location allows Anna Maria Porter to continue to anatomise true chivalry.

Throughout the book Porter's politics are as clear as those of her hero, Charles, who bemoans the 'destructive system, and thirst of universal dominion' that supposedly distinguish the Republicans.[16] Distancing herself from revolution, Porter is more concerned with another political danger, the harm that the aristocracy can do to itself. Prince Nuremberg, for instance, tries to prevent Demetrius marrying his niece, condemning the 'levelling' that such a union would involve. Porter implies he has misunderstood the term. His pride in rank without pride in function is as culpable as republicanism.[17] The danger of such hubris is made evident when the machinations of the prince and the villain Wurtzburg lead to Demetrius's imprisonment. Wurtzburg has manufactured a casket of traitorous letters, leading to Demetrius's arrest as a spy and to a secret mock trial (recalling the practice of the *lettre de cachet*). Ultimately, the young man is forced to labour in the mines. Yet it is Wurtzburg himself, who eventually turns out to have betrayed the Austrians and to be in 'correspondence with a French officer; to whom he revealed every military operation of which he gained intelligence'.[18] While Genlis had suggested that a corrupt aristocracy and the oppressions of 'arbitrary power' can generate revolution, here Anna Maria Porter is more cautious. Irresponsible behaviour is displaced onto an envious military officer but it can still further the terrible cause of revolution.[19]

Having exposed the dangers of corruption, what Porter tries to provide is a redefinition of chivalry, that quality that for Robertson introduced 'humanity' into warfare and distinguished 'ancient from modern manners'.[20] Robertson had used the term 'gallantry' in his paean to chivalry's influence: Porter finds this disturbing and is particularly concerned to emphasise that this behaviour should not descend into (aristocratic) licentiousness or uncontrolled, sexualised feeling.

The warnings regarding gallantry begin immediately. After making the romantic gesture of marrying an orphan, the brothers' father succumbs to 'licentious passions' which make 'ruins of his once admirable figure' – and his fortune.[21] The two brothers are left to cope, with Charles, the elder, trying to protect the younger, Demetrius, from the financial truth. Porter is, in effect, masculinising the model of contrasting characters, one rational, one governed by feeling, seen in, for instance, Maria Edgeworth's *Letters for Literary Ladies* (1795), Jane West's *A Gossip's Story* (1796) and, eventually, Jane Austen's *Sense and Sensibility* (1811). Edgeworth's *Letters* had begun with an epistle from 'a gentleman to his friend upon the birth of a daughter' in which the writer remarks that 'the days of chivalry are past and . . . modern gallantry permits men to speak, at least to one another, in less sublime language of the fair'.[22] In contrast, Anna Maria Porter suggests that the problem is that men themselves are in danger of falling prey to vices associated with women, such as vanity. Charles spends considerable time warning Demetrius against 'the hazard of having a handsome person', a warning that 'seems laughable; and a century or two ago, would have been a work of supererogation'. Now, he remarks, 'the free manners of the present day render it indispensable'.[23]

Charles proves right. Demetrius is asked to sit for a sculpture of 'Paris' (despite having a deep 'contempt' for him) and during the process develops feelings for the married Madame de Fontainville, sculpted by the same artist as 'Cleopatra'.[24] This sign of the woman's potential moral weakness is reinforced by the fact that her father 'took an active share in the Revolution' and that her husband is also suspected.[25] Tellingly, one of the heroines, Adelaide, has already warned that 'sensibility' is a 'misfortune' for the vulnerable woman. While dangerously close to being drawn into a lawless passion, Demetrius finds himself tested by the revolutionary philosophy of Colonel Wurtzburg. On the one hand, the officer suggests that given her husband's potentially traitorous behaviour, 'how could she be considered as still his wife; the *wife* of an apostate, a traitor to his God and his king?'[26] On the other, he argues that Demetrius's 'pure affection' means there is no danger, no need for 'irresolution' when it comes to spending time with his mistress.[27] Demetrius still resists. However, it is notable that Wurtzburg's military and sexual behaviour are equally culpable.[28] Corrupt sexuality undermines duty along with other ties.

Porter is not repudiating heterosexual romance altogether. It is valuable when it involves waiting, self-denial and heroism (Demetrius, for example, disinterestedly rescues the Princess of Nuremberg and Duchess di Felieri from a fire and learns to respect both the older and the younger woman before falling in love).[29] Still, friendship forms a stronger focus. It is no coincidence that when Charles returns from an interval of five years of warfare to meet his inexperienced brother Demetrius, Demetrius volunteers, 'I am *sure* we shall like each other!'[30] The extent of the brothers' mutual affection and the flamboyant way in which it is displayed is, Porter admits, potentially problematic. In the preface her 'friend' defensively remarks that although the 'strong painting of some of the characters, to many of her readers, might appear inappropriate and preposterous', 'all who have travelled over the Continent, must recollect the animated salutations which pass between relations and friends of either sex', 'extraordinary', as she says, 'to us'.[31] By the time of the Standard Novels edition Anna Maria herself apologises, blaming such enthusiasm on her own youth. The behaviour of her brothers certainly forms a strange contrast with, for instance, John and George Knightley, who greet each other in Jane Austen's *Emma* (1816) 'in the true English style, burying under a calmness that seemed all but indifference, the real attachment which would have led either of them, if requisite, to do every thing for the good of the other'.[32] Like the actions of the Knightley brothers, Demetrius's and Charles's behaviour is also positioned as a feature of national character. Such affection is something Porter wishes to transplant: sensibility need not be primarily sexually focused but can, she insists, be fraternal or connected with friendship.

The emphasis on friendship as opposed to sexual impulses is reinforced by a series of letters sent to Charles by a mysterious correspondent. The identity of this correspondent (attracted to Charles because of the soldier's virtue and bravery) causes the brothers considerable speculation. When Charles first becomes recipient of the letters around 1793, having won the favour of Marshal Wurmser, his vanity encourages him to think the writer is a woman. As a result he falls in love with Signora Berghi, facing a conflict between love and duty that leads him to be court-martialled (although the conflict is such that, we are assured, he has still behaved honourably). Lacking Charles's salutary experiences, Demestrius later sees one of the messages and immediately asks, 'Is it a love-letter?'[33] The letter writer must be 'as beautiful as an angel', he supposes, to which Charles replies: 'But can't you conceive the possibility of this 'dearest creature' having whiskers and a bald head?'[34] Although Demestrius suggests he would not give a 'rush' for such an advisor, both brothers have to learn to insulate their judgement against sexual desire. The mysterious friend (eventually revealed as Marshal Ingersdorf) tests Charles by exposing him to Wurtzburg's corrupt mistress, warns the elder brother about Demetrius's temptation, and ultimately even provides Charles with a wife – Adelaide Ingersdorf, whom Charles providentially already loves. Although matchmaking can be a dangerous business, desire should be preceded by friendship and sanctioned by it.

Above all, Porter wishes to emphasise the chivalric importance of the 'humanity' mentioned by Robertson.[35] Hence in her narrative both war and patriotism become a kind of qualified moral medicine. Away from Wurtzburg's influence, Demetrius is guided by the noble Forshiem 'skilled in his profession'.[36] He finds his days 'given to interesting employment' and patriotism aids him in overcoming his passion for Zaire de Fontainville.[37] The narrator remarks: 'As those that have been sick best know how to estimate health: so, it is only the penitent sinner who can tell the unspeakable joys of a reconciled conscience.'[38] Although 'judicious praise' may be an 'aliment' to virtue, here military activity is also medicinal. Yet to position warfare as curative for the nation is obviously problematic: Porter must shape her narrative carefully. As Demetrius 'oppos[es] his genius' to Forshiem's 'experience', the two attempt 'wild experiments' to discover 'Greek Fire', and also reinterpret the landscape in military terms: Demestrius forgets 'to remark its beauties in the ardour with which he canvassed the advantages and disadvantages it presented for attack or defence'.[39]

References to 'experiment' and 'system-mak[ing]' recall the ideas of the 'New Philosophers' (criticised elsewhere in the book) but, unlike such ideas, these experiments are 'lessons' in 'a science which it was now patriotism to study'.[40] Nonetheless, the search for 'Greek Fire' is too destructive to be carried out seriously: Demestrius's 'heart was too humane' to 'add another to the many tremendous engines invented for human destruction'.[41] As Demetrius becomes distracted by the military potential of the landscape, he falls into error like other 'system makers' and as a result Forshiem is injured.[42] For Porter, true military heroism must attempt to mitigate suffering. Forshiem's accident leads the pair to seek aid from a nearby cottager. There, Demetrius learns that 'it had always been the benevolent system of Charles to visit his sick soldiers after every engagement' – the aging cottager is the mother of one of these soldiers, 'restor[ed]' by Charles' help to 'her own country'.[43] Combined with virtuous love (Constantia herself frequently visits 'the sick and aged'), this form of martial heroism benefits the country both in war and peace.[44]

Having examined the relationship between virtue, chivalry and the nation in *The Hungarian Brothers*, Anna Maria Porter becomes increasingly anxious about how such lessons apply to royalty. *Don Sebastian or the House of Braganza, An Historical Romance* (1809) probes the limits of useful Christian zeal and in the process attempts to shape a vision of right chivalric rule. The novel parallels political crisis in the present with (what Porter suggests is) usurpation in the past. The introductory frame narrative describes the Portuguese Prince Regent's departure for Brazil in 1807 following the French invasion of his country. In November 1806 Napoleon had brought in the Berlin Decree, embargoing British trade. But to Napoleon's irritation, Prince John of Braganza proved unwilling to place restrictions on Portugal's sea trade with the United Kingdom, provoking the invasion (which might also have been motivated by a French wish to use Portugal in future operations against Spain). At a military disadvantage, the Prince and his courtiers departed for the New World on 29 November 1807. In providing a frame that references these events, Porter makes her anti-Napoleonic stance clear. However, in order to provide instruction to royalty in this moment of imperial revolution, Porter rapidly shifts from the present moment of breakage to a narrative of past rupture. The bulk of the book focuses on the story of Sebastian I (1554–78), who died (or, according to Porter, only disappeared) at the Battle of Alcácer Quiber (4 August 1578).

*The Critical Review* disapproved of the device of the frame narrative. The reviewer 'lament[s] that the poor prince regent . . . should have been burthened with so unconscionable a roll of paper . . . in the inside of his waistcoat'.[45] The critic's use of a sardonic tone and the bathetic intrusion of the waistcoat is unfair. Porter does not commit such a solecism – the Prince only draws 'from his breast a large roll of written paper'.[46] Still, the remark highlights the vast expansion of the historical record that Porter has undertaken. Even though the fiction is pleasing, the reviewer finds that historical *vraisemblance* must not be expected – and presumably the idea of the Portuguese royal family hearing Sebastian's fictional adventures after Alcácer Quiber produces an unsettling mix of romance and reality. But Porter's comparison has a purpose. The Prince Regent is travelling 'to stamp the future character of an unborn nation'.[47] While continuing to police the concept of chivalry, the younger Porter sister also wishes to underline the importance of royalty even under a modern state formation.

Porter's narrative testifies that the enterprise is a surprisingly awkward one. Benedict Anderson speculates that early political units are connected to the name of a monarch or noble family but this connection becomes tenuous when the modern nation is in question.[48] Even as Porter seeks to reinforce the connection between royalty and state, her very insistence on the importance of correct conduct suggests the precarious nature of royal authority. In Porter's narrative, Prince Sebastian survives the religiously motivated battle of Alcácer Quiber but then, presumed dead, struggles to have his identity acknowledged, making this a story first of Christian hubris and then of usurpation. It is only when he has learnt the lessons of true chivalric humanity that he is fit to rule. For Don Sebastian, the knowledge comes too late. He eventually has to give up all hope of regaining his throne; circumstances, indeed, suggest such renunciation is the ultimate chivalric gesture. Like Prince John's departure in the face of Napoleonic law and military might, Don Sebastian's fate in fact marks a potential separation between monarch and modern state. Why should the Portuguese family listen to such a story? For Porter, moral character and commercial prosperity are both at stake – and so 'the history of an illustrious ancestor, more unfortunate than ourselves, but for whom misfortune was a blessing' is a 'most precious' 'state treasure'.[49] The role of 'historical romance' is to show how the connection between royalty and nation might be re-interpreted, even at a moment of apparent failure.

The historical Prince Sebastian, born heir apparent, succeeded to the throne at the age of three. This circumstance allows Porter to focus on the Prince's education. Rather like Emily in *The Mysteries of Udolpho* or Demetrius in *The Hungarian Brothers*, Sebastian exhibits an excess of sensibility and (as in *St Leon*) this excess is channelled so that, 'His head was soon filled by visions of future greatness, and his heart fired with holy zeal: he meditated the conquest and the conversion of half the globe.'[50] In this case, while Sebastian understands the importance of 'the laws', informing 'his people that nothing was so valuable in his eyes as their rights', his Christian zeal is excessive. First it leads him on a 'secret excursion' to 'Tangier' which almost ends in disaster when he has to fight off 'the Turk'.[51] Then it leads him to make a vow to fight a Holy War in Africa before he marries. When Sebastian tries to circumvent the laws he had originally supported in order to marry the already affianced Gonsalva, these impetuous behaviours combine to bad effect. In order for the Pope to agree to this marriage, Sebastian must fulfil his vow, drawing his nation into a dangerous and destructive war while leaving his throne unprotected.

The ill-fated expedition allows Porter to distinguish between types of supposedly chivalric behaviour. Sebastian admires the British knight Sir Thomas Stukeley who has killed his brother in a hunting accident but whose chivalric bravery in fact only reflects the 'extremity of despair' (the historical Stukeley [1520–78] was a financially desperate mercenary).[52] Meanwhile, de Castro (formerly affianced to Gonsalva) avoids the 'romantic sanguineness of the inexperienced Sebastian', as well as Stukeley's 'indifference to life' and the aristocratic pleasure-seeking of Sebastian's other friend, Crato. Rather, he gives cautious military advice which is ignored: Sebastian has confused foolhardiness with bravery and the result is military disaster. Tellingly, de Castro, Gonsalva's original fiancé, has also previously resisted Sebastian's attempts to marry his bride. 'I promise', he says, 'never to invade this prerogative in the person of another, and for that reason expect never to have it invaded in my own.'[53] Accuracy, a true belief in equality before the law and a Christian knowledge of the human cost of fighting are all key to Porter's definition of proper knightly behaviour.

The strongest lessons in correct behaviour are, however, provided by some of Sebastian's Muslim opponents. Although the 'Moorish princes' 'Muley Hamet' and his brother-in-law, 'Cid Albequerin' (supposedly Christian converts from Islam), tell their ally Sebastian not to listen to the enemy 'Xeriff Muley Moloch', Moloch writes a moderate letter in support of his own continued rule. 'He laboured to shew that his right to the crowns of Fez and Morocco, was superior to that of his nephew; and that even were it otherwise, the later had forfeited his claim by acts of cruelty and oppression.'[54] Later, Hamet betrays Prince Sebastian and switches faith again. Moloch's probity and his recognition that good rule is defined by the welfare of the people mark him as the better choice. Religious difference is less important than virtue, as Porter underlines by having Sebastian rescued by a 'benevolent' dervish, seeking 'for such Christians as yet might remain capable of receiving assistance'.[55] It must be admitted that Sebastian himself is later converted to Protestantism by his Moorish bride, rather compromising the message of tolerance. Still, at this point, revived by 'balsam' and 'cordial', Sebastian finds that 'Africa has already taught me a lesson I shall never forget.'[56]

The cure is only partial. Sebastian is not fully ready to accept the dervish's suggestion that there is a difference between 'his prophet's laws' and the conduct of 'his spiritual superiors', between what God requires and Rome commands.[57] It is only when, in a scene that echoes Mrs Montgomery's search for her husband in Charlotte Smith's *Ethelinde*, Sebastian returns to the battlefield to search for his fallen comrades that he gains a fuller understanding. There he sees the 'divine image' ravaged by wild animals.[58] Here an important shift has taken place: in *Ethelinde* the widow experiences the aftermath of war; in Porter's work, the ruler himself must grasp the human cost of religious and monarchical ambition. Sebastian's Christian desire to free Africa from supposed Muslim tyranny is dangerously unrealistic. High principles, the dervish suggests, can be quickly become translated into fanaticism and religious persecution. Sebastian has to learn that religion has its place in a nationalist discourse but only in terms of self-protection and inspiring charity to others. Captured and forced to work as a slave, compelled (like Demetrius in *The Hungarian Brothers*) to understand the horror of labour, Sebastian experiences the importance of such charity and is finally helped to escape with the help of the Muslim woman, Kara Aziek (whom he eventually marries). Nonetheless, when Braganza reappears in Portugal, he finds his supposedly Christian aristocrats, his former mistress and the new ruler unwilling to acknowledge his identity – besides his faithful dog, only de Castro has shown willingness to acknowledge him. Porter suggests that probity, compassion and the religious feeling (whether Muslim or Christian) that underpins them are more important than sectarian differences. Such qualities are, Don Sebastian must learn, more important than the throne he no longer possesses.

Charlotte Smith and other radical writers repeatedly tried to imagine an ameliorative space outside present social conditions where an ideal community might be set up and new behaviours practised. In Porter's novel such a space is occupied not by progressive thinkers but by the Portuguese royal family. This conjunction of historical fact and fantasy offers the hope that royalty itself will learn (through Don Sebastian's narrative) how true chivalry can operate even under conditions of slavery – the difficulties of work, explored so thoroughly in historical novels of the recent past, must now be understood and dealt with by the compassionate Christian ruler. A response to the displacement at the upper end of society caused by Napoleon, Porter's figuration of royal exile also foreshadows Scott's fascination with Jacobite displacement and attempted return. Porter, though, is more confident of the displaced royal family's ability to adapt. Braganza gains a new understanding of chivalry and for Porter this wisdom makes him fit to rule; on the other hand, those who deny his heritage remain relatively unsympathetic. In contrast, Scott's Jacobites retain their old-fashioned courtly understanding and their return is, in part, thwarted by the presence of another, more modern royal family. For Scott, modernisation, albeit painful, can occur at home. For Porter the social improvement associated with re-educated royalty remains in the space of fantasy.

Anna Maria Porter's attempts to rehabilitate the chivalric proved highly problematic. Having attempted to broaden its appeal in *The Hungarian Brothers*, creating a kind of sympathetic, virtuous patriotism, Porter feels obliged to spell out the ways such religious virtue might itself malfunction – not only the reader but royalty itself needs to understand the lesson and such re-education seems unlikely in the Old World. For Anna Maria's sister, Jane, the survival of chivalry under conditions of commercial modernity appeared similarly unlikely, as the struggles of her hero in the England of *Thaddeus of Warsaw* suggest. A new way of connecting the values of the past with the present was necessary. How could the heroism, which both sisters (but particularly Jane) were obsessed by, function in the present? Jane Porter pursues the idea of an extended heroism, a practical chivalry for the masses to far greater extent than her sister, yet in her writing such heroism remains at once essential and hazardous. Both sisters are anxious about the brutality and jingoism that might accompany identification with the nation. Jane Porter adds to this a concern with what happens after the patriotic moment of national defence is over. Although commercial existence presents a series of affronts to Thaddeus's chivalric way of being, he finally finds his place amongst the aristocracy. But this absorption into the propertied ruling classes is hardly possible for heroic returnees more generally. Commercial society has to be defended but those very defenders potentially put it at risk.

In *The Scottish Chiefs* (1810) Porter's need at once to extend and to control the chivalric impulse is immediately visible. The title page has an epigraph from James Macpherson's *Ossian*, a series of poems which (in a narrative Dafydd Moore complicates) invokes and recreates the relationship between Ireland and Scotland in terms that discredited the former's version of history.[59] Yet when Porter draws on these works, with their potential to create strife amongst the home nations, the emphasis is different: 'There comes a voice that awakes my soul. It is the voice of years that are gone; they roll before me with all their deeds.'[60] The inspirational rather than the divisive potential of the past is key. In the preface she moves on to the conflict between Scotland and England, coding it in terms of opposing families, the 'long race of Douglas, or the descendants of the Percy'.[61] This was a site of strife that John Home had previously tried to neutralise in the prologue to the play *Douglas* (1757). Home's 'Prologue' suggested that the Scottish Douglas and English Percy were in fact 'generous rivals' who 'loved each other well'.[62] It insists that the battles between the nations are distant (although the play was first performed on 14 December 1756) and that the affective bonds have, at any rate, always been strong. Porter similarly acknowledges the 'contending arms of these two brave families' but adds that it is 'happy' that the 'destiny' that once made them fight has now 'also consolidated their rival nations into one'. Although Porter's claim is that this is a dynastic union (legitimated by the presence of 'the heir of Plantagenet and of Bruce upon the British throne'), her concept of nation is wider. Just as the descendants of Douglas and Percy are inspired by the nobility of their past not to division but to glory, the populace also has its models: 'But where is the Englishman who is not proud of being the countryman of Nelson? Where the British sailor that does not thirst to emulate his fame?'[63] Aspiration as well as inspiration, talent as well as ancestry, inform Porter's idea of the virtuous and unified nation. This is an extended idea of chivalry but it is also one in which conflict has already been foreclosed.

A certain unease concerning Edmund Burke's more restrictive idea of chivalry and right rule enshrined in 'ensigns armorial' registers in the body of the text. In a parallel to the systematic destruction of the documents of Irish history from the Elizabethan period onward mentioned in the national tale, Porter's King Edward I of England has 'not left a parchment, either of public records, or of private annals, in any of the monasteries or castles around Montrose'.[64] Similar depredations have, we are told, been carried out 'from the eastern shores of the Highlands to the farthest of the Western Isles' by the 'faithless Earl of March' with Lord Soulis – aristocratic lineage alone is no guarantee of national loyalty. Wallace insists that such destruction is in vain: 'Do the traitors think . . . that by robbing Scotland of her annals, and of that stone, they really deprive her of her palladium?' These are 'talismans', superstitious, even potentially blasphemous, idle tokens. 'Scotland's history is in the memories of her sons; her palladium is in their hearts.' Wallace and Porter direct the (eighteenth-century) fascination with sentiment to the patriotic – and historical. Aristocratic insignia are inadequate when it comes to defending the nation.

Nonetheless, events surrounding the mysterious casket which Monteith gives Wallace suggest that the destruction of documents is not merely symbolic. The box is to be opened when Scotland '*be again free*', but after Wallace suggests it may contain treasure, Monteith wishes to retain it.[65] His anxiety leads to the chest being seen by English soldiers, who, also supposing it is treasure, determinedly pursue it. In this way, Porter signals that the destruction of history is also a destruction of property. Yet as she wishes to construct the nation as a unified mass without a radical agenda, the issue of property must be handled carefully. In this narrative, only the corrupt and cowardly aristocracy feel greed. The property-rights of the other righteous landowners are coded in sentimental and historical terms, while Porter's emphasis on the devastation of the land and its food sources make it clear that it is the interest of the peasantry to defend aristocratic rights. The pursuit of the mysterious box, its identity suspended between relic and treasure, causes the death of Wallace's wife, Marion, and hence precipitates his fight to expel the English.

To contrast (and undercut) the struggle over wealth that national conquest in fact involves, Porter sets up another series of exchanges. The box is moved, unopened, inviolate, from hand to hand, even held by a trustworthy Englishman, Gilbert Hambledon (later Lord Montgomery). Whatever the mysterious package of national identity is, the honourable citizen knows that the contract must be kept. No investigation is possible during the conflict. It is only at the end of the novel, when

Bruce comes to throne and the heroine, Helen, dies on Wallace's coffin, that the box is revealed to contain the regalia of Scotland. This kind of exchange, without profit or ownership, only entailing self-sacrifice, is supplemented by the movement of other tokens. The bugle, which sounds 'a summons so dear to every Scottish heart' is given by Halbert, the retainer, to Wallace as a sign from the Earl of Mar.[66] Like the legends told by 'Thomas of Ercildown' (as Porter refers to him), its sound is readily understandable to the masses, galvanising them to action, but its call is, of course, immaterial. Wallace gives a lock of his bloody hair to Halbert to take to the Earl of Mar. The lock is then sewn by Helen into a banner used to lead the troops, a banner which reads '*God armeth the patriot*'.[67] The sentimental token is transformed into a national one as Wallace pledges his affection to a persistently feminised Scotland; the lock of hair no longer signals ownership by another individual but by the wider community of the nation.

The idea of exchange without personal ownership also has its peculiar echo in relation to the novel's sexual politics. If certain radical thinkers (like Mary Hays) had interrogated the use of women as property within marriage and encouraged ideas of greater sexual freedom, Porter emphasises modesty and sexual self-denial as a form of patriotic freedom. After the death of Wallace's wife, Marion, sentimental affection and peaceful privacy in the novel are blocked: no ownership of the heroine, Helen, is possible. Captured and threatened with rape and torture by the corrupt Soulis, Helen is rescued by an unknown stranger (Wallace). Her ignorance of her rescuer's identity sanctions sexual desire but on the discovery of his name this longing must be redirected towards the ideal of patriotism. As Helen is exchanged from father, to church, to Wallace, to Edward, and even when she travels, disguised as a boy alongside both Wallace and Bruce, she remains inviolate, as unopened as the casket. Hence her disguise as a page, a junior but masculinised figure in the national drama meets with narrative approval. On the other hand, Joanna Mar disguises herself as the Knight of the Green Plume because of her sexual jealousy towards Wallace and subsequently betrays her country. The problem is not only that she (successfully) impersonates a mature male warrior but that she does so for the wrong reason. Personal sexual fulfilment is impossible – and this is obvious to all but the most corrupt. In this symbolic economy, where Helen forms the human equivalent to the casket containing national identity, the heroine's death at the end of the novel is suggestive. At the end of the struggle for national identity the quasi-sexual charge of patriotism is dissipated. It only carries its full force as a mysterious, un-investigated trust, drawn on in times of crisis. When national identity is exposed, captured in the solid form of the regalia, such tension vanishes and the normal laws of possession resume. Logically no space for exchange without ownership exists and so Helen must die.

For all its omnipresence in the book, Porter's national identity has a subtly elusive quality. When it is fully invoked, it creates a kind of state of exception that, she implies, cannot and should not be maintained. Patriotism (a kind of extended chivalric sentiment) is too dangerous to be constantly followed to its logical end; it involves mass engagement with the nation and yet the people are notoriously unreliable. When virtuous, the masses are capable of hearing the call of the 'heart' that Porter sees as vital to national identity and this is fortuitous since they must be mobilised in war.[68] Yet groups of (English) soldiers are capable of indulging in excessive consumption (drunkenness for instance) and vice. During the period of national defence, the masses should become animated by a spirit that acknowledges no property but the common property of the nation. During this period, too, (the conqueror's) law is suspended, with no application to the common people. When Wallace is called a 'rebel' and a 'blasphemous leader' by Beck, the Lord of Durham, and emissary of the king, Wallace exclaims 'Does [God] not read the heart?'[69] Such mass engagement, disregard for the law and sense of common property are dangerous tendencies to civil society and must come conveniently to an end when the need is over. Nonetheless, in case the crisis reoccurs, the potential for patriotic self-sacrifice has to remain, dormant but ready to be swiftly invoked. This act of prestidigitation – the 'now you see it, now you don't' of heroism – is performed by the historical novel.

The uncertain status of the hero and the fluctuating value of chivalry itself did not prevent, indeed it arguably facilitated, the satirical use of romance. The idea that the nobility of the past had been truly chivalric was easily overstrained, since even if works like Anna Maria and Jane Porter's claimed an educational dimension, such fictions tended to glorify the contemporary aristocracy by association – to create a rhetoric of aristocratic service. The refusal of this type of narrative is evident in Sarah Green's *Private History of the Court of England*, where romance's more negative associations are used to attack both the luxurious aristocracy and a supposedly corrupt radicalism. Green does not explicitly mention chivalry in her first volume, although pageants, honour and gallantry all form part of the feudal backdrop. Instead, in Green's essentially static narrative of universal history, a corrupt past mirrors the corrupt present. Green appeals to those readers who 'are fond of tracing the characters of mankind, and their close similarity in every age'.[70] Superficial behaviours have altered but the underlying reality, the pursuit of individual desire, remains: 'The late ferocious violator of all the rites of hospitality, who murdered the husband, that he might possess the wife in uninterrupted security, is now the smooth-tongued adulterer.'[71] In 'wound[ing]] the *mind*' this adulterer eschews the direct violence of the loosely evoked feudal age. Modern violence is linguistic or metaphoric but the destructive impulse remains. If modern manners derive from the (chivalric) past, that continuity has not dignified the character. The worst elements seem to predominate. In particular, the corrupt behaviour of the 'heir apparent' Prince Edward (1442–83) (that is, the Prince of Wales, later George IV) is reflected on every social level. Green details Edward's affair with Maria de Rosenvault (Mary Robinson), bemoans his illicit marriage to Lady Elizabeth Grey (the Catholic Mrs Maria Fitzherbert) and deplores his conduct to Bona of Saxony (Princess Caroline). Green displays what the Porters struggle with: the difficulty of convincingly applying any kind of chivalric template to the early nineteenth-century aristocracy and its followers.

## Healing the Nation: Science and History

As well as lamenting the death of chivalry, in his *Reflections* Edmund Burke draws on the language of natural science. During recent events in France, he writes, the 'strong principle' of the spirit of liberty acted 'like a wild gas': 'The fixed air is plainly broke loose: but we ought to suspend our judgement until the first effervescence is a little subsided, till the liquor is cleared, and until we see something deeper than the agitation of a troubled and frothy surface.'[72] With this metaphor (alluding to Dr Joseph Priestley's *Directions for Impregnating Water with Fixed Air* [1772]), liberty is at once vital but volatile. It seethes, disturbs and dissipates. Only after a period of observation, when the reaction is finished, can its effect be assessed. In Burke's rhetoric, as the Revolution becomes an experiment, history is transformed. No longer a matter of tradition, it becomes a science in which the past provides experimental data. Burke's shift in metaphor recalls Priestley's supposed suggestion that: 'The English hierarchy [. . .] has [. . .] equal reason to tremble even at an air-pump, or an electrical machine.'[73] The political status quo, in other words, is challenged by scientific practice, by a clear examination of data and by experimentation and its results. Whether Priestley made this remark or not, he certainly insisted on the connection between natural science and history. In his *History and Present State of Electricity* (1767) Priestley had explored the close relationship between '*civil, natural* and *philosophical* history', emphasising that philosophical history combines the benefits of the other two classes.[74] The implication is that his own work, as a history of 'Natural Philosophy,' is particularly valuable.[75]

In some ways, the close association between natural science and human history was uncontroversial. As Rosemary Sweet notes, there was overlap between the Royal Society and the Society of Antiquarians, even under the 'resolutely mathematical presidency' of Isaac Newton.[76] The tendency to connect the two is suggested by the title of the 1778 work *Remarkable Ruins and Romantic Prospects, of North Britain with Ancient Monuments, and Singular Subjects of Natural History.* For the work's writers, both these two 'subject[s] of investigation' contributed to the understanding of 'system', that is, to the organisation of knowledge.[77] Both antiquarianism and natural history potentially rely on a form of collection; the experimental method that characterises physical science is not always seen as fully separate from this kind of data gathering. A similar alliance between human history, broadly conceived, and natural history is also suggested in educational works, such as Ann Murry's *Mentoria; Or the Young Ladies Instructor* (1796), which establishes 'different classes' of history, including '*Sacred History*', '*Profane History*', '*Natural History*', and '*Biography*'.[78] Murry's pupil will first peruse sacred and natural history which 'tend to increase . . . love and admiration of the Deity'. Only then will her pupil learn to compare former 'arbitrary measures' with contemporary 'lenity' and celebrate the British constitution.[79]

However, while the term 'science' has a certain flexibility in the late eighteenth century, Burke was undermining the radical appropriation of the term. In *An Historical and Moral View of the French Revolution*, for instance, Wollstonecraft suggests that 'political science' and 'philosophy' have 'simplified the principles of social union, so as to render them easy to be comprehended'. Written from this perspective, her history suggests that 'ensanguined regal pomp' has enslaved the 'multitude'; that hereditary rights harm the state; and that 'war' is pursued 'by the idle'. But without exercising the understanding, Wollstonecraft suggests, 'ignorant people . . . grow romantic . . . like croisaders [sic] and like women'.[80] Here science, broadly understood, can debunk chivalry and the feudal institutions that accompany it; poor education, conversely, leads to romantic and superstitious misapprehensions. It is notable that Charlotte Smith, who shares Wollstonecraft's anti-chivalric sentiments, turned with works like *Minor Morals, Interspersed with Sketches of Natural History, Historical Anecdotes, and Original Stories* (1798) increasingly to the botany that had always interested her. Her decision to write educational works might in part have been financially motivated but her invitation to examine the natural as well as the human world is linked to issues of perspective and clarity of vision. For Smith accurate observation of the natural world enriches economic understanding and at the same time broadens a child's sympathies.[81] In *St Leon* Godwin, more equivocal about chivalry, has his hero conduct both alchemical and social experiments. Against a hostile, often Catholic backdrop, alchemy operates as a kind of proto-science, a step (or stage) on the journey towards true scientific and social rationality.

There were several ways to respond to this radical discourse. On the one hand, the stadial model could be used to suggest that chivalry itself had generated the conditions for scientific knowledge. Writing in a *'philosophical* view' the author of *A Protest against T. Paine's 'Rights of Man'* (1792) insists:

> The decline of literature, the extinction of the arts and sciences, must surely follow, when the supreme power is in the hands of the illiterate Many; before whose Gothic ravages, the monuments of fame and merit, the depositaries of learning and the archives of science, will speedily appear.[82]

Here the New Philosophy, elsewhere accused of painting a gothic view of an oppressive past, itself becomes a destructive force, generating decay and ruin. A return to the past, to 'a new age of romantic chivalry' will be necessary to bring about 'a more perfect civilization'.[83] Also claiming a connection between chivalry and science, in 1815 Eleanor Anne Porden writes a romance, *The Veils*, a poetic allegory of the elements and of the types of scientific minds. The romance was published by Murray, the conservative editor of the *Quarterly Review*.[84]

On other hand, it was possible to imply continuity between the excesses of chivalric superstition and radical enthusiasm – and to reject both. In Maria Edgeworth's novel *Belinda* (1801) as Lady Delacour plays Queen Elizabeth, Clarence Hervey, the hero, responds to Dr X–'s desire to take her pulse:

> Look through the door at the shadow of Queen Elizabeth's ruff – observe how it vibrates; the motion as well as the figure is magnified in the shadow. – Cannot you count every pulsation distinctly?[85]

In Edgeworth's empirical and progressive approach, modern science interprets the historical masque, seeing through the pageantry in order to diagnose illness. But if chivalry is suspect, another of the novel's episodes suggests radical readings of the environment are equally so. When the cursed figure of the obeah woman appears in the room of the West Indian slave, Juba, he is persuaded that he is marked for death. But Belinda realises that the figure has been painted in phosphorus by the manly Harriot Freke (often identified as Wollstonecraft). Edgeworth suggests that while radicals use the discoveries of science to excite superstition and panic, and to trick the people, a training in first-hand observation and experiment will defeat them. Science interprets both the past and the natural world, correcting chivalric longings and assuaging revolutionary fears. Moreover, in an appendix to *Practical Education* (1798) Maria Edgeworth and her father, Richard Lovell Edgeworth, include the suggestion that education be considered an 'experimental science' and 'recur to a passage in Dr Reid's *Essays*': 'If we could obtain a distinct and full history of all that hath passed in the mind of a child from the beginning of life and sensation till it grows up to the use of reason . . . this would be a treasure of natural history.'[86] As Edgeworth's educational works suggest, she imagines that this biographical form of natural history itself works to dispel false associations, political and customary.

Similar ideas inform the work of the novelist and educational writer Elizabeth Hamilton. Interested, like Edgeworth, in the association of ideas, Hamilton suggests that superstitious pseudo-science must be utterly rejected, whether it is a product of paganism or of radical abstraction. Although *Memoirs of the Life of Agrippina* focuses on the classical rather than the feudal world, it insists that false notions of the external world, or false associations, lead to false religion. Conversely, Hamilton argues, correct observation and Christianity (implicitly, perhaps, Protestantism) go hand in hand to ensure social progress. For Hamilton, as for Wollstonecraft, the reader must be familiar with the right kind of history in order to understand this. Completing this sequence, in *The Loyalists* Jane West would reclaim the association between science and social rationality for the Church of England. Ultimately, instead of radicals producing a false or gothicised history to fool the masses, the Anglican loyalists will be able to use such mechanisms against the enthused and superstitious radical dissenters.

While Edgeworth imagines a natural history of the developing child's mind, in *Memoirs of the Life of Agrippina* Elizabeth Hamilton attempts to develop a similar profile of the passions in relation to a historical figure. Like William Godwin, Maria Edgeworth and Joanna Baillie, Hamilton was interested in the educational and socially ameliorative effects of studying character. Encouraged by 'D- S-' (the Scottish philosopher Dugald Stewart), Hamilton wrote *Agrippina* as an 'illustration of principles' set out in her *Letters on Education*.[87] Having constructed an educational theory, in other words, Hamilton gathers the empirical data concerning Agrippina's life (or speculates when data is lacking) in order to provide a kind of scientific demonstration. Although Hamilton unsurprisingly asserts that *Agrippina* is not a novel, the results of the experiment are too interesting to be passed over here. Hamilton outlines her scientific approach to the passions in her preface. For Hamilton, the exploration of their 'origin and progress' (a project reminiscent of Joanna Baillie's, as outlined in her introductory discourse to *Plays on the Passions*), is a 'complex' matter, requiring accurate observation of their gradual development.[88] This difficulty is not, however, grounds for discouragement:

> The metaphysician may indeed separate the passions from each other, as the experimental philosopher separates the rays of light by the prism, and represent each singly to our view in one uniform colour. But in human character it is not thus that the passion are found to appear. Every passion, even that which predominates, is there seen blended with those which gave it birth.[89]

Baillie's project had been to examine the development of one passion in each of her plays. Hamilton's response serves at once to distinguish her own work and to suggest (and ultimately restructure) the connection between potentially radical metaphysics and empirical science. In *Translations of the Letters of a Hindoo Rajah* (1796) she had parodied the modern 'Philosophers' who failed in their 'knowledge' 'moral or natural': a 'Sceptic' decides to change sparrows into honey bees with disastrous results.[90] This wariness concerning poor science remains. Instead of splitting 'rays', Hamilton wishes to shed 'light'.[91] As her comparison suggests, for Hamilton, the practical applications of any theory are always key.

Aiming to reap the practical fruits of observation, in the *Memoirs of the Life of Agrippina* Hamilton explains her choice of genre carefully – and in the process she argues for a strange model of historical distance. Whereas Godwin had briefly made the suggestion in 'Of History and Romance' that the historical romance could provide a more useful insight into individual motivation than history, Hamilton, in contrast, suggests that while a successful novel must be emotionally engaging, these very 'feelings' mislead the reader.[92] Unable to judge from 'experience' the accuracy with which character is delineated, readers will, she imagines, be converted by emotion into a belief in erroneous 'system[s]' (clearly Hamilton is once again attacking radical thought).[93] Thus she suggests *Agrippina* is not a novel but a biography, a genre which makes a deeper impression of truth. Yet even with biography, there is a problem of distance, albeit this time historical: 'The writer who speaks from his own knowledge, . . . may describe with the faithful accuracy the personal defects, the incidental weaknesses of a departed friend, and by his philosophical impartiality entitle himself to rank with the investigator of nature.' In doing so, he becomes 'One who could peep and botanize / Upon his mother's grave!'[94] Like other sciences, the investigation of character must not only by based on accurate observation; it must also avoid indelicacy and prurience.

In contrast, the classical past might seem to offer too much distance. However, Hamilton raises and rejects this objection. When ancient history is under consideration, distance and 'detail' can, she argues, be combined. This position in part relies on Hamilton's supposedly minute historical researches (albeit via translations) and her investigation and insertion of information regarding Roman familiar 'manners': the element of conjecture in the work is considerable. Significantly, though, her assertions concerning the usefulness of the classical past also rely on the belief that 'we shall find [human nature] in every clime and situation invariably the same'.[95] Drawing on the idea of universal history, Hamilton suggests that the same causes produce the same effects (without explicitly using such wording, perhaps because of its connection with the systemising she had condemned in the 1790s). Thus, human character operates like a physical substance that reacts in a reliable way to particular stimuli. All this enables Hamilton to offer a kind of displaced observation as the most socially ameliorative form of knowledge.

Hamilton wishes to use this combination of proximity and detachment to correct her reader's understanding of the classical past. Probably thinking of Gibbon's *Decline and Fall of the Roman Empire*, Hamilton suggests that the 'colouring' of the historian has ensured that Roman progress from banditti to imperial power has been celebrated and the real 'merit' of the society exaggerated.[96] In contrast, for Hamilton, the end of the empire is not a story of violent breakage in which virtuous Romans are replaced by despicable successors. Hamilton proposes an alternative narrative, one of a society in some respect admirable but ultimately flawed by mistaken associations. She frames her biography with a large-scale stadial account of Roman society, remarking that 'Political institution is to society what early education is to the individual' – in other words, the mode of government can be thought about in terms of its impact on the association of ideas.[97] One of the most important of these ideas is 'liberty', a source of the 'generous motives' that 'purifies the heart'.[98] In Rome the 'idea of liberty' generates 'manly virtues', working through the very 'institutions' of the Republic.[99] Notably, this particular 'idea of liberty' encourages laudable ambition:

> every idea of glory was associated with the idea of Rome: not with Rome, as the place of his birth, or the seat of his residence, but as the community of which he formed, not a nominal, but an essential part. The strength of this sentiment is evident throughout the Roman history; where we have many

proofs, how entirely the idea of *self* may be annihilated in the fervour of patriotic zeal.[100]

Shaped by institutions which give him a stake in the society (even, in the barbarous ages, in its plunder), the Roman identifies with the political unit. What Hamilton imagines is not a liberty of individual political rights but a liberty of identification with (what will become) the nation.

Nonetheless, the Roman ability to connect love of liberty and the nation in the proper way is flawed. In Hamilton's account, this is because of mistaken religious associations, which generate an inaccurate perception of the external world. Classical 'credulity with regard to supernatural events' leads the priesthood to enlist:

> all the striking phenomena of nature into their service, they made every change in the state of the elements, every movement of the feathered tribes, nay even the very garbage from which the eyes of delicacy turns abhorrent, means of working on the hopes and fears of the deluded multitude.[101]

In effect superstition generates a kind of pseudo-science and this in turn leads to mistaken policy, corruption and ultimately the loss of that liberty which was so highly prized. Hamilton emphasises the bad consequences of 'constantly viewing objects as connected, that have in reality no connection'.[102] Exploiting the poor associations of superstition to govern the populace, the Roman magistrates come themselves to believe in such inaccurate perceptions: it proves 'almost impossible for the mind of man to remain uninfluenced by the prejudices which he imposes upon others', she insists. Even Tiberius himself is affected. After 'heathen philosophy' fails to comfort Tiberius in exile, he becomes 'addict[ed]' to the 'science of astrology, which the superstition of the times had brought into repute': brutally, he tests successive astrologers' grasp of futurity by seeing if they can predict his plans to kill them.[103] Hamilton's seemingly stray observation when discussing Agrippina's leisure, that the Roman matron had no knowledge of how silks were produced and no interest in natural science, is consistent with this account of superstition. Accurate observation of the external world is, like proper morality, alien to the heathen mind. The link between 'pretended science', failed religion and false philosophy is as strong a theme in Hamilton's treatment of ancient past as it is in her discussions of contemporary radical science and philosophy in *A Hindoo Rajah*.[104] When such beliefs take hold, government, morality and liberty are all weakened.

Dugald Stewart had proposed to Elizabeth Hamilton that *Agrippina* should mark the start of 'a series of comparative biography' that would 'balance the ancient with a modern character'. Stewart wished her to undertake the life of John Locke but Hamilton found the 'skip from Agrippina to Locke' too dizzying.[105] Instead, she imagined moving from Agrippina to the 'Princess Palatine, daughter to James I', then tackling 'Seneca' before finally coming to the writer of *An Essay on Human Understanding*.[106] Although this extended project was never undertaken due to Hamilton's misgivings, the plan and *Agrippina*'s echoes between past and present scepticism suggest that the memoir is more than an 'illustration': it is also a lesson about the operation of association in the present.[107] Part of what Hamilton wishes to correct is the mindset of the modern young reader of classical history, who arises with feelings of esteem for the Romans and disgust for their successors. Such a reader has also been exposed to 'the improper use of epithets': 'the clemency of Augustus' has been the theme of eulogium to authors, ancient and modern', Hamilton writes, 'yet ... the *mild*, the *polite* AUGUSTUS, with his own hands tore out the eyes of Gallius'.[108] Such epithets, coupled with such actions, perplex the reader's 'ideas of right and wrong', something for which Gibbon (significantly criticised by contemporaries for his 'irreligion') is, Hamilton suggests, particularly to blame.[109] This is symptomatic of a deeper problem. Hamilton suggests that the introduction of Christianity into the Roman world was hampered by superstitious and inaccurate associations – and that this effect will take a long time to wear off. The implication is that, underpinned by false history, such poor associations continue to hamper Christian thinking in the modern world. To observe the external world properly and to rewrite history accordingly (as *Agrippina* seeks to do) is to enable a better religious sense.

In attempting to create this improved Christian impulse, Hamilton's project is not only scientific (to do with accurate observation) but in some sense medicinal. When Germanicus is suffering from what is possibly 'an affection of the liver', he believes he is being poisoned by his enemies.[110] But even as they appeal to 'infernal deities' for his death, 'superstition did more in their behalf than the stars could have effected': 'horror' and dismay contributes to Germanicus's fatal illness.[111] Further, the ignorant physicians, unable to observe nature, think the poison has been successful. Wrong associations and failed medicine together lead to Germanicus's demise and, facing it, he lacks 'the cj160
almness of resignation' that the Christian faith would have given him. His death and that of Agrippina's is placed by Hamilton in contrast with Christ's execution – and resurrection. The Romans 'saw the Saviour of the world burst the bands of death', a new event which gives rise to new 'ideas' and moves the reader beyond chronological time to 'everlasting joy'.[112] For Hamilton, this Christian perspective (even operating

'imperfectly') makes it possible to correct the 'pride' connected with the idea of national liberty. It has, she argues, 'removed the barriers which before its introduction separated man from man'.[113] Whereas the Romans looked with scorn on the 'barbarian' Germans, the British will be able to combine an emphasis on liberty with cross-cultural sensitivity. Self will be safely offset by the idea of generous national freedom.

Jane West's works similarly suggest the complexity of the use of science and history in the post-French Revolution debate. Frequently positioned as, in Gary Kelly's words, one of the 'most notable Anti-Jacobin novelists', West's function in critical works has been largely to provide a stable conservative touchstone against which the complexities of radical writers can be measured.[114] Yet, as her thoughts concerning the meaning and purpose of history suggest, she is a more complex political thinker than has usually been assumed. Although West's anti-Jacobin works of the 1790s ostensibly concentrate on the contemporary, these novels nonetheless register an interest in the uses and, particularly, the abuses of history. Suspicious of radical abstraction and of gothic reconstructions of history, in these novels West also, more surprisingly, begins to query the efficacy of chivalry. Searching for a proper historical mode, in *Letters Addressed to a Young Man* (1801) she examines history's relation to the natural sciences. History provides a source of data that not only 'elucidate[s] the human character' but also provides empirical evidence on which to base political thought.[115] West's shift in 1812 to historical fiction can be seen as a logical outcome of her interest in the validation of custom by history. *The Loyalists* sees West reject chivalry as constitutional defence in a way that is far from Burkean. Instead, in this novel, while she equates what are for her the evils of dissent and radicalism, she also reclaims science – and an allegedly scientific approach to history – for the Church of England. For West, this conjunction of history, science and religion is emphatically not a solely masculine matter. As has been explored elsewhere, West's early works expand female authority by using domestic metaphors of 'cooking' and ingestion.[116] In *The Loyalists* it is women, as well as the church, who, by their knowledge of history and science, will doctor the unhealthy social body, curing its over-consumption.

There is a clear but often overlooked the connection between West's anti-Jacobin project of the 1790s and her later choice of the genre of historical novel. In her early works, although West agrees with Burke's implicit argument that liberty and the correct attitude to the past are linked, she begins to query his chivalric narrative of 'manly freedom'.[117] A close reading of works such as *A Gossip's Story* (1796) and *A Tale of the Times* (1799) suggests that, even as West attacks radicalism, she remains suspicious of the sexualised model of power associated with chivalry. In *Letters Addressed to a Young Man* Jane West repairs this breach with Burke by exploiting another strand of his rhetoric, a strand which Burke himself had co-opted from the radicals. Reusing the metaphor concerning the 'wild gases' of revolution, West quotes 'Dr Priestly' [sic]: 'real history resembles experiments made by the airpump'.[118] For the student of history, the events of the past are a source of information about the likely outcomes of political experiment.

Warning her nephew against the 'slight compendiums of literature' used by 'our anarchists', West suggests he 'devote [his] leisure hours to some author who clearly enters upon an improving subject, and treats it methodically, in a train of reasoning'.[119] No subject is better for this than 'history', she contends, although 'Natural Philosophy, is, indeed, a highly improving pursuit'.[120] This last can be advantageous because it increases admiration 'of the great First Cause who actuates his subordinate agent, Nature' – West's language is not only scientific but has a deistic tone that recalls the suggestions of dissenters like Priestley.[121] However, 'natural philosophy' involves expensive apparatus and the need for instruction. History has a similarly moral impact without these disadvantages. More expertise can be acquired with less reliance on an instructor:

> Experience, which determines on the present by inferences drawn from the past, is our substitute for wisdom; and where can this be so fully acquired, as from those details of past events which are preserved in the pages of authentic history?[122]

History provides a bank of experimental data and is, also in the words of 'Dr Priestly' [sic] 'an exhibition of the conduct of Divine Providence'. It provides the evidence where fiction provides only the philosophy. West has firmly co-opted Priestley's experimental model.

West also attacks a number of radical errors, which historical evidence, when properly weighed, disproves. A more scientific approach to history will enable her nephew to dismiss Rousseau's erroneous idealisation of the state of nature. He will also reject the suggestion that 'war originates from the rapacity, ambition, selfishness, or inconsiderateness of rulers' – 'savages', she insists, are far more often at war.[123] In these instances, radicalism distorts history. 'It has of late been a prevailing custom', West writes, 'for the novelists of the democratic school to avail themselves of the obscurity which has enveloped remote times for a very insidious purpose.'[124] While 'a novel really written in the age of Coeur de Lion would be invaluable', modern fictions cannot provide accurate information about the past. West probably had in mind James White's humorous *Adventures of King Richard Coeur-de-Lion* (1791), a work which, in undermining chivalry, also made monarchy itself ludicrous.[125] Worst of all are tales of atrocity 'heaped upon the back of some monk', taken by democratic novelists and inaccurate historians 'as a faithful representation of the clergy of past times'.[126] When West eventually turns to historical fiction, it will be to correct such misreadings of the role of the church and king.

In *Letters to a Young Man* West suggests that engaging in the 'science of politics' her pupil should 'turn your eyes from the present state of your country, till you have obtained a clear knowledge of the past'.[127] Involved in such studies, he should 'consider whether public liberty was most religiously protected by those whom our constitution had appointed to be its guardians, or by those who surreptitiously acquired that envied privilege'.[128] *The Loyalists* fictionalises that experiment. West's usual anti-Jacobin message is clearly present in the novel: radicalism is presented as a form of insubordination that generates social chaos, while the book's civil war setting gives West an unprecedented opportunity to connect such radicalism with religious dissent. Despite West's title and premise, *The Loyalists* is more critical of monarchical and court behaviour than West's anti-Jacobin past has led commentators to assume. In particular, West argues that aristocratic weakness is facilitated by adherence to a false code of chivalry which is in turn generated by a misreading of history. As West immediately makes clear, this chivalric code is dangerous because it affects even true loyalists like the youthful hero Eustace and his father, Colonel Evellin. Both misread history; both reject female interpretations of it and both are threatened by danger and disgrace.

Although West is suspicious of Burkean chivalry, connecting it with 'voluptuous' behaviour and unnecessary expenditure, she is determined to support the status quo.[129] The Church of England, the episcopacy and the subordination, which, for West, these represent, must be reinforced. In order to do this, she re-appropriates some of the associations of radical dissent for the church, making the organisation seem progressive and rational as well as structured and orderly. In the Birmingham riots of 14 to 17 July 1791, Joseph Priestley's house had been attacked by an angry mob, apparently prompted by a small group of local magistrates. West's novel rewrites these events. In *Desmond* Major Danby had referred to the dissenters' riots only to be reminded by Bethel that the dissenters were the victims rather than the perpetrators of the disturbance. *The Loyalists* fictionalises history to support Danby's suggestion (a rewriting which has a curious and distorted echo in the confusion of the rioters themselves, who are popularly supposed to have shouted anti-papist slogans). In this narrative, it is Davies, the dissenting village schoolmaster, who leads the rioting villagers against the house of Dr Beaumont, the Church of England clergyman. Davies has 'laboured under the pressure of poverty', a pressure that generates both metaphysical confusion (he mistakes the 'cravings of want for spiritual illumination') and a desire for material comfort.[130] Rather than the home of a leading scientist and radical dissenter being destroyed by a king and church mob, the property of the Church of England is attacked by a dissenter.

Joseph Priestley had suggested that, circumventing the restrictions of the Royal Society, 'several companies' be established to allow free experimentation.[131] In *The Loyalists*, on the contrary, scientific rationality belongs to a minister of the established church, while the Anglican suspicion regarding dissent and insubordination is reconfirmed.[132] As well as attacking classical learning ('See you that bust? It represents Diana of the Esphesians . . . who endangered Paul's life', Davies angrily exclaims), the ill-informed and narrow-minded schoolmaster mistakes 'mathematical exercises' for 'necromancing figures, . . . squares and triangles, and the sun, moon and stars, which Job said he never worshipped'.[133] Priestley had written church histories; Davies, on the other hand, denounces Dr Beaumont's: 'Touch not his books, dearly beloved; they will prove the Devil's bird-lime, teaching you to despise my godly ministry . . . Do those church histories tell us about saving faith?' For the mistaken Davies, the answer is an emphatic 'nay'.[134] The cultural destruction of the Reformation is restaged but it is now not the Church of Rome but the Church of England, supposed home of hierarchical and historically validated learning, which is in danger.

For West, the solution lies, not only with the Church of England itself, but with its loyalist worshippers. Mrs Mellicent, Dr Beautmont's sister, and Lloyd, a medical doctor, both suggest accurate knowledge of the natural world is connected with right religion and a healing that is social as well as physical. Mrs Mellicent (who resembles Mrs Prudentia Homespun, the narrator of some of West's earlier works) is 'fully occupied by the villagers, many of whom were hurt at the riot'.[135] Although somewhat irascible, Mrs Mellicent finds 'her cordial waters, lotions, and plaisters . . . in a constant state of requisition'.[136] The symbolism of Mrs Mellicent's healing is made clear by Dr Beaumont. Suggesting that his own suffering parallels that of King Charles, Dr. Beaumont observes: 'When the head suffers grievously, the members must be indisposed.'[137] The metaphor of the body politic suggests that Mrs Mellicent's medicinal efforts have a broader symbolic importance, catering, albeit indirectly, to the unity of the community. Similarly, when De Vallance is filled with guilt about his family's treatment of the hero Eustace, presumed dead, Dr Lloyd offers him a 'cordial': 'I see your disease, and know my remedy will complete your cure.'[138] Eustace is alive and De Vallance is morally and physically restored. West also insists that this masculine medical and social authority can comfortably coexist with the healing herbals associated with female moral aid. Marriage is not necessary to unite the two forms of political power: 'History does not warrant [her] in adding, that [Mrs Mellicent] afterwards consummated the happiness of Dr Lloyd.'[139] In fact, the independence of Mrs Mellicent's single state allows the two practitioners to remain 'sincere friends': as an unmarried woman, Mrs Mellicent can remain confident about 'superiority of her own cordials and ointments', and does not have to subscribe to 'the efficacy of those medical nostrums which were not found in the British herbal'.[140] Although West believes in subordination, then, she also indicates the significance of a space for female authority, separate from masculinised scientific and religious hierarchies.

In *The Loyalists* West argues that the correct interpretation of history is reached through such masculine and feminine loyalist medicines. In particular, the practitioners can manipulate and correct the gothic rhetoric of radical history, rewriting the past to support loyalism in the present. Carried out by Mrs Mellicent and Dr Lloyd this kind of rewriting mirrors West's project in her own historical novels. In *Letters Addressed to a Young Man* West argued that the 'democratic school' had 'avail[ed]' themselves of the obscurity which has enveloped remote times'; such historical tales are full of 'bloody tyrant[s]', 'cruel marauders' and 'loathsome dungeon[s]'.[141] The gothic was, according to West, a radical perversion of history that had to be contested. In *The Loyalists* she answers such democratic gothicisms: the gothic is not connected with oppression but rather with a failure to interpret the evidence of the past. While Cromwell's followers and dissenters like Davies misinterpret history, loyalists like Mrs Mellicent and Dr Lloyd have more accurate vision. As such, in *The Loyalists* comic hauntings play an important role. When Sedley (later De Vallance), is lodging with the Beaumonts at Waverly-Hall, he hears the tale of the 'illness' of the dissenter Farmer Humphreys.[142] Humphreys has had 'a vision, in which he had seen the ghost of Sir William Waverly in torment, complaining that there was a royalist in his grave who would not let him rest'.[143] Lady Bellingham, Cromwell's ally, also sees the supposed spectre and, feeling the 'agony only the guilty can feel', gives 'a loud shriek' before fainting.[144] Yet neither can rely on the evidence of their senses. The spectre is in fact the living loyalist, Colonel Evellin, who is in hiding from the authorities. Rather than being a genre which reveals the oppression of the feudal system to encourage progress, the gothic is only a sign of the radicals' guilty consciences. They are the ones who encourage oppression. They may consider that loyalism is dead at their hands but, West implies, like Evellin himself, it is in fact still living.

Those with what West considers the correct political perspective are the only ones who can realise that loyalism is a still vital tradition. When De Vallance converts from the Parliamentarian to the Royalist cause, he is able to discover the cause of Humphreys' sickness, finding Colonel Evellin's hiding place. Meanwhile, Mrs Mellicent, who knows the truth, is quite willing to call strategically on the gothic fears of the radicals. Confronted with the hysterical Lady Bellingham, she 'gravely allowed the possibility of ghosts inhabiting ruins; . . . and wondered at the Lady's alarm, since from the little she had said the preceding day, it was plain she considered herself as a favourite of Heaven'.[145] Having 'sorted her simples, compounded her medicines, and examined her patients', Mrs Mellicent is capable of some humorous deception in supporting the Royalist cause.[146] The link between accurate history, natural science and loyalism is evident. Such connections are also reinforced by the confused but well-meaning labourer Jobson. Jobson, whose political naïvety supports West's argument about the importance of subordination, accidentally fights for the wrong side before falling into depression. As De Vallance discovers, the cause of the illness is Jobson's belief that he has experienced 'a supernatural intimation that England was ruined': 'I met Fido in the streets of Worcester the night before it was taken by Old Noll – Mr Eustace's own poor Fido, and I then said the King would be beat.'[147] Actually, the dog, far from being 'oracular', is alive and well in the care of Dr Lloyd. The Welsh doctor is not, as Jobson supposes, an anatomist, who gathers bodies to dissect them. Instead, he has rescued Eustace and is eventually able to reveal the truth. Science re-examines the past and saves the Loyalist political body.

Connected with clear, scientific vision, the church itself also provides a kind of cure for both chivalric luxury and dissenting confusion. When the chivalrous and historically mis-educated Eustace arrives at court, he encounters 'shallow courtiers, known only for polished manners, habits of dissipation, and an excessive regard to their own interest'.[148] These courtiers 'hang like leeches' on the 'exhausted frame of Royalty', draining the 'scanty resources of the public treasury'.[149] But if luxury damages the nation, the Anglican Church prevents such misapplied medicines, simultaneously ensuring liberty against the envy-driven disorder of dissent. When Barton, a virtuous dissenter, sees the 'fury of fanatic mobs' in destroying 'exquisite remains of antient art', consecrated to the worship of God he addresses the crowd with the suggestion that 'the

plainness and poverty' of the early church 'were no rule for her government in future ages':

> How are curious craftsmen to flourish, if there are no purchasers of their
> handy-works; and if we admit these into our houses, why not into the places
> where we hold our religious assemblies? Are paintings and carvings less
> likely to carnalize our hearts in our halls and banqueting-rooms than in our
> chapels? Is a golden cup on the Lord's table the accursed spoil of Achan; and
> doth it become purified by being removed to the buttery and used in a private
> carousal?[150]

Although this is a comparative argument, its length implies that the
church is in fact a more appropriate destination for high-end consumer
products than the home. The church is able, according to Barton, to
absorb the superfluities of the market without the danger of over-
indulgence (the 'carousals') that afflict ordinary individuals. By implication, then, its tithes have a moral effect – eventually used to stimulate
production without the evils of consumption. Here, private vices are not
necessary to ensure public benefit. As the surplus of wealth is channelled
into the church (or into moral and charitable activity) West imagines
that the envy and social unrest that accompany more straightforwardly
capitalist free-markets, will be removed. This belief in the church allows
West, in this fictional space at least, to avoid the model of economic
progression found in Scott, in which individuals' more vicious impulses
are controlled, not so much by morality, as by the uncertain operation
of the law. For West, the church is the guarantor of morality and hence
of liberty.

Jane West's suspicion of chivalry and her attempt to reclaim the
radical emphasis on science must be understood as an intervention in a
complex debate about political morality. As a system of signs and a set
of practices, chivalry had itself from time to time been seen as a scientific
system of knowledge. In E. M. Foster's *Duke of Clarence: An Historical
Novel* (1795), set in the fifteenth century, for instance, the guardian of
the youthful hero is 'desirous, that Edgar should become an adept in that
noble science'.[151] However, once read as a deceptive show or as sign of
radical quixotism, this supposedly systematised code of conduct needed
a lot of monitoring and adjustment to perform meaningful political
work. Genlis attempts to use the language of chivalry to underline the
moral need for the monarchy to listen to the 'people'. In more safely
reformist mode Anna Maria Porter suggests that the humanity of the
code could guide aristocracy and monarchy, while Jane Porter in some
sense reverses Genlis's point, suggesting that an adapted chivalric narrative can enhance the moral capability of the people. In *The Scottish
Chiefs* chivalry is reinvented as nationalist sentiment, a feeling which

encourages ordinary citizens to see their interests as united with those of the ruling class. The surprising political malleability of chivalry also continued to worry Jane West, who, after undermining its connection with effeminate luxury in *The Loyalists*, turned to a project of chivalric redefinition in her next novel, *Alicia de Lacy: An Historical Romance* (1814). Characteristically, her redefinition focuses on religion. Although 'the habits of the age' are at once 'pious and martial', Jane West wants to distinguish proper religious behaviour from Roman Catholic practice.[152] Rome, she suggests, tends to disrupt private ties by emphasising solitude. True religion, on the other hand, supports private ties of affection and, as religious and historical portraiture shows, prevents (female) vanity, fashion and luxury.[153] It is thus crucial to patriotism.[154] If there is a problem with luxury, if property is an obstacle difficult to negotiate in relation to nation, for West religion provides the solution. Religion is the pure source of (corrupted) chivalric values.

Even if chivalry could be associated with the humanitarian and medicinal (as Anna Maria Porter had suggested), its connection with inherited property and power made it fragile, vulnerable to radical reinterpretation. But the idea of scientific experiment offered a different way of looking at political actors, political process and the materialities of national life. In the nineteenth century the idea of history as a form of science would prove particularly influential. Yet this idea is rarely associated with the post-French Revolution debate in Britain. It is more commonly identified with the German historian, Leopold von Ranke.

In his 'Inaugural Lecture on the Study of History' (1895) Lord Acton described Ranke as 'representative of the age which instigated the modern study of history'. Requiring, as Acton described it, history to be 'critical', 'colourless' and 'new', Ranke argued that his discipline should aim to show 'simply how it was' (*'wie es eigentlich gewesen'*).[155] Acton notes Ranke's:

> course had been determined, in early life, by *Quentin Durward*. The shock of the discovery that Scott's Lewis [sic] the Eleventh was inconsistent with the original in Commynes made him resolve that his object thenceforth should be above all things to follow, without swerving, and in stern subordination and surrender, the lead of his authorities.[156]

On his part, Ranke recalls being 'offended' by Scott's historical portraits, which:

> seemed, even in particular details, to be completely contradictory to the historical evidence. I could not forgive him for accepting in his narrative biased tendencies which were totally unhistorical, and presenting them as if he believed them.[157]

This 'subordination' to the historical sources led the publication of Ranke's *History of the Latin and Teutonic Nations, 1494–1514* (1824) to be seen as a 'crucial moment' in the 'development of modern professional, "scientific" history'.[158] As a result, not only Scott's fictions but the whole of eighteenth-century historiography came to be superseded, rejected as amateurish and inaccurate.[159] It is perhaps ironic, then, that the idea of a relationship between science and history had been mooted by Joseph Priestley, developed by radical thinkers like Wollstonecraft and Godwin, and reclaimed by Elizabeth Hamilton and Jane West. Although these writers have the 'biased tendencies' Ranke dislikes, they also have something he would have found more acceptable, a 'purpose'.[160] Writing in response to the French Revolution, Hamilton proposes a relation between Christianity, science and the interpretation of the past in which individual psychology and 'manners' generate the freedoms of a rational society. More conservatively, West's revisionist position leads her to position history as a true science, one which reveals the centrality of church, king and subordination to the social system.

## Notes

1. C. Butler, *The Age of Chivalry*, p. 1.
2. C. Butler, *The Age of Chivalry*, np.
3. De Genlis, *Knights*, 2: 236. For further information about Genlis see Dow, Stéphanie-Félicité de Genlis and the French Historical Novel'.
4. Genlis, *Knights*, 2: 239.
5. Genlis, *Knights*, 2: 240.
6. C. Butler, *The Age of Chivalry*, np.
7. Priestley, *Lectures*, pp. 129–30.
8. Anna Maria Porter, *The Hungarian Brothers* (1807), 1: v. Unless stated, all other references are to this edition.
9. A. M. Porter, *The Hungarian Brothers* (1807), Standard Novel Edition, vi.
10. A. M. Porter, *Hungarian Brothers*, 1: 49.
11. A. M. Porter, *Hungarian Brothers*, 1: 59.
12. A. M. Porter, *Hungarian Brothers*, 1: vi.
13. A. M. Porter, *Hungarian Brothers*, 2: 195.
14. A. M. Porter, *Hungarian Brothers*, 3: 236.
15. A. M. Porter, *Hungarian Brothers*, 1: vi.
16. A. M. Porter, *Hungarian Brothers*, 1: 181.
17. A. M. Porter, *Hungarian Brothers*, 2: 156.
18. A. M. Porter, *Hungarian Brothers*, 3: 266.
19. Genlis, *Knights*, 1: 161.

20. William Robertson, *History of Charles V*, p. 71.
21. A. M. Porter, *Hungarian Brothers*, 1: 3.
22. Maria Edgeworth, *Letters for Literary Ladies*, p. 1, p. 3.
23. A. M. Porter, *Hungarian Brothers*, 1: 26.
24. A. M. Porter, *Hungarian Brothers*, 1: 98.
25. A. M. Porter, *Hungarian Brothers*, 1: 107.
26. A. M. Porter, *Hungarian Brothers*, 1: 225.
27. A. M. Porter, *Hungarian Brothers*, 1: 226.
28. A. M. Porter, *Hungarian Brothers*, 2: 152.
29. A. M. Porter, *Hungarian Brothers*, 2: 120–2.
30. A. M. Porter, *Hungarian Brothers*, 1: 18.
31. A. M. Porter, *Hungarian Brothers*, 1: vii.
32. Austen, *Emma*, p. 99.
33. A. M. Porter, *Hungarian Brothers*, 1: 45.
34. A. M. Porter, *Hungarian Brothers*, 1: 45.
35. William Robertson, *History of Charles V*, p. 71.
36. A. M. Porter, *Hungarian Brothers*, 2:92.
37. A. M. Porter, *Hungarian Brothers*, 2: 93.
38. A. M. Porter, *Hungarian Brothers*, 2: 94.
39. A. M. Porter, *Hungarian Brothers*, 2: 95–6.
40. A. M. Porter, *Hungarian Brothers*, 2: 97; 2: 96.
41. A. M. Porter, *Hungarian Brothers*, 2: 95.
42. A. M. Porter, *Hungarian Brothers*, 2: 97.
43. A. M. Porter, *Hungarian Brothers*, 2: 100–1.
44. A. M. Porter, *Hungarian Brothers*, 1: 43–5.
45. 'Art. II. *Don Sebastian*', p. 363.
46. A. M. Porter, *Don Sebastian*, 1: viii.
47. A. M. Porter, *Don Sebastian*, 1: xv.
48. Anderson, *Imagined Communities*, p. 12, p. 20.
49. A. M. Porter, *Don Sebastian*, 1: xv.
50. A. M. Porter, *Don Sebastian*, 1: 16.
51. A. M. Porter, *Don Sebastian*, 1: 15, 1: 23.
52. A. M. Porter, *Don Sebastian*, 1: 110–11.
53. A. M. Porter, *Don Sebastian*, 1: 83.
54. A. M. Porter, *Don Sebastian*, 1: 123–4.
55. A. M. Porter, *Don Sebastian*, 1: 151–2.
56. A. M. Porter, *Don Sebastian*, 1: 160.
57. A. M. Porter, *Don Sebastian*, 1: 158.
58. A. M. Porter, *Don Sebastian*, 1: 170.
59. Moore, '"Caledonian Plagiary"', pp. 92–108.
60. Jane Porter, *Scottish Chiefs*, np.
61. Jane Porter, *Scottish Chiefs*, p. 42.
62. Home, *Douglas A Tragedy*, np.
63. Jane Porter, *Scottish Chiefs*, p. 41.
64. Burke, *Reflections*, p. 121; Jane Porter, *Scottish Chiefs*, p. 54.
65. Jane Porter, *Scottish Chiefs*, p. 55.
66. Jane Porter, *Scottish Chiefs*, p. 88.
67. Jane Porter, *Scottish Chiefs*, p. 116.
68. Jane Porter, *Scottish Chiefs*, p. 88.

69. Jane Porter, *Scottish Chiefs*, pp. 404–5.
70. Green, *Private History*, p. 5.
71. Green, *Private History*, p. 5.
72. Burke, *Reflections*, p. 90.
73. Qtd in Knox, 'Lunatick Visions', p. 444.
74. Priestley, *The History and Present State of Electricity*, ii–iii.
75. Priestley, *The History and Present State of Electricity*, iii.
76. Sweet, *Antiquaries*, p. 10.
77. Cordiner, *Remarkable Ruins*, ii.
78. Murry, *Mentoria*, pp. 140–1.
79. Murry, *Mentoria*, p. 143, p. 141.
80. Wollstonecraft, *Works*, 6: 14–15.
81. Charlotte Smith, *Minor Morals, Interspersed with Sketches of Natural History, Historical Anecdotes, and Original Stories*, 2nd edn, 2 vols (London: Low, 1799), 47, 31.
82. [John Bowles], *A Protest*, p. 33.
83. [John Bowles], *A Protest*, p. 33.
84. See Johns-Putra, '"Blending Science with Literature"'.
85. Maria Edgeworth, *Belinda*, p. 89.
86. Maria Edgeworth and Richard Lovell Edgeworth, *Practical Education*, 2: 734–5.
87. See 'Letter to Dr. S-', 14 September 1802, in Benger, *Memoirs*, 2: 28–9.
88. Baillie, pp. 67–113. Hamilton, *Agrippina*, 1: ix.
89. Hamilton, *Agrippina*, 1: ix.
90. Hamilton, *Letters of a Hindoo Rajah*, pp. 266–8.
91. Hamilton, *Agrippina*, 1: ix.
92. Hamilton, *Agrippina*, 1: xii
93. Hamilton, *Agrippina*, 1: xii, 1: xi.
94. Hamilton, *Agrippina*, 1: xx.
95. Hamilton, *Agrippina*, 1: xxiv.
96. Hamilton, *Agrippina*, 1: 2.
97. Hamilton, *Agrippina*, 1: 4–5.
98. Hamilton, *Agrippina*, 1: 6.
99. Hamilton, *Agrippina*, 1: 6–7.
100. Hamilton, *Agrippina*, 1: 7.
101. Hamilton, *Agrippina*, 1: 39, 1: 36–7.
102. Hamilton, *Agrippina*, 1: 37.
103. Hamilton, *Agrippina*, 1: 143.
104. Hamilton, *Agrippina*, 1: 144.
105. Benger, *Memoirs*, 2: 47–8.
106. Benger, *Memoirs*, 2: 48.
107. Hamilton, *Agrippina*, 1: vii.
108. Hamilton, *Agrippina*, 1: 34.
109. Hamilton, *Agrippina*, 1: 34; Whitaker, *Gibbon's History*, p. 12. See Womersley, *Gibbon and 'The Watchmen of the Holy City'*.
110. Hamilton, *Agrippina*, 2: 185.
111. Hamilton, *Agrippina*, 2: 196.
112. Hamilton, *Agrippina*, 3: 282.
113. Hamilton, *Agrippina*, 2: 21.

114. Kelly, *English Fiction*, p. 62. See Wood, 'Bachelors and "Old Maids"'; Wood, '"This Maze of History and Fiction"'; and Thame, 'Cooking up a Story.

115. Mark Salber Phillips, *Society and Sentiment*, p. 21; West, *Letters Addressed to a Young Man*, 1: 152.

116. Thame, 'Cooking up a Story'.

117. Burke, *Reflections*, p. 121.

118. West, *Young Man*, 1: 154.

119. West, *Young Man*, 1: 148–50.

120. West, *Young Man*, 1: 150.

121. West, *Young Man*, 1: 151.

122. West, *Young Man*, 1: 153.

123. West, *Young Man*, 1: 180.

124. West, *Young Man*, 1: 125–6.

125. West, *Young Man*, 1: 125.

126. West, *Young Man*, 1: 127.

127. West, *Young Man*, 1: 157.

128. West, *Young Man*, 1: 160.

129. West, *Loyalists*, 2: 20.

130. West, *Loyalists*, 1: 122.

131. Priestley, *The History and Present State of Electricity*, xiv. For further discussion, see Wood, *Science and Dissent*, p. 114; Jasper, 'A Poetics of Dissent; or, Pantisocracy in America', paragraphs 14–20.

132. John Kent, *Wesley*, p. 72

133. West, *Loyalists*, 1: 168.

134. West, *Loyalists*, 1: 169.

135. West, *Loyalists*, 1: 176.

136. West, *Loyalists*, 1: 176.

137. West, *Loyalists*, 1: 175.

138. West, *Loyalists*, 3: 117.

139. West, *Loyalists*, 3: 337.

140. West, *Loyalists*, 3: 338.

141. West, *Young Man*, 1: 126.

142. West, *Loyalists*, 2: 241.

143. West, *Loyalists*, 2: 250.

144. West, *Loyalists*, 3: 82.

145. West, *Loyalists*, 3: 83.

146. West, *Loyalists*, 2: 229.

147. West, *Loyalists*, 3: 102.

148. West, *Loyalists*, 2: 11.

149. West, *Loyalists*, 2: 18–19.

150. West, *Loyalists*, 1: 341, 1: 346–7.

151. E. M. Foster, *Duke of Clarence*, 1: 12.

152. West, *Alicia*, 1: 330–1.

153. West, *Alicia*, 2: 52.

154. West, *Alicia*, 2: 75.

155. Lord Acton, 'Inaugural Address', in Acton, *Lectures on Modern History*, p. 18; Curthoys and Docker, *Is History Fiction?*, p. 70.

156. Acton, *Lectures on Modern History*, p. 19.

157.  Von Ranke, 'Autobiographical Dictation', p. 38.
158.  Curthoys and Docker, *Is History Fiction?*, pp. 69–70.
159.  See Mark Salber Phillips, *Society and Sentiment*, xi.
160.  Von Ranke, 'Introduction', p. 58.

# Chapter 5

# The End of History? Scott, His Precursors and the Violent Past

Writing to her sister in 1821, Jane Porter makes a claim concerning her influence on Scott, which she repeats in the 1831 Standard Novels edition of *Thaddeus of Warsaw*.[1] Recounting a conversation between 'Sir Andrew Haliday', the King and Walter Scott on the 'admiration' felt for *Tales of my Landlord* and *Waverley*, she has 'Haliday' interject:

> 'Well Sir, who ever may be the author of those Novels; you, Sir Walter, must allow that the foundation of them all were laid by Miss Porter in her *Scottish Chiefs*.' 'I grant it;'/ replied Sir Walter, 'there is something in what you say.'[2]

In Porter's letter, Scott's 'I grant it' occurs at the end of a line. Along with the reporting clause, 'replied Sir Walter', this lends emphasis to Scott's affirmation; without these devices, his remarks dwindle to a polite nothing of good-natured agreement. The element of wish-fulfilment in Porter's remarks reflects her growing annoyance: the success of *Ivanhoe* followed hard on the failure of her play 'Switzerland' in 1819.[3] When Porter writes in relation to her sister's novel, *The Knight of St John, A Romance* (1817), 'Surely this Great Author, does not keep his hands from picking & stealing',[4] her frustration is thus understandable but inaccurate. No one who reads *The Knight* alongside *Ivanhoe* could accuse Scott of plagiarism. However, the novels share a focus on Judaism, an urgent drive to adapt the chivalric, a motif of national healing and a stadial approach to historical narrative. Scott is in dialogue with other historical fictions. But such dialogue is forgotten. Porter laments how one reviewer of *Ivanhoe* suggests that 'the universal merits of "Ivanhoe" as a romance, by embracing all subjects of romance, set at nought all romances which had ever been written'.[5] Her wording, 'set at nought', suggests an erasure that Peter Garside also remarks on. From the 1820s, the reviewers, who had initially compared Scott's works to other romances, tended to view him as 'the founder of a new historical fiction' and to compare him (not always favourably) to himself.[6]

For Garside, *Waverley*'s 'relation to other contemporary novels' still 'invites reappraisal'.[7] Yet, although it is well established that the title *Waverley* refers to historical novels by Charlotte Smith and Jane West, the role of earlier historical fiction in shaping Scott's fiction remains obscure.[8] The apparent scarcity of direct reference to these earlier works in the Waverley Novels is perhaps explained by Scott's approach to political risk. Although Scott was traditionally considered (by Andrew Lang, for example) as an author generous in his acknowledgements, and although Hazlitt for one comments on the extent of reference to contemporary literature in his works, there is also what Garside calls a tendency to 'exclusivity' in his writings, a distance from contemporary sources provided by the historical and editorial frames.[9] Exclusivity is a canonising and commercial strategy, but it is also a political one. Carried out largely in the realm of fiction rather than history, the debates about the status, method and reading of history that occurred after the French Revolution were highly politically charged and, by 1814, damaging to the reputation, as the reception of Frances Burney's *The Wanderer* suggests. For John Wilson Croker, famously, Burney's last novel is 'Evelina grown old'. His dislike stems from his ideas concerning Burney's radicalism – he suggests Burney has written the book under what she sees as 'the mild and beneficent government of Napoleon the Great'.[10] Skirting such dangers, Scott as novelist achieves authority, Richard Cronin notes, 'by maintaining a political position so determined to distance itself from faction that it refuses any political content'.[11]

In this context, what does Scott achieve by entitling his first novel *Waverley*? The feckless character Waverly in *Desmond* had allowed Charlotte Smith to reinforce Thomas Paine's suggestion that monarchical government and consequently the people under it had 'no fixed character', changing 'with the temper of every succeeding individual'.[12] Writing in reply on the other side of the political spectrum, Jane West has her Sir William Waverly arrange 'a scheme to secure Waverly-hall and its dependencies whichever party finally predominated'.[13] Wavering is, West hints, a feature of democracy and republicanism, both of which she considers close neighbours of anarchy. In *Letters Addressed to a Young Man* she had suggested that, having been 'for some years the seat of anarchy', France makes all other countries subservient to its 'capricious alterations'.[14] For West, history underlines the lesson. Even the republican form of government found in Rome generated 'violent domestic factions'.[15] But while Smith and West quarrel over whether monarchy or democracy is the most fluctuating form of rule, Scott's reference to wavering combines and transforms their terms. In his narrative of Jacobite struggle against Hanoverian dominance, the only choice is monarchy – and the Hanoverians carry a moderated form of the progressive hopes implicit in Smith's position. The security of property that Smith had highlighted as key to liberty (with the narrative of the unfortunate Breton) is highlighted by Scott. However, the struggle over the mode of government has, momentarily, receded.

The contest for the political past in which West and Smith were participating refuses to be easily laid to rest. The 'plain, communicable signs' (circulated, redefined and recuperated) found in the battle over history are foregrounded in *The Antiquary*.[16] There the historical quarrels between the titular character and his chivalric neighbour are for much of the narrative of greater prominence than the return of the disinherited heir. True, Oldbuck and Sir Arthur Wardour fight about everything historical except the specific use of history in the post-French Revolution debate. Nonetheless, as the fierceness of their disputes indicate, *The Antiquary* is an attempt to work through the strong political feeling that the early historical novel registers. And while *The Antiquary* restages the fierceness of historiographic combat, *Ivanhoe* (supposedly a manuscript possessed by one of the disputants) marshals the tropes found in the earlier historical novels that had been the site of controversy. *Ivanhoe* is a tour de force of rearrangement, bringing together different subgenres of the historical novel in order to imagine a liberty that might be defended both by the people and their government. Yet, despite such flamboyant reorganisation, the social and fictional equation refuses to balance: state and nation remain unsettlingly violent. Aggression persists in *St Ronan's Well*, the only one of Scott's fictions set later than *The Antiquary*. In this historical novel of the recent past, Scott recycles the tropes of the post-French Revolution debate in order to re-examine the relationship between commerce and the aristocracy that had proved so troubling in works like *The Wanderer* and *Desmond*. But whereas in *The Antiquary* Scott had attempted to save the discourse of history by siphoning off the rage caused by the post-French debate, in *St Ronan's Well* it is too late: history has been irreparably damaged. It can no longer protect any liberty worth preserving.

## 'Dogs in Couples': Quarrelling for Liberty

In 1795 Governor Pownall decided to entitle his new work *An Antiquarian Romance*. A fellow of the Royal Society, Pownall had earlier seen '*Antiquarian* learning' 'as *a commentary to history*' but by 1795 his perception has shifted.[17] The practice of collecting and cataloguing becomes almost fused with the conjectural or philosophical approach: 'the philosophic antiquary' can 'recompose the history of the human race by the principles of its system': 'some parts may be lost, others broken, and all lying in confusion of ruin' but through combining such fragments he can construct 'the original' whole.[18] As Pownall's comments suggest, in the process of weighing the relationship between fragments of evidence and wider narrative, older doubts about the fictionality of history (often previously confined to the speeches historians invented) resurface more acutely. Thus the work is given the title of romance, a title which 'need not stagger the reader's faith; for all history might equally have the same title given to it' when it looks at 'the first ages of nations'.[19] Tensions between philosophical and antiquarian history, and the potential blurring of such categories, had consequences for the epistemological value of history. Such doubts opened a fertile space for early writers of historical fiction, who interrogated the political meaning of the past and whose quarrels form the substance of *The Antiquary*.

Pownall's attempt to establish historiographic harmony between the different approaches distinguishes *An Antiquarian Romance* from many of the historical novels in the marketplace. In the historical novel the contest over historical method and interpretation was at once fierce and politically nuanced. After Burke used both the language of chivalry and of science in relation to history in *The Reflections*, not only was the correct (stadial) approach to chivalry interrogated, but both radicals and conservative thinkers struggled to claim the empirical or scientific high ground in relation to historical data and interpretation. The selection and use of material evidence (a much broader matter than antiquarian practice) was a political issue since, differently interpreted, 'data' could be used to support different narratives of stadial 'progress'. Although *The Antiquary*'s relation to historical thought, particularly to Burke's rhetoric in his *Reflections* and to the tensions between stadial and antiquarian thought, has been explored, the novel's relationship to this wider struggle has received less attention.[20] *The Antiquary* attempts to figure the end of any political impact to the debate over history, a debate which was carried out in historical fiction as well as in more traditional modes of writing the past. Scott's novel renders the idea of an alternate history from below less threatening by replying to the debunking of chivalry carried out by Wollstonecraft and Smith and it also attempts to neutralise the subversive potential of historical data, a potential emergent in the opposing thought of Godwin and West. But this process of reduction and neutralisation ultimately worries Scott in ways that foreshadow his later, more pessimistic rearrangement of history in *St Ronan's Well*.

Just as he had done in *Waverley*, Scott signals his debt to other historical fiction with his hero's name. As Angela Wright has noted, Scott's hero in *The Antiquary* shares his *nom de guerre* 'Lovel' with the initially dispossessed hero of Clara Reeve's *The Old English Baron*.[21] (The name 'Mr Lovel' also occurs in Burney's *Evelina* but while, as Oldbuck suggests, the name may be a common choice for the stage, it is found far less frequently in the novel.)[22] It has also been acknowledged that, like *Waverley*, *The Antiquary* contains an echo of Jane West's *The Loyalists*.[23] West's dispossessed heir (also somewhat marginal to the narrative) is Allan Neville, also known as Colonel Evellin; Scott's hero's actual (though not his final) name is Captain Neville, while his mother's was Eveline. (Additionally, West's Colonel Evellin marries an 'Isabel', while Scott's hero, Neville, marries an 'Isabella' or 'Miss Isabel').[24] The plot of *The Antiquary* and the reinstatement of Scott's hero is therefore bracketed by these two most loyalist and English of historical novels, novels which stretch across the debate concerning civil liberties from the Declaration of American independence to the closing years of the Napoleonic Wars. These are loyalist novels which speak very explicitly of England; Scott transplants them to Scotland but his choice also signals his desire to impose an ending to the quarrel. West's hero can only take the name Neville when the restoration of the monarchy takes place; Scott's when civic, national and familial order has been re-established.

Beginning in 1794 but ending in a way that invokes fears of invasion felt in 1804,[25] the subject matter of the novel reflects the extent and dominance of the historical debate that took place after the French Revolution. Superficially at least, it evacuates this debate of much of its political meaning, instead using the repeated disputes as a distraction from the conflict rather than an extension of it. For much of the novel, disputes concerning the past and its material remains push aside the matter of the possible French invasion and even the plot of the returned heir.[26] It is only after Lovel's and Oldbuck's conversation concerning 'Gordon's *Itinerarium Septentrionale*'; after the prolonged description of Oldbuck's fragment-jammed study; and following Edie's contradiction of Oldbuck's reading of supposed Roman remains, that the post-French Revolution debate and the threat of invasion are introduced at all.[27] Even then the mention of the 'two parties which then divided' the kingdom, the 'aristocrat[ic]' 'Royal True Blues' and the democratic 'Friends of the People', occurs only in passing in relation to the mystery of Lovel's identity.[28] For Nicola Watson, the novel's atmosphere reflects the 'post-Napoleonic insubstantiality of the romance of restoration'; for Duncan it is the Revolution itself that must be avoided.[29] Yet the attempt to separate contemporary events from the heat of historical dispute suggests that Scott is trying to neutralise an ongoing politico-historiographic threat with its roots in the 1790s.[30] 'Invasion from abroad, and insurrection at home' are bracketed and contained by history, by 'old books' and 'abstruse' philology, not foregrounded by them.[31]

A comparison with the historical debates in Charlotte Smith's *Desmond* highlights Scott's strategy. In this work, set in the period from 1790 to 1792, political discussion between the hero and Abbé de Bremont necessarily becomes a debate concerning the meaning of history. Desmond's radical perspective on the feudal and chivalric past explains the need for revolutionary progress in the present: Desmond is thankful that 'The days of chivalry' are over: 'the ravings of a fanatic monk will never again prevail on the French to make a crusade'.[32] In *The Antiquary*, in contrast, the transformational reading of history proceeds more subtly. While Smith's Abbé de Bremont supports the *ancien régime* against Desmond's radicalism, Sir Arthur is (in his imagination, at least) a Jacobite and Oldbuck a progressive descendent of a typographer. (Wollstonecraft's claims for the progressive science of printing in her *Historical and Moral View* offer a contemporary reminder of the radical value of the profession.)[33] Yet when the two talk politics, remarking upon the 'military frenzy' introduced by the fear of a French invasion, division is less apparent. Sir Arthur's fearful 'dreams of standing armies and German oppression' do not, as Oldbuck teasingly suggests they should, lead him to doubt the need for establishment of defensive militia.[34] Unlike Desmond, the old friends do not consciously try to use history to provide a fresh perspective on the events of the day; repeatedly canvassed, their positions are both unshifting and often pointedly irrelevant to public events.

Despite this deflationary sleight of hand, the historical battles in *The Antiquary* provide as strong a guide to public events as the heated controversies of *Desmond*. The companions' debates about Pictish and Saxon etymology or their quarrels regarding the 'good fame of Queen Mary' might initially seem to be primarily concerned with national identity rather than with the individual political liberties of the post-French Revolution debate.[35] In shifting the subject of historical dispute, Scott mirrors the tendency of hegemonic discourse in wartime, when threats to the nation are used to overwrite internal discontents. Yet, despite this distracting shift in the focus of historical dispute, the pain of the struggle for personal liberty, explored so fully by the earlier historical novel, still echoes. The 'good fame of Queen Mary' recalls not only the disagreements of Hume and Robertson, but also Sophia Lee's *The Recess* or Rossetta Ballin's *The Statue Room*, raising the question of monarchical tyranny and the freedom of the individual subject.[36] The 'Ragman-roll' evokes not only Edward I's imperial ambitions in relation to Scotland, but, as a register of property, also foreground the issue of taxation.[37] Even the echo between the name of the hero of *The Loyalists* (Colonel Evellin Neville) and Scott's hero's mother, Eveline Neville, suggests the struggle for political freedom. In Jane West's novel Colonel Evellin has been deprived of his inheritance by the machinations of his sister and her husband, first at the court of King Charles I and then under Cromwell. Civil war lurks behind the story of Scott's hero's admittedly more private dispossession.[38]

Scott's narrative repeatedly alludes to pressure points in wider debates concerning individual liberties. And these historical hints have their contemporary echo: in the Fairport area the threat to personal liberty and the anxiety caused by radical historiography among the lower classes remain. Where Oldbuck sees traces of the battle between Agricola and the Caledonians, Edie Ochiltree, the bedesman, allegedly sees a ditch dug for a wedding. Edie has made a resistant reading of history but his rereading is a much milder debunking than those critiques of chivalry offered by Wollstonecraft and Smith, pointing as it does to the domestic and celebratory.[39] Nonetheless, when challenged, Oldbuck remarks upon the 'church wardens and dog whips' which would make short work of the beggar in England.[40] Edie's reductions of historical conflict suit Scott's deflationary agenda but they still provoke a political unease that Scott is keen to suggest is unnecessary. Certainly, Sir Arthur's hostility appears excessive when he responds to Edie's supposed suggestion that 'Willie Howie's Kilmarnock cowl covered more sense than all the three wigs in the parish'.[41] The bedesman's disrespect for individuals becomes a disrespect for the system, for heritage and the wisdom of age that (as well as the *ancien régime*) the wig symbolises. Consequently, Sir Arthur directs 'the constables to take up that old scoundrelly beggar . . . for spreading disaffection against church and state through the whole parish'; 'the rogue', he exclaims, 'shall be taught better manners'.[42] Although his daughter exclaims against the notion of the beggar receiving such treatment, Sir Arthur's description of Edie recalls Miss Fairfax's denunciation of 'the scum of the people' in *Desmond*. As radical historiographer, Edie recalls the early historical novel's concern with the political role of the 'mass'. Such anxieties had directed Edgeworth and, in *Lioncel*, Louis de Bruno to consider the issue of work – perhaps the right form of economic production might bind the ranks together. In this context, Scott's choice of Edie's profession, beggar, bedesman and alternative historian, is provocative.

But Scott takes this extreme and potentially anxiety-provoking case and minimises it, rewriting the climate of fear in the 1790s. He does this by providing Edie with both a social role (of which more later) and, in the 'Advertisement' which begins the first edition, a heritage. He also, crucially, counters the threat of radical historiography that Edie foregrounds. By creating a stadial vision of history that is at once chivalric and progressive, Scott contains the threat represented by Edie's historical resistance. Following the rather sexualised account of the age of chivalry in Burke's *Reflections*, and the critique of the knightly code by Wollstonecraft and Smith, even reformist and conservative thinkers struggled with William Robertson's notion that the 'humanity', 'gallantry' and 'honour' which 'distinguish modern from ancient manners' were the result of chivalry. The Porters had attempted to reinvent (and in Jane's case) to broaden the concept of a (newly re-Christianised) chivalry but their attempts suggested the notion's potential lack of application to the present. In 1817, a year after the publication of *The Antiquary*, in *The Knight of St John* Anna Maria has the anti-heroine Beatrice chased through the woods and rescued by one of the heroes, Giovanni: '"O, save me! sir," she cried; "You are a knight – protect me – hide me!"'[43] Almost immediately, he finds that his knight-errantry is unnecessary – the episode is a matter of 'disguise' and deception, staged for entertainment; in everyday life chivalry is in danger of becoming play-acting.[44]

In *The Antiquary* Scott finds a reply to this sort of critique. While Sir Arthur's chivalric credentials are announced by his name, Oldbuck, as 'descendent of a Westphalian printer', seems to be a representative of modernity, perhaps likely to reject the chivalric.[45] In fact, Scott offers some teasingly contradictory hints about Oldbuck's affiliations. Although Oldbuck has the 'humanity' Robertson assigns to the chivalric (he stops for a lame horse), presented as a 'misogynist', he initially seems to lack the gallantry Robertson requires.[46] Later, it becomes evident that the reverse is true: his whole character has been shaped by a 'disappointment in love'.[47] As for 'honour' Oldbuck is conscious of the credit of other, ancient families and of his own. Aldobrand Oldenbuck printed 'the rare quarto of the Augsburg Confession', for which he was 'expelled from his ungrateful country' and Oldbuck invites Lovel to look upon Aldobrand's 'venerable effigies' 'and respect the honourable occupation in which it presents him, as labouring personally at the press for the diffusion of Christian and political knowledge'.[48] The descendant of the printer and reformist is not a revolutionary – the religious and political progress Godwin envisioned in *St Leon* does need not lead to the radicalism of *The Enquirer* but to an alternative sense of tradition.

Having retained his phallic walking stick (an updated sword stick perhaps) since 'when [he] did not expect always to have been a bachelor',

Oldbuck represents not a break with chivalry but a more cautious contemporary version of it.[49] Although he is 'much more scrupulous in receiving legends as current and authentic coin' than Sir Arthur, whose 'faith' is 'boundless', he does not reveal what for Wollstonecraft are the shows of feudal historiography.[50] He might not carry his book-collecting exploits to such an expense as 'Don Quixote de la Mancha', but it later becomes evident he is willing to exchange 'fields and farms', if not for 'folios', then for the ruins themselves.[51] In short, he is just quixotic enough, indicating the innately chivalric nature of historical study. The radical historicism of a Wollstonecraft, a Smith or a Godwin has been subsumed. Neither Edie or Oldbuck will write a history that fundamentally threatens the social order. This progressive chivalry is also continued into the younger, practical generation. Hector is not willing to pine over Lady Isabel but his quixotic attack on the 'phoca' is prelude to him 'rising rapidly in the army'.[52] Most importantly, given Porter's idea of chivalry as a masque (and West's criticism of the incorrect performances of history in *The Refusal* [1810]), Lovel is not an actor, as Oldbuck at first assumes. A Protestant member of an old Catholic family, Scott's hero is in fact a true and updated representative of an old feudal system rather than a player staging a set of bygone manners to fool the multitude. Wollstonecraft's suspicions of the shows of chivalry as well as conservative dislike of such aristocratic play-acting are proved false.

Within this stadial framework of the progress of chivalry, Scott also deals with the early historical novel's anxiety concerning historical evidence. The antiquarian habits of Oldbuck and the first-hand witnessing of Edie triumph over a false of idea of history as science.[53] Here Scott seems to respond to Jane West, who had recuperated the radical emphasis on history as data, suggesting that both science and the correct interpretation of history belonged to church and king. In West's novel *The Loyalists*, Joseph Priestley had been the implicit subject of attack. In *The Antiquary*, in contrast, Scott associates Dousterswivel, the alchemist, with a faulty model of 'science', recalling Godwin's *St Leon*. Godwin had implied that a chivalric attitude, connected with an unjust model of imperial gain, causes the urge to speculate. The adventures of Scott's fiscally irresponsible Sir Arthur can be read as a reply to Godwin's suggestion. Both St Leon and Sir Arthur are risk-takers who damage the position of their families and who turn to someone with alchemical powers to aid them. In Godwin's novel, St Leon eventually fuses the roles of aristocrat, alchemist and social experimenter, attempting to build upon the comparative knowledge gained by living through history. In *The Antiquary* the roles of alchemist and aristocrat remain separate. Sir Arthur can receive no genuine powers from Dousterswivel (as St Leon does from the false 'Zampieri'): the German's version of history is an illusion.[54]

Whereas *The Enquirer* and *St Leon* suggest the possibility of individual experiment through the rational medium of reading, in *The Antiquary* Scott denies the possibility. When Lovel, the antiquarians and Dousterswivel visit St Ruth's Priory, the characters consider the past from their own isolated perspective. Except Lovel's more measured reasoning concerning the nature of historical records, no genuine development of historical and social knowledge is possible. Only desperate greed brings Sir Arthur and Dousterswivel together. This alliance is particularly dangerous, since if Edie represents the threat of mass unrest and Oldbuck the (false) threat of printing and intellectual reform, Dousterswivel is the worst of the novel's potential radicals. When the 'German' says with 'a low bow, "the monksh might also make de vary curious experiment in deir laboraties, both in chemistry and *magia naturalis*"', he confuses science and magic, presenting the past as gothic, a manoeuvre that loyalists like Reeve and West had fearfully associated with revolutionary philosophy.[55] When Dousterswivel, like St Leon, experiments (divining first for water, then for gold), his performances are not for the social good – but for economic gain. Issuing from the 'other side of the water', Dousterswivel is neither Jacobite nor Jacobin but, in his fraudulent activity, a negative representative of the age of 'sophisters, oeconomists and calculators' narrowly conceived; there is no genuine political radicalism.[56] 'High' revolutionary philosophy and historiography is a sordid matter, a misreading of the data of history as gothic rather than scientific which ultimately leads even the experimenter himself astray.

Oldbuck's role in exposing Dousterswivel is significant. Scott bypasses the scientific by choosing an alternate model of historical evidence, the antiquarian. In doing so, he again shifts his ground from the narrative of individual rights to that of national history. Yet this shift generates its own difficulties. The antiquarian had played an often painful role, a role anything but academic in matters of national dispute. Oldbuck boasts that 'if you want an affair of consequence properly managed, put it into the hands of an antiquary' because he is like the corps that is frequently drilled upon 'parade'.[57] The potentially controversial nature of antiquarianism had been registered in the early historical novel and the national tale: particularly in the Irish context the possible overwriting of history was deeply contentious, as both White's *Earl Strongbow* and Owenson's national tales indicate. Moreover, the Ossian debate referred to by Hector and Oldbuck suggests another, more contemporary robbery of Irish history and Irish reputation.[58] That the removal of 'manuscripts, . . . records . . . annals' has a material, as well as cultural, consequence is indicated in Godwin's *Mandeville*, published the year after *The Antiquary*: James I pursues his system of colonisation 'by many forfeitures, and by a vexatious inquiry . . . into the titles by which the Irish chieftains held their estates'.[59] The destruction or falsification of antiquarian records is clearly a serious matter both culturally and economically.

In *The Antiquary* Scott goes to considerable lengths to neutralise the subversive potential of antiquarianism. Far from the destruction of records or their absence causing a loss of property, the chivalric frame ensures that Oldbuck's antiquarian interests involve him in comic disadvantage. When the town clerk offers Monkbarns 'the carved through-stanes' in exchange for 'bringing the water frae the Fairwell-spring through a part o' your lands', Oldbuck's enthusiasm leads him to succumb to the ruse.[60] An interest in the past is not connected with a possessive sense of belonging but becomes more generalised and thus more profitable to the community. Anxiety concerning private owner-ship is diminished. The 'chaos of maps, engravings, scraps of parchment, bundles of papers, pieces of old armour, swords, dirks, helmets, and Highland targets' in Oldbuck's study, even as they literalise the weight of controversy concerning ownership, also comically reduce such legal and physical battles.[61] The only threat that remains is from the 'three ancient calthrops, or *craw-taes*', 'dug up in the bog near Bannockburn', thus coming 'in process of time to endamage the sitting part of a learned professor of Utrecht'.[62]

In line with this, the historical material suggests that even invasion itself can sometimes ultimately become a matter of little note. Printed in Edinburgh, the 1798 work *The Genius of Caledonia: A Poem on the Threatened French Invasion* had emphasised the geographical limits imposed on invaders of Scotland (it mentions Grampian, 'the boundary of the Roman incursions into Scotland' and Largs, where the Norwegians were defeated in 1236). These limits are meant to inspire the 'descendants' of 'Scotia's honour'd heroes'.[63] In contrast, Scott sug-gests the evidence of occupation: the Roman 'Praetorium', would be prized by Oldbuck, if only he could read its traces on the landscape. Oldbuck pressures Lovel to write the 'Caledoniad' but, typically, the celebration of native courage is not even commenced – only the notes are written, testimony to the antiquarian passion and to the wider com-munity's indifference.[64] The illegibility of ancient invasion is also sug-gested by the dispute concerning the word *Benval*, in relation to which William Camden himself had remarked 'little can be inferred from the language'.[65] Sometimes the 'fragments' of the past cannot be fitted into a convincing larger picture – this is the area of 'romance' mentioned by Pownall.

The modern irrelevance of ancient invasion provides a perspective on the equally migratory ancestors of the disputants. Sir Arthur's ancestor Sir Richard Wardour ('the first o' the name ever was in this country') came from the 'south' and gained his land through a forced marriage with 'Sybil Knockwinnock' ('for marry him she maun it's like').[66] Oldbuck is 'the descendant of a Westphalian printer' yet his title of 'Monkbarns' associates him with the land and the property that stands upon it.[67] This is a history of dispersion, invasion and amalgamation. The past renders the Hanoverian displacement of the Stuarts and the Union itself more acceptable. In doing so, it also minimises the danger of the rumoured French invasion. The fact that the narrative makes so much of an invasion that never happens is, though, telling – it implies that there are some types of incursion that are too radical to be imagined.

In *The Antiquary* Scott sets up a series of historiographic distractions. If Edie's behaviour evokes (in attenuated fashion) the threat of radicalism and its critique of history, the stadial narrative of shifting chivalry contains the threat. Within that stadial framework, Oldbuck's and Sir Arthur's antiquarian disputes shift the focus from political rights to national ones. In turn their discourse relies on a vast number of fragments, which themselves work to distract and defuse, undermining the passion of nationalism. But this almost complete ronde bears witness to two specific historiographical problems: that of inflation (not only a monetary issue in the novel) and of a deflation so complete that it leads to despair.[68] The inflationary or hubristic chivalric impulse registered by Godwin finds its correlative in Scott. It is Sir Arthur who facilitates Dousterswivel's criminal manoeuvres, while Elspeth Mucklebackit's 'Ballad of Roland Cheyne' suggests that the feudal relation itself causes this vulnerability. There the dependent gives the nobleman bad advice (echoing the corrupt relation between Elspeth and the countess in the present):

> If they hae twenty thousand blades,
> And we twice ten times ten,
> Yet they hae but their tartan plaids,
> And we are mail-clad men.[69]

Recalling the inflated armour of Alfonso in *The Castle of Otranto*, the exaggeration of the power of 'lowland' weaponry against the 'Gaelic' numbers is disastrous. Superior technology cannot make up for the lack of living labour.[70] The tendency to assign an inflated value, to desire profit without additional labour is connected not with commerce, but with the sycophancy (and desire for mobility) present even in the feudal system. Even Oldbuck is infected. It is no coincidence that even while Oldbuck dreams of an antiquarian find that will double in value at each point of exchange, he cannot strike a good bargain with Mrs Mucklebackit over the price of fish. For all his caution, this quixote gives neither historical data nor objects their correct value. Tellingly, it is he who lights the fire (to destroy the trickster Dousterswivel's artefacts) that supposedly signals the French invasion.

Like the passion for liberty or nation, the chivalric impulse can prove dangerously inflationary and distorting. Yet it represents a necessary attempt to struggle against erasure by another increasing tide. Without a narrative to connect them and give them value, the fragments of the past found in Oldbuck's study become a kind of overwhelming detritus. Referred to by Oldbuck as a 'mare magnum', these fragments symbolically echo the sea that threatens to rise and overwhelm Sir Arthur and his daughter as representatives of a past order.[71] Trapped above the turbulent waters, finding the land around them rapidly devoured, the Wardours face both physical and financial annihilation. The past forms a rising tide that is curiously without value or coherence, faintly foreshadowing the chaos that Ian Duncan traces in Scott's *Castle Dangerous*.[72] In *The Antiquary* Scott attempts to moderate the passion of the politico-historiographic debate that accompanied the French Revolutionary and Napoleonic Wars. However, as he moves from one approach to another, inflating, foregrounding and then distracting and deflating, he points to an epistemological problem – in the space of narrative experimentation, evidence itself may be evacuated of all meaning. The reduction of the passionate historical quarrels of the French Revolution to the squabbles of 'dogs in couples' itself generates a threat to continuity.[73]

It is against these two opposing threats that Edie stands. Refusing the money that is offered him so readily, Edie, anti-inflationary in both his humour and his attitude to exchange, also suggests the price for his loyalty is exceptionally reasonable. Although he deliberately chooses to have little by way of property, he will fight for the property of others who help him – for 'the country', the 'burnsides' 'and 'the hearths o' the gudewives that gie me my bit bread, and the bits o'weans that come toddling to play wi' me when I come about a landward town?'.[74] The 'bit' of bread, the 'bits o'weans' are fragments in line with Edie's deflationary tendencies. What is worth celebrating, what is truly valuable is the minute, the domestic and the affective. Instead of the war-torn communities and enforced wandering felt during the Napoleonic Wars, and reflected in, for example, Charlotte Smith's *Letters of a Solitary Wanderer* (1800–2), Edie's wandering binds these small parts of the community together in an affective pattern. Free but fixed within a particular circuit, performing work without labour, he generates the fantasy of social coherence which Oldbuck's fragments of history fail to provide. But the Magnum Opus edition insists that Edie himself belongs to the past, that is, to a space where, *The Antiquary* suggests, evidence has very uncertain value.

## The Increasing Murmur of Conflict: *Ivanhoe*

It is perhaps a sense that the post-French Revolution dispute concerning history has not been detoxified which causes Scott to revisit *The Antiquary* in the 'Dedicatory Epistle' to *Ivanhoe*. There, Laurence Templeton, *Ivanhoe*'s supposed editor, writes to the Rev. Dr Dryasdust, F.A.S. (mentioned in *The Antiquary* as Oldbuck's 'literary friend in York').[75] Laurence insists that his text, the 'Wardour MS', has been 'preserve[d]' unread by Sir Arthur in 'the third draw of his oaken cabinet': a direct – and I would argue symbolically accurate – relationship is established between the two novels.[76] While *The Antiquary* reimagines the combatants at war in the 1790s quarrel over history, in *Ivanhoe* we enter into one of the disputed historical fictionalisations that multiplied during the debate. As Scott had attempted in *The Antiquary* to reconcile (at least) two approaches to history, to combine a stadial narrative of chivalry with an emphasis on data, here he attempts to combine the chief tropes of several kinds of historical novel. The clash between Normans and Saxons, which Scott outlines in the novel, has been interpreted both in terms of conjectural history and in relation to the Norman Yoke.[77] However, given the rich tradition of historical fiction that precedes Scott's 1819 work, *Ivanhoe* can also be read as staging a clash between the novel of ancient liberties and that of chivalry and nation, combining the radical trope of the alternative community on one hand and the recuperated and adjusted conservative narrative of history as science on the other.

Like *The Antiquary*, *Ivanhoe* employs a strategy of displacement and disguise. The 'Dedicatory Epistle', the invocation of the Wardour manuscript and, after the 1830 Magnum Opus edition, the further antiquarian frame provided by the introduction, all make it easy to miss *Ivanhoe*'s entry into the political/historical dispute. In the same way that Sir Arthur's and Oldbuck's antiquarian disputes are far less directly embedded in contemporary political controversy than those in, for example, *Desmond*, *Ivanhoe* is represented (albeit coyly) as an original manuscript far removed from the contemporary historical novel. The

perhaps unreliable romance of a gothic scrivener, *Ivanhoe* is rendered
even more untrustworthy since Sir Arthur's gullibility is well known to
readers of *The Antiquary*. While antiquarian playfulness establishes the
novel's literary sophistication, it disowns any political authority with
a flourish that is almost suspicious. Scott foregrounds the antiquarian
in order, rather curiously, to hold out the possibility of access to an
authentic, even unmediated past. 'Laurence Templeton' emphasises the
physicality and changed technologies of writing that characterise the
MS – he has promised, he tells his correspondent, to 'designate it by
some emphatic mode of printing, as {The Wardour Manuscript}; giving
it, thereby, an individuality as important as the Bannatyne MS, the
Auchinleck MS'. This concentration on the material befits the antiquarian but also serves playfully to highlight his distance from the meaning
of the object. Sir Arthur 'scarcely allow[s] anyone to touch it . . . being
himself not able to read one syllable of its contents'.[78] For Sir Arthur,
the MS is given value by rarity and not by meaning. Curiously, though,
his misuse (or rather failure to use) the object that is *Ivanhoe* propels
the reader towards an alternate mode of access to the past, one that
bypasses the physical object and that attempts to grasp distant events
unquestioningly, leaving matters of probability and sceptical weighing
of historical material out of the question – it directs the reader, in other
words, towards 'romance', that exercise, as Pownall had suggested, in
building a whole out of fragments.

Even so, the materials out of which the romance is constructed can be
traced amongst the displacements of the 1830 Magnum Opus introduction. The source Scott cites which is chronologically nearest to *Ivanhoe*
is 'Logan's tragedy of Runnamede'. Scott emphasises that *Runnamede* is
not a stadial narrative (he does not 'recollect that there was any attempt
to contrast the two races in their habits and sentiments'). Indeed, with
his suggestion that he 'had seen the Saxon and Norman barons opposed
to each other on different sides of the stage', he implies the differences
sketched in the play are a matter of spacial origin.[79] But *Runnamede*
is deliberately not a stadial work (taught by William Robertson Logan
could have written one but chose not to). Instead, responding to the
context of the American War of Independence, Logan has both the
Saxons and the Normans emphasise a shared commitment to 'ancient
rights'.[80] That Scott challenges such narratives of ancient liberties in
*Ivanhoe* has long been clear but the precise way in which he manipulates
them is less obvious. Like *Runnamede* works including *Son of Ethelwolf*
(1789) and Anna Maria Mackenzie's *Danish Massacre: An Historic Fact*
(1791) highlight discontent and touch upon the need to 'cashier' rulers,
but also sheer way from such social disturbance. In Mackenzie's *Danish*

*Massacre: An Historic Fact*, for example, 'Ethred, a British prince' leads the Danes to take 'every occasion to distress his subjects'. In response, the Duke of Mercia 'disguise[es] the deep plots of a wary statesman under a pretended zeal for the happiness of his countrymen'.[81] But the revolution is sidestepped – in *Ethelwolf* Alfred will return; in the *Danish Massacre* the issue of liberty is worked out via a romance plot.

Scott's work is in some ways bolder in its presentation of discontent but he is able to achieve this safely by exploiting the emphasis on cultural invasion in such narratives. In Ian Duncan's words, Scott 'divert[s]' the 'problem of class difference', translating it into racial tension.[82] In *Feudal Events* Ann Maria Mackenzie had mentioned tensions between Stephen and Maud in relation to Saxon and Norman descent, but had concentrated on Maud's oppressive tendencies and unfitness to rule. In contrast, *Ivanhoe* extends the idea of oppression beyond the individual to the nation, at the same time minimizing the issue of rank. Cedric is (relatively) oppressed because he is Saxon against Normans rather than because he is a thane. Scott can then use the complex patterns of invasion described by such novels to offset tension. Writing about the Norman invasion of Ireland in *Earl Strongbow*, for example, James White emphasises the complicated tribal make-up of society and the colonial fate of both Saxon and Irish. But whereas White recalls what he feels is easily forgotten to undermine the idea of English superiority, Scott plays on the idea of forgetting itself. In *Ivanhoe*, as in *The Antiquary*, the fading 'murmur' of oppression caused by invasion (rather than class) is emphasised: such tensions pass away.[83] And having made these gestures of containment, Scott can be more audacious in his treatment of social discontent.

Such discontent is magnified, ironically, in order to attack the very narratives of ancient constitutionalism that had become a vehicle for radical thought. Although Scott mentions the 'milder . . . spirit of the Saxon constitution', the use of the comparative suggests a reservation: Anglo-Saxon ancient liberties are flawed.[84] In line with this, dividing between them the features of Edie Ochiltree, Wamba and Gurth find their situation harsher and more precarious than the bedesman. Whereas Bailie Littlejohn the magistrate temporarily jails Edie in *The Antiquary*, in *Ivanhoe* it is Gurth's loyalty that leads Cedric himself to call for the 'gyves, the gyves' and to attack Fangs, Gurth's dog.[85] In *Rokeby* such an attack causes the populace to riot.[86] Here Cedric's behaviour suggests he is almost as vicious as old Hubert, 'Sir Philip de Malvoisin's keeper of the chase' who 'struck off two of [Fangs'] fore-claws'.[87] Mistreated by Saxon as well as Norman, Gurth, as temporary squire to Ivanhoe, recalls contemporary concern with the fate of the returning soldier, a concern also registered in *The Antiquary* and in Joanna Baillie's *Count Basil* (1798). His justified withdrawal of loyalty is thus all the more provocative.

If the narrative of Anglo-Saxon return offers radicals and reformists no hope, neither does another variety of ancient constitutionalism, the idea that the Norman Yoke was removed by Magna Carta and Barons' Revolts. For Scott, the barons deserve little credit. 'It is grievous', he remarks, 'to think that those valiant barons, to whose stand against the crown the liberties of England were indebted for their existence, should themselves have been such dreadful oppressors.'[88] Although he cites Robert Henry's *History of Great Britain* (reprinted by Cadell, Davies and Strahan in 1799–1800), his remarks also correspond to a fairly radical position, one held, for instance, by Charlotte Smith. She writes in *Minor Morals*: 'the proud and spirited Barons, who felt how unworthy such a man was to govern them, took advantage of the cowardly and abject character of John', 'extorting from him a greater degree of freedom than they had enjoyed since the Conquest' 'though they had no just ideas of political liberty'.[89] For Smith, Magna Carta's protection of ancient liberties was an instance of history advancing by the bad side. In Scott, similarly, no nostalgia is felt for the time before the Conquest and little admiration is given to the rebellious nobility after it.

This bleakness allows Scott to give Norman crimes against person and property a particular shape. In *The Antiquary* Edie had refused to connect money with freedom, insisting that the possession of gold would end his peripatetic occupation. For Gurth, Cedric's 'thrall', on the other hand, the connection between money and freedom is far more direct.[90] The item he needs to purchase is himself. But if the Anglo-Saxons see an equivalence between money and liberty, the Norman system is, for Scott, more sinister. In the early historical novel William the Conqueror is associated with the confiscation of property: the depopulation of villages to make way for the New Forest is usually the incident dwelt upon. 'For ten leagues he has demolished churches, abbeys, castles, and houses, to convert it to a forest, and habitation for wild beasts; and he would more readily pardon the killing of a man than of a stag' complains a character in *Edwy, Son of Ethelred*.[91] But Scott suggests that the Norman barons indulge in something harsher than dispossession. Ivanhoe's identity has to be kept secret in case he is tortured by Front-de-Boeuf for his lands, while the Norman knight also threatens to give Isaac 'a long and lingering death' if he is not given his prisoner's silver.[92] Isaac's fate loosens the likely connection between poverty and unjust treatment; it suggests that wealth itself is not enough to guarantee freedom. The issue is not the suffering caused by financial inequality, an issue that might be solved by the redistribution of wealth. Instead, security of property is key. Without this, Scott's imagery implies, there is no liberty. Personal safety vanishes and robbery or fraud, murder, and torture, the gravest of crimes against the individual, become possible.

Having rejected ancient constitutionalism and highlighted security of property, Scott uses another motif central to the historical novel to underpin this security: chivalry. As Dyer notes, the chivalric rhetoric used after the 1819 Peterloo Massacre informs *Ivanhoe*.[93] After eleven civilians were killed by troops while attending a peaceful meeting to extend the franchise, radicals suggested that they, not the government, were the true inheritors of chivalry. But (largely written before the massacre) *Ivanhoe* exploits a longer debate concerning the nature of chivalry itself: following Burke's *Reflections*, the code had been attacked by radical historical novelists, reclaimed by reformists and repeatedly reimagined. In *Ivanhoe*, such constant redefinition becomes, not a matter of nineteenth-century historiographical debate, but an essential (and politically useful) feature of the code itself. In *The Knight of St John*, for example, Anna Maria Porter had suggested that the redefinition of chivalry in secular society had impoverished it. But when the Adimaris are legally deprived of property they 'kept quiet possession of for two centuries', Giovanni Cigala, son of the victor and Knight of St John, finds Cesario Adimari's dispossession 'unjust'.[94] Both participate in the Siege of Malta, implying that Christian dispossession is more important than private loss, but Adimari ultimately looks likely to have his estate restored through marriage to Cigala's sister. When attached to a Christian order, fixed in meaning, chivalry safeguards property; when detached, its meaning fluctuates disastrously. In his *Essay on Chivalry* (1818) and in *Ivanhoe* Scott disagrees, questioning the code's association with the institutional power of Christianity. If the 'Knight Bachelor' was possibly 'a resource for the weak', 'restless and intolerant zeal' characterises both Templars and Hospitallers.[95] The ambiguity and danger that previous historical novelists had tried to police are foregrounded by Scott. Brutality and change become part of our imaginary of rule, albeit apparently chronologically bracketed in *Ivanhoe* by the Conquest and Magna Carta.[96]

Against this dark institutional backdrop of knightly and religious orders, the fantasy of the lone chivalric figure (St Leon without his fall to alchemy and social experiment), is crucial. The ambiguity of both king and code become essential to the reformulation of the state in *Ivanhoe*. Richard's own duality (he is 'open, frank', but 'revengeful, domineering', according to Hume) exacerbates chivalric instability.[97] Positioned by the comic opera *Richard Coeur de Lion* as hero of 'British' liberty, in

James White's *Adventures of Richard Coeur de Lion* (a work owned by Scott) Richard is adherent to a ludicrous code.[98] Exploiting this instability, in *Ivanhoe*, Richard, generous and violent, becomes the figure of an impossible compromise, between nations and between classes. It is not only that he joins Norman and Saxon by using the words 'English' and 'Englishman' or that he comes from over the sea, like the Stuarts, but is from a line new to the throne (like the Hanoverians).[99] It is also that his volatility and that of his code generate a moment of social exception, of potential (but limited) change.

Earlier, Wollstonecraft and Smith had tried to remove chivalric 'shows' to expose unfair distribution of property and power. But at the Ashby Passage of Arms both the rituals of chivalry, and its privilege of anonymity allow the 'Disinherited Knight' and '*Le Noir Faineant*, or the Black Sluggard' to begin their attempt to reclaim what is, or what seems to be, theirs.[100] Ivanhoe and Richard have the right of previous ownership (somewhat qualified by successive moments of invasion) on their side. Chivalry allows rearrangement, Scott typically suggests, because, while it is something that is over (its 'escutcheons' and 'evanescent symbols of . . . martial rank', its very 'historians of honour' no longer with us), it is also not fully formulated: 'armorial bearings were then a novelty among the Norman chivalry themselves'.[101] The very chivalry that for Burke contained social change, establishing 'ensigns armorial' implicitly linked to property, is seen in flux (social mobility is possible). But the code is also simultaneously positioned as a mechanism of return, encompassing the idea of stability as well as the possibility of political change. Symbolically, its incognitos and ambiguities perform the restitution that the trope of ancient liberty cannot.

Matthew Rowlinson suggests that Scott's monarchs' fondness for 'masquerade, concealment, and bluff' is an extension of Scott's concern with anonymity as a mysterious source of profit.[102] But in *Ivanhoe* such incognitos also allow an (apparent) reimagining of the operation of power itself. It is not only that Richard follows what Scott in 1830 asserts is the global motif of the 'disguised sovereign', an equalising trope also associated with Alfred and Wallace in the earlier historical novel.[103] It is also that Richard's outlawry suggests the monarch's violent potential to adapt. In *Robin Hood: A Collection* (1795) (a major source for *Ivanhoe*) Joseph Ritson suggests that Robin has reigned 'in these forests' 'for many years . . . like an independent sovereign; at perpetual war, indeed, with the king of England, and all his subjects, with an exception, however, of the poor and needy'.[104] Ritson continues: 'what better title King Richard could pretend to the territory and people of England, than Robin Hood had to the dominion of Barnsdale or Sherwood, is a question humbly submitted to the consideration of the political philosopher'.[105] Scott confronts this radical reading of Richard's illegitimacy. Breaking the game laws associated with Norman tyranny (laws revisited in the 1790s historical novel), Richard gradually enters the type of alternative community that had been explored in *Caleb Williams*, *Arville Castle*, and *Montford Castle*. In 'Scott and the Outlaws' Helen Phillips argues that Robin is himself monarch, limiting reformist implications. However, by moving the disguised monarch into the alternative radical space, Scott implies the reverse manoeuvre, where reform can be brought into the centre of power.

Having suspended knowledge of Richard's and Robin's identity, Scott uses the bouts of drinking and arms between the Clerk of Copmanhurst and the Sluggish Knight (suggestive of initiation rituals), the siege of Torquilstone; and Richard's participation in the forest court, to establish a symbolic parallel between the two. He exploits this similarity to cancel out the fear of mass political activity, on the one hand, and the fear of monarchical tyranny on the other. In *Ivanhoe* both commoner and king are tainted by illegality (Richard's claim to the throne is as underpinned by violence as Robin's). But Robin's care for the poor, his concern for equitable taxation (robbing those who come through his territory only to the right degree) and his fair distribution of property amongst his workers all suggest a model for the national kingdom that legitimises Richard who accepts Robin's temporary rule. Thus Richard's willingness to suspend the law (albeit a willingness which he seems ready to revoke violently at any moment) curiously provides evidence of Richard's fitness to rule. And as the people legitimise the king, so the king legitimises the people. Richard's presence sanctions the behaviour of Hood's men when they tackle tyranny and transform the Barons' Revolt by laying siege to Front-de-Boeuf's castle. By taking the historical novel's interest in the alternative community within his work, Scott creates a dynamic space where suspension and alteration of the law is possible. This is, though, a tense imagining of the civic arena. Alfred gets his ears boxed by a peasant and, whether because of this or despite it, learns about the need for universal justice. King Richard exchanges buffets with Tuck and lays him flat. The people should be aware of the ruler's superior force.

In this fantasy of Robin Hood, what was threatening to the social order becomes merely what should happen. Fighting together against injustice (in the siege), monarch and people are part of a chivalric enterprise which will ensure the freedom of security of property (and hence of person). But in this progress of chivalric liberty, for Richard, Ivanhoe and the people to regain their rights, both credit and the mechanism of exchange must be protected. Underlining the importance of money and credit, Scott links it to the medicinal, using the father–daughter relationship of Isaac and Rebecca. In creating this curative connection, Scott transforms tropes seen in the earlier historical novel. In Anna Maria Porter's *Knight of St John* the Jewish character 'Reuben' suffers from 'feebleness' of character and stereotypical avarice but aids the hero.[106] In *Ivanhoe*, Isaac shares some of Reuben's avarice – and helpfulness – and as a result finds himself threatened. And whereas in *The Loyalists* West's Christian Mrs Mellicent is able to use her medical and historical skills to promote the Royalist cause, in *Ivanhoe* Rebecca's salve puts her in danger. The potential cure can be interpreted as healing (by the virtuous) or as destructive (by the bigoted Templars). Through Rebecca's trial for witchcraft, Scott alerts us by analogy to the need for interpretative caution when considering Isaac's more morally ambiguous money. If his silver is capable of supporting John's corrupt followers, it is also capable of healing the realm. In helping Ivanhoe, Isaac and Rebecca suggest that both portable property and intellectual inheritance are potentially socially beneficial.

Equally, the chivalry that proves so dangerous for Rebecca and of which she is so suspicious ultimately benefits her. Although Rebecca denounces the bloodthirsty nature of the chivalric code, which causes 'travail and pain' and generates valueless history (the 'glory' of a 'rusted mail' or the valueless 'rhyme[s] of a wandering bard'), she is vindicated when her tormentor de Bois-Guilbert falls during the trial by combat.[107] In 'Waging Battle' Schoenfeld connects Rebecca's trial to the contemporary case in which Abraham Thornton claimed the right to trial by combat after being challenged by the brother of the murdered Mary Ashford.[108] But the episode also suggests a shift in Scott's position concerning credit. In *The Antiquary* Lovel/Neville had melted down Glenallan plate to support the Wardours: the circulation of wealth happens within a closed aristocratic circuit. The Godwinian Dousterswivel and his false magic have no part to play. In *Ivanhoe* the medicinal (even apparently magical) power of finance is acknowledged – but, in a strange quid pro quo, such finance relies on aristocratic protection. The aristocrat and the provider of money do not fuse into one as they do in *St Leon* but together Ivanhoe and Isaac represent a somewhat happier relationship between commerce and the aristocrat than do Sir Arthur and the alchemist in *The Antiquary*.

Disturbingly, though, money is still connected with suffering. Of course Isaac and Rebecca are used by Scott to overwrite further the idea of class with cultural difference, while when Isaac is tortured for his wealth, the notion that those without property are likely to experience the harshest injustices is obscured. Yet Isaac's pleas in the dungeon at Torquilstone ('I must beg as a mendicant at the door of our synagogue ere I make up so unheard-of a sum'), and even his desire to bargain when trying to maintain his daughter's chastity, also suggest the psychological pain of precarity.[109] Fear of poverty operates as sharply on Isaac as it ever did on St Leon with his starving children. Connected with the rootlessness of Isaac's people, money signifies tragic loss. When Rebecca mourns her country, her narrative is not only one of religious persecution and military defeat. It also contains buried within it the concerns of the previous historical novel. It is as if the dispossession that accompanies formal subsumption and the emergence of capitalism, is transplanted to a yearning for the nation: in a case far more extreme than that of the 'unfortunate Breton' in *Desmond*, the loss of land is lamented as the loss of homeland. Ultimately, the narrative of national compromise and reintegration proves painfully impossible. Unlike the invasions and displacements in *The Antiquary*, this is a displacement which continues agonisingly to reverberate. As such it foreshadows *St Ronan's Well*, where the consequences of English influence are tragically played out in nineteenth-century Scotland.

### Violence, Commerce and the History of the Recent Past: *St Ronan's Well*

*St Ronan's Well* is the only one of Scott's novels to be set definitively in the nineteenth century and the closest in temporal setting to *The Antiquary*. Weinstein suggests that the majority of the references place it between 1809 and 1812, yet the anxieties of the revolutionary period linger on.[110] Perhaps as a result, the novel was not given a positive reception. The *Monthly Review* complained that in this narrative of spa life: 'Blue-stockings, fat widows, old bachelors, coquets, and exquisites, occupy the room of chieftains, statesmen, warriors, and those half unearthly beings', generated by Shakespeare.[111] Effeminacy, that is (in the eighteenth-century definition) closeness to the feminine, had replaced the proper masculinity evoked by the historical novel. Writing in a way previously associated with the 'brilliant and talented names of Edgeworth, Austin [sic], Charlotte Smith and others' (as Scott notes in the introduction to the Magnum Opus edition of 1833), it seemed that the author of *Waverley* had inevitably declined.[112]

Scholarly work on the novel also emphasises its anomalous nature. According to Ina Ferris, in the Waverley Novels Scott had successfully employed history to masculinise the romance of reconciliation found in the national tale.[113] This gesture is, Emily Allen suggests, undone in the 'feminizing' space of *St Ronan's Well*.[114] In such a reading, romance, already feminine when opposed to history, somehow becomes doubly and enervatingly so when situated in the modern Scottish spa town. Even when romance is valorised by critical discourse, its place within Scott's schema proves hard to isolate. Ian Duncan, for instance, finds that 'history comes to a stop' in Scott's novels, replaced by a romance that is always 'modern' while for Burgess it is this romance rather than history which provides a new legitimacy for the nation.[115] Acknowledging Scott's generic complexity, such manoeuvres still recall the long tradition of seeing history and romance as in some sense polarised.[116] Yet Scott's female precursors challenge the gendering of history and romance, while both they and Scott acknowledge that the two forms are anything but opposites.

Scott himself is in part responsible for the tendency to downplay the historical sense of his predecessors, even as he generously acknowledges their influence. Suggesting in the introduction to the Magnum Opus that the 'ladies' are 'gifted by nature with keen powers of observation and light satire', he suggests that 'reckoning from the authoress of *Evelina* to her of *Marriage*, a catalogue might be made'.[117] This is a kind of invitation to see the works themselves as each representative of a particular moment of contemporary vision. To extrapolate from Burgess's reading of Scott, the romances that end Burney's, Austen's and even Smith's novels usher in a national cultural legitimacy, a legitimacy that from *Evelina*, to *Ethelinde* to *Emma* becomes increasingly bourgeois. Burney's Lord Orville gives way to Smith's Montgomery (descendant of Stuart supporters) who is in turn replaced by Austen's significantly titled *Mr* Knightley. In the feminised 'novel of manners', history is what happens between the works rather than within them.

Yet only a few lines before, it has been the 'shifting manners of our own time' that Scott hopes to depict, while fearing his inability to rival 'the many formidable competitors who have already won deserved honours in this department'.[118] The historical dimension of such works should be taken seriously; these novels attempt to capture the felt breakage in history connected with the French Revolution and they draw upon stadial history's ability to posit historical change even in the present. The stadial interest in changing manners so clear in Edgeworth's work, is also present in Burney's *The Wanderer* and Charlotte Smith's *Desmond*, historical novels of the recent past which begin to account for the feeling of breakage stemming from the Revolution. Even in Austen's novels, where the breakage of the Revolution has been exchanged for the distant background of the Napoleonic Wars, the sense of historicity, of 'alteration', if not 'improvement' has begun to be discerned by critics,[119] while Susan Ferrier's 1818 novel *Marriage* sketches the contrast between *ancien régime* style aristocracy, the frivolous modern, and the dilapidated 'hoose', 'gude Glenfern Castle'.[120] In *St Ronan's Well* Scott follows his female forebears by writing a historical novel of the recent past; also like his forebears (with their critique of chivalry), he realises that romance itself is a historical category. Romance is endemic both in history's subject matter and in its practice. First, both romance and chivalry have their own stages; they are a key element of the changing system of manners. Second, as Oldbuck's adventures in *The Antiquary* demonstrate, study of the past, with all its antiquarian practice, involves a certain quixotic knight errantry.

However, set against the background of the decayed 'Aul' Town' and the new, superficial and selfish spa, the main plot of *St Ronan's Well* transforms the post-Revolution historical novels of the recent past.[121] Such novels had, by and large, suggested that a refigured, affective heterosexual romance would replace the narratives of lineage. In these works the emotional relationship between the workers and the aristocracy is rethought; the class system is probed but revolution is usually imagined as contained. In contrast, Scott presents an aristocracy painfully, even unfairly imperilled by the shifting times, an aristocracy that is its own worst enemy but that also damages its replacement, commerce. In *The Antiquary* the aristocracy proves self-supporting with no need for commerce; in *Ivanhoe* the usury that supplies trade, war and fine living is equivocal – it can work to support either a vicious or a virtuous aristocracy. But in *St Ronan's Well*, the aristocracy and commerce collapse together, to bad effect.

Radical thinkers had suggested the dangers of fusing modern commercial conditions with the uneven playing field of aristocratic privilege. Wollstonecraft, for example, had suggested that despite prejudices to the contrary, 'a state will infallibly grow old and feeble, if hereditary riches support hereditary rank'.[122] On the other hand, 'Men exclaim, only noticing the evil, against the luxury introduced with the arts and the sciences when it is obviously the cultivation of these alone, emphatically termed the arts of peace, that can turn the sword into a ploughshare.'[123] The civilising influence attached to the commerce necessary for the arts and the sciences is in some sense opposed by the hereditary principle. *St Ronan's Well* darkly refigures both such suspicions and the radical hopes that accompanied them. For Scott trade has its chivalric stages, stages which replace the original chivalry of the aristocrats. Tragically, the nobility itself has corrupted this new scene of progress. As the study of the past is itself corrupted by the feminisation attendant upon modernity, the romance of history fails. The result is a new gothic, manufactured not in an absolutist past but in the present moment.

One cause of this reduction is the sexual and contractual confusion generated by Tyrrel's father, in marrying abroad and then making a bigamous alliance at home. Producing two sons, Tyrrel and then Bulmer, this betrayal of the 'ensigns armorial' that support the traditional chivalric order is associated with *ancien régime* France.[124] Yet the newer, affective order of heterosexual and national romance which replaces the old system fares no better. Six or seven years before the action of the novel begins, a romance between Clara Mowbray and Francis Tyrrel comes to ruin when the heroine is tricked into marrying his illegitimate brother, also the usurper of his title, Valentine Bulmer. Clara is gradually maddened by guilt, not (as to be assumed used on Lockhart's evidence) because the marriage with Bulmer is consummated, but because she has had premarital relations with Tyrrel.[125] The affair is now usually linked to the case of John William Henry Dalrymple versus Johanna Gordon: in Edinburgh, an officer, Dalrymple, slept with Johanna Gordon, promising her marriage but later returned to marry another woman. The judge's ruling suggested that coitus accompanied by intent to marry was the equivalent of marriage itself. According to this ruling, Clara is never married to Bulmer but to Frank – her only problem would be proving the absence of bigamous intent. Nonetheless, the affair eventually ends in Clara's death when Bulmer returns to try officially to (re)marry her in order to gain an estate.

But Scott's novel of breakage in the recent past also revisits a literary motif common in the novel of ideas in the post-French Revolution debate: the motif of female sexual freedom. The twenty-four lines from the manuscript suggesting Clara and Frank's fall (reinstated by Weinstein in the Edinburgh edition) were cut due to James Ballantyne's scruples – apparently about the class content. Building on Scott's suggestion that the publisher 'would never have quarrelled with it . . . had the thing happened to a girl in gingham', Fiona Robertson rightly notes that 'eighteenth- and early nineteenth-century literature is strewn with seduced women, but of a lower social class'.[126] However, the post-French Revolution debate saw some exceptions to this rule. Attempts to treat the idea of sexuality outside the boundaries of marriage were made with some seriousness by precariously middle-ranking writers like Mary Wollstonecraft and Mary Hays and (sensitively but less positively) by Mary Brunton, Elizabeth Inchbald, and Amelia Opie. In particular, the eponymous heroine of Mrs Opie's *Adeline Mowbray* (1805) shares a surname with Scott's Clara and there is also some similarity of situation. Adeline first makes a love match with the young philosopher, Frederic

Glenmurray, to his horror believing the arguments against marriage he has made in a youthful publication. After Glenmurray's death, her social vulnerability forces her (with Glenmurray's pre-death agreement) to marry the commonplace Mr Berrendale. Although the novel has been read as a conservative attack on the idea of female sexual freedom, it in fact creates a contrast between social ostracism with affection outside marriage, on the one hand, and the pain of incompatibility within it, on the other. Scott historicises the pattern. Replacing the faltering aristocratic concern with lineage, the progressive sentimental ties of the French Revolutionary debate are themselves corrupted. The loving relationship is a source of guilt; the supposedly orthodox relationship a source of horror. But rather than denouncing revolutionary free love, Scott seems more concerned with the legal context, in which a private marriage contract can stand in for a public one. Affective ties are under threat because of Scottish legal modernity.

Moreover, the decline of affect and the corruption of aristocratic chivalry are linked. In Susan Ferrier's *Marriage* the Earl of Courtland, seeking to form a dynastic alliance through his daughter, Lady Juliana, tells her that 'love was now entirely confined to the *canaille*'.[127] His *ancien régime* language at once signals the affective indifference of the aristocracy and hints at its dangerous results. Unexpectedly, Scott makes a similar point. When Touchwood attempts to reason with Captain Jekyl, Bulmer's associate, about the duel fought with Tyrrel, the military man begins 'to whistle an opera air'.[128] This reminds Touchwood of the 'Marquis, another dear friend' who 'whistles all the time you talk to him – He says he learned it in the reign of terror, when a man was glad to whistle to shew his throat was whole'.[129] The Marquis's behaviour suggests a certain bravado, but the episode links Jekyl's honour and the exclusivity of his code to a consequence – revolutionary violence. How much worse, then, Bulmer's 'gallant attempt to murder his elder brother or his more lawful brother'.[130] The book suggests that on every level the chivalric code has been debased: the lover, who should protect his mistress, indulges in license with her; the false knight (Bulmer) falsely marries her; a duel is fought over property rather than love; the weak are not sheltered by those who profess the code of honour; and (unlike Sir Arthur who at least regrets that his extravagant ways may hurt his daughter) Mowbray attempts to sell his own sister. It is no wonder Touchwood's humour in dealing with Captain Jekyl is decidedly sardonic. In *The Antiquary* the grandiose chivalric impulse can be reduced by humour (as with the phoca). Here, at least as far as the aristocracy are concerned, the code of chivalry is already too reduced to admit of much uncomplicated amusement.

As in earlier historical novels, the chivalric aristocratic decay identified by Scott has its effect on corrupt followers. *Lioncel*, for example,
had compared the possibility of reform where good workers and aristocracy cooperate to the possibility of corruption when such relationships are lacking (the theme, inflected with the idea of gratitude versus
ingratitude, is also a familiar one for Edgeworth). In *St Ronan's Well*
the idea of the mass, central in *Ivanhoe*, has been largely erased. Elspeth
and Ulrica have been transfigured into Hannah Irwin, who, along with
the valet Solmes, recalls the motif of the corrupt body servant tainted by
aristocratic envy. The negative idea of the relationship between ranks
is much more strongly in evidence than any reforming bond. In addition, more positive modes of labour are also undercut in *St Ronan's
Well*. Whereas in 'Madame de Fleury' Maria Edgeworth had compared
the corrupting work of servants to labour in the market place, Scott
outlines in greater detail the stages of commerce and suggests that they
are themselves chivalric. However, these stages are in decline because of
aristocratic meddling.

Meg Dods is the novel's 'keeper of feudal loyalty' but she is also the
second-generation owner of her own business and other Mowbray land
besides.[131] Her self-sufficiency and property ownership is the first (chivalric) stage in the development of trade. The old Mowbray dwelling has
been replaced with the mansion which Meg now operates as a public
house. Thus the business is at several removes this Scottish woman's
'Castle' – trade has replaced the aristocratic order but, more than that,
as Meg reigns with the 'despotism of Queen Bess herself', business has
its own chivalric accompaniments, its own feudal moment.[132] With the
merchant-capitalist Touchwood, Scott includes a more advanced stage
in this narrative of the new chivalry of trade. Touchwood contends
'there is as good inheritance in house as in field – a man's partners are his
fathers and brothers'.[133] This is a new financial and affective relationship
that provides its own martial insignia. The new code of trade is not as
grand as the older form of chivalry (Touchwood is quite willing to listen
at doors, for example) but its moral code is improved, less concerned
with empty names and more concerned with conduct. It is notable that
the few truly humorous moments of the novel concern Touchwood and
Meg, signalling that they are the genuine bearers of chivalry in the novel.

But the chivalry of trade finds itself helpless in relation to aristocratic
speculation. The trouble begins when Touchwood's relative Scrogie
misunderstands the stages of trade. His failure to see that 'there is as
good inheritance in house as in field' and his desire to ally himself to the
ancient name 'Mowbray' transform Clara into a valuable commodity.
In the past, his father's bigamous marriage allowed Bulmer to continue

in the possession of Tyrrel's estates and in the present his illegal union would allow him to enjoy those of Scrogie. Uncovering both past and present scandal, Touchwood is still unable to stop events. Rather like a character in *Ivanhoe*, the merchant would like to manage the fate and reveal the identity of the disinherited knight, Tyrrel, and to make Clara's impoverished brother Mowbray 'a free man of the forest'.[134] But his behaviour is too quixotic and meandering. In deciding to celebrate his own cleverness by explaining all to Mowbray, Touchwood gives Clara time to escape Shaws-Castle, thinking that Bulmer is coming for her. Thus she ultimately dies.

Touchwood is symbolically defeated by the aristocratic corruption that produces a new, third stage of trade. Touchwood thinks in terms of the means of production and the commodity (at one point saying to Mowbray that you 'think yourself a mill-stone, and turn out a sack of grain'; commodities may dance by having different places in the chain of supply and demand but, with Old Whig bullishness, Touchwood insists one should know one's identity and stick to it).[135] Mowbray, in contrast, refers to his money as 'stock'.[136] That which was representative of goods or services to a certain value becomes in itself an object of trade and as such its value fluctuates, as the act of gambling indicates. When Mowbray is forced to put his remaining acres in feu to the developers of the spa, he ignores the land's use value in favour of creating further stock for speculation. The inflationary effect of the spa town draws attention to, and begins to operate as a metaphor for, fluctuations not in the price of this or that commodity but in the value of money itself.

Moreover, the 'tontine' by which St Ronan's spa hotel is constructed, continues the pattern of speculation. The tontine ('sinful presumption', as Meg has it) is a form of partnership in which whoever lives longest eventually owns the company and its assets.[137] It relies on the death of other partners, that is, on the demise of what Touchwood describes as the trading alternative to the aristocratic family. It therefore echoes in relation to trade the barrenness produced amongst the aristocracy at the end of the novel. This barrenness is the result of Bulmer's marital trickery. In Godwin's *St Leon* the chivalric gambler later turns alchemist and social experimenter. But whereas in *The Antiquary* Scott critiques this by distinguishing between the chivalric Sir Arthur and the alchemical trickster, Dousterswivel, in *St Ronan's Well* the characteristics are once more terribly united in the figure of Valentine Bulmer. Chivalry does not eventually lead to progress, as Godwin hopes, but to ruinous speculation and it is the aristocracy who are themselves responsible.

Under such circumstances, although *St Ronan's Well* does not exactly depict the end of history, it certainly suggests that the overlapping codes of history, chivalry and romance are in decline. Although Scott's revisions soften the portrait of the Reverend Cargill, there is little doubt that his mistakes, product of an overly active historical imagination, precipitate disaster.[138] If Oldbuck is a debased Baron Bradwardine, the Reverend Cargill represents a further reduction. Absorbed by his researches into the Crusades, he initially weds Clara to the wrong bridegroom and later, by misreading an Indian shawl as a badge of identity, partially exposes the secret of her marriage. Concerned with the aristocratic chivalry that provided the origin of romance, the historian proves impractical, unable to protect either dynastic or affective union in the present. Whereas Oldbuck had been financially careful, the Rev. Cargill husbands his antiquarian learning like a 'miser's concealed hoard' (recalling Sir Arthur's treatment of the *Ivanhoe* or Wardour manuscript).[139] Chivalric knowledge remains idle, even when Mr Touchstone supplements it, answering the priest's question 'From Acon, Accor, or St. John d'Acre, to Jerusalem, how far' with the laconic 'twenty three miles'.[140] Touchwood's practical knowledge fails: the legal and historical evidence held by the house of Touchwood, Scrogie, and Co. proves ineffective. By the time Tyrrel has proved his title, the heroine is already dead.

The historical fragments which in *The Antiquary* had been found in Oldbuck's study (and which were always of dubious value) have been transmuted and feminised. The 'trash and trinketry' 'accumulate[d]' by 'old maids' for a century resist arrangement by Mowbray and his maddened sister. The '*chiffonerie*' hypothesised by Scott recall the Alhambra hangings of Lady Clonbrony in Edgeworth's *The Absentee* or the mixture of classical and biblical tapestries found in West's *A Tale of the Times*.[141] But while Lady Clonbrony cannot discriminate between tyranny and freedom and West's Monteiths confuse classical and Christian, Scott's bric-a-brac signals family disarray. 'The great grandsire's thumb-ring couchant with the coral and bells of the first-born – and the boatswain's whistle of some old naval uncle', or his 'tobacco-box, redolent of Oronoko, happily grouped with the mother's ivory comb-case' form a history jumbled in terms of chronology and gender.

The quotidian replaces the legal and chivalric; the imperial overwrites the national. History itself has become feminised in an extension of Adam Smith's thought. In his *Theory of Moral Sentiments* Adam Smith had described the 'awful' and the 'amiable' virtues, implying that a luxurious, modern and late stage society would be softened and feminised – both Wollstonecraft and Baillie, in different ways, make the point that this feminisation is societal rather than necessarily characteristic of female behaviour.[142] Scott, in contrast, suggests that in this late stage history will itself be infected – and the nation with it. The disorganisation of the past – and its impact on the nation – is underlined by a play enacted at Shaws-Castle. As John Wilson Croker suggested in relation to Scott's use of the supernatural in *Guy Mannering* and *The Antiquary*, *A Midsummer Night's Dream* 'mixes up fairies, witchery, mythology, and common life in a brilliant extravaganza which affects no historical nor even possible truth'.[143] Imported to Scotland, this English play signals that cultural history is in as much confusion as family tradition.

Under such circumstances, national and personal healing is contaminated by the gothic. Whereas Jane West's loyalists had proved able to manipulate the gothic for their own healing ends, and whereas even in *Ivanhoe* the motif of medicine is equivocal, here no healing will take place: the gothic is out of control. Dr Quackleben speaks in praise of *Midsummer Night's Dream* as a kind of the '*placebo*' – illusion, not medicine, is his stock-in-trade.[144] The Well is similarly fallacious. When the *British Critic* laments the replacement of 'some haunted fountain, connected with . . . a knightly race' by 'a watering place of nineteenth century', the reviewer fails to grasp that this is Scott's point.[145] The parallel between Wordsworth's 'Hart-Leap Well' and *St Ronan's Well* suggests a place of merciless pursuit, transformed into a site of hollow gaiety, then into a ruin.[146] In the case of Scott's novel, knightly errors have led a fantasy of healing which inevitably fails. The well, Shakespearian sign of female purity, familial wholeness, and political virtue, is as trivialised and ineffective as one of Dr Quackleben's cures, its healing as illusory as Dousterswivel's powers when he divines for water.

While Godwin had imagined that chivalric ambition might generate a social experiment that would appear gothic to outsiders, it was the idea that radicals might paint the past as a place of gothic tyranny that proved more troubling to conservative writers like West and Reeve. Thus the royalists tried to regain control of the fictional past – by promoting the supposedly historical, by privileging the romance, or making gothic work to the benefit of the aristocracy. In *St Ronan's Well*, the aristocracy becomes associated with gothic in a way that reverses West's technique in *The Loyalists*. When the 'sick woman', Bulmer's confidant, Hannah Irwin, makes her deathbed confession to Cargill, she suspects she hears movement in the otherwise empty room. Suddenly 'the figure of Clara Mowbray, her clothes and long hair drenched and dripping with rain', appears, like an 'apparition'.[147] Colonel Evellin's ghostly appearance keeps him safe, allowing his ultimate return; but Clara's wraithlike shape places her amongst the living dead.[148]

Curiously, such a gothicised aristocracy might have proved initially pleasing to the sorts of radicals that Reeve and West had imagined.

But in *St Ronan's Well* the connection between the aristocracy and the gothic is not the result of their past oppressive practices but of present failure. Trying to retain their prestige in the face of change, they harm themselves and the commerce (itself chivalric) that could replace them. As they struggle to maintain their status in the face of social change, they are subsumed by the gothic. Even a more moderate approach cannot prevent this gothic erasure: post Clara's death and the failure of aristocratic regeneration, Mowbray tries to stop history – the new town is demolished. But in vain – the process of erosion, which is coupled with the even more troubling attrition of national identity, continues. Ultimately, the sole marriage finalised in the novel is the bourgeois and debased union between Dr Quackleben and Mrs Blower. Even the best representative of the old order, Francis Tyrrel, inherits his title only to become a wandering painter. This is a disenfranchisement, a homeless wandering in which aesthetic ownership is no substitute for actual possession. It is rather as if Lovel, the hero of *The Antiquary,* had after all proved to be a player.

In *The Antiquary* Scott contains the threat of radical history and politics from below within a stadial narrative of the progress of chivalry. He also attacks a more formally intellectual radicalism, associating it with an emphasis on science and opposing it with antiquarianism. As he recycles the methodological quarrels of the post-French Revolution debate about history he tries to diffuse tension by a strategy of displacement: the struggle for political liberty is overwritten by a sense of national competition, yet this is one in which faded memories of repeated past invasions undercut the need for passion; nationalism is invoked and ready but is rendered unnecessary by the final absence of threat. Yet, even as tension dissipates, there is a concern that a history without tension will be no history at all. The energy of debate, of competing nationalisms, even of radicalism is necessary to avoid ennui. Hence in *Ivanhoe,* Scott's attempt to recombine the tropes of the historical novel to form one whole, imaginary polis, violence is disturbingly inscribed as part of the political system. *Ivanhoe* rewrites the historical novel to undermine ancient constitutionalism; it inhibits the very idea of the radical alternative community (ironically by placing a king in the greenwood); it exploits the fluctuating definitions of chivalry in order to stage social readjustment and to foreclose further change. The novel seeks to accept a limited form of violence as a necessary part of political life.

But as fast as it rearranges the tropes of historical fiction, the violence those tropes contain spills out, refusing to be neatly contained. When ancient liberties are undermined, an unexpectedly sympathetic space of radical protest opens and now radical discourse is presumably no longer confined by a need to present reform in terms of the past. As, like *The Antiquary*, *Ivanhoe* replaces political tensions with issues of national identity, it also suggests that the process of invasion is not necessarily followed by integration. Again, when Scott adapts the motif of history as medicine found in Jane West's work, Isaac and Rebecca do not only reveal the healing potential of money and of alternative forms of traditionary knowledge. They do more, too, than foregrounding the importance of security of property. Father and daughter encode the painful fear of poverty and alienation, the uncertainty of justice and the fragility of personal and religious liberty. Despite suggestions to the contrary, since chivalric violence has exacerbated their condition, it seems unlikely ultimately to protect them. The alliance between the aristocracy and commerce, disallowed in *The Antiquary* but encouraged here, seems unlikely to provide a solution to social ills.

By the time of *St Ronan's Well* Scott's preoccupation with violence and his concern regarding the relationship between commerce, finance and the aristocracy register still more darkly. In this historical novel of the recent past the stages of chivalry, once associated with the aristocracy, are now a feature of commerce. The post-French Revolution concern regarding the role of the workers has been transformed by Scott into a positive interest in trade. However, as in the earlier historical novels of the recent past, it is aristocratic hubris (and the ambition of the nobility's body servants) which threaten the social order. Wollstonecraft had suggested that the rulers had 'fenced round' their property with partial laws and religious and courtly shows. But Scott suggests that the removal of those fences, the erosion of social status, generates social difficulty. The false wealth promised Sir Arthur by Dousterswivel has become not the ambiguous silver of Isaac, but something potentially far more wholesome. Yet the aristocracy see money as 'stock' and irreligiously, even brutally, speculate with it. It is this speculation that disrupts the potential nobility of trade and threatens the stages Scott now traces in relation to capitalism. As a result, even the violence Scott finds necessary to the social order has deteriorated, becoming petty and dishonourable, manifesting as a murderous attack against a brother, the robbing of the mails or the cruelty of inaccurate gossip.

Gothic desperation characterises the actions of the aristocracy in the present, not the past, in a distorted reflection of earlier radical fears, and national identity is itself the victim. David Hume had proposed the erosion of such national character by commerce in relatively cheerful terms, but for Scott the process is marked by corruption.[149] Jumbled family mementos of imperialist luxury now form the substance of history, poor substitutes for the healing matrilineal inheritance possessed by Rebecca. When Clara's mention of Burns is brushed aside by her brother and when 'Dryads and Naiads', and Greek and Roman gods, inhabit the literary space of the Well, it becomes clear that the erosion of Scottish identity by a kind of cultural melange is being registered.[150] Invasion, which fails to happen in *The Antiquary* and is already a half-digested memory in *Ivanhoe*, now becomes a sharply painful part of the Scottish present. Scott remains haunted by the historical anxieties of his predecessors.

## Notes

1. For Porter's public claim see Jane Porter, *Thaddeus of Warsaw*, Standard Novels, 4: vi.
2. Jane Porter to Robert Ker Porter, 23 September 1821, Long Ditton, Surrey, MS, Jane Porter Papers, POR2045, Huntington Library, CA. In this letter Porter refers to Haliday both as 'Andrew' and as 'John'. She may have been thinking of Sir Andrew Halliday.
3. See McLean, 'Jane Porter', pp. 147–59.
4. Jane Porter to Anna Maria Porter, 20 February 1820, MS, Jane Porter Papers POR1781, Huntington Library, CA.
5. Jane Porter to Anna Maria Porter, 24 February 1820, Brighton, MS, Jane Porter Papers POR1782, Huntington Library, CA.
6. Garside, 'Popular Fiction', p. 31.
7. Garside, 'Popular Fiction', p. 48; See Fiona Robertson, *Legitimate Histories*, Gamer, *Romanticism and the Gothic*; Ferris, *The Achievement of Literary Authority*, and Trumpener, *Bardic Nationalism*, amongst others.
8. Cross, 'An Earlier Waverley', pp. 88–90. Garside, 'Walter Scott and the "Common" Novel', np.
9. Lang, intro. *Waverley*, p. lxxxvi; Hazlitt, '35. Hazlitt and the Spirit of the Age' in Hayden, *Walter Scott*, p. 289; Garside, 'Popular Fiction', p. 52.
10. See Croker, *Quarterly Review*, p. 124; See also the anonymous review by Hazlitt, '*The Wanderer*', p. 336.
11. Cronin, *Paper Pellets*, p. 27.
12. Paine, *Political Writings*, p. 163.
13. West, *Loyalists*, 1: 222.
14. West, *Young Man*, 3: 334.
15. West, *Young Man*, 3: 339–40.
16. Marilyn Butler, *Jane Austen*, p. xvi.
17. Pownall, *An Antiquarian Romance,* v. See Sweet, *Antiquaries*, pp. 23–6.
18. Pownall, *An Antiquarian Romance*, p. 7.
19. Pownall, *An Antiquarian Romance*, vi–vii.
20. For *The Antiquary* and Burke see Goode, 'Dryasdust Antiquarianism' and for the tension between amateurs and the University discipline of conjectural history, see Ferris, 'Pedantry'.

21. Angela Wright, 'Scottish Gothic', p. 80.
22. Scott, *Antiquary*, p. 27.
23. Garside, 'Walter Scott and the "Common" Novel', np.
24. West, *Loyalists*, 1: 72.
25. Scott, *Antiquary*, xv.
26. As Shaw notes, 'Amazingly, for a novel set in the turbulent political climate of the 1790s, *The Antiquary* is unusually silent about the threat of dissent' ('Walter Scott', p. 63).
27. Scott, *Antiquary*, p. 18. For Scott and the false alarm of French invasion see Lockhart, *Life*, p. 149.
28. Scott, *Antiquary*, p. 49.
29. Scott, *Antiquary*, xvii; Duncan, 'Scotland and the Novel', p. 260. See also Duncan, *Scott's Shadow*.
30. Scott, *Antiquary*, p. xvii.
31. Scott, *Antiquary*, p. 61, p. 63.
32. Charlotte Smith, *Desmond*, p. 137.
33. Wollstonecraft, *Works*, 6: 18.
34. Scott, *Antiquary*, p. 61.
35. Scott, *Antiquary*, p. 64, p. 53.
36. Scott, *Antiquary*, p. 53.
37. Scott, *Antiquary*, p. 66.
38. For Scott's movement from public to private legitimacy see Burgess, *British Fiction*, pp. 186–234.
39. For a possible origin see Hogg, *Familiar Anecdotes* (1834), p. 131.
40. Scott, *Antiquary*, p. 47.
41. Scott, *Antiquary*, p. 61. It is noteworthy that Edie is not a hairdresser and that Caxon, the wig-dresser, desires to retain the fashions of the past. In contrast, see the aspiration of hairdressers in *Memoirs of Modern Philosophers* and 'Madame de Fleury', as well as the satire by 'A. Scott, citizen and hairdresser', *Plain Reasons* (1793).
42. Scott, *Antiquary*, p. 61.
43. A. M. Porter, *Knight*, 1: 228.
44. A. M. Porter, *Knight*, 1: 230.
45. Scott, *Antiquary*, p. 66.
46. Scott, *Antiquary*, p. 25.
47. Scott, *Antiquary*, p. 25.
48. Scott, *Antiquary*, p. 108.
49. Scott, *Antiquary*, pp. 296–7.
50. Scott, *Antiquary*, p. 52.
51. Scott, *Antiquary*, p. 34.
52. Scott, *Antiquary*, p. 430.
53. For associations between Scott's antiquarianism and Anti-Jacobin politicians see Gamer, *Romanticism and the Gothic*, p. 174.
54. Godwin, *St Leon*, p. 159.
55. Scott, *Antiquary*, p. 163.
56. Scott, *Antiquary*, p. 358; Burke, *Reflections*, p. 170.
57. Scott, *Antiquary*, p. 340.
58. See, however, Moore, '"Caledonian Plagiary"', pp. 92–108, for complexities in Macpherson's treatment of Ireland.

59. Godwin, *Collected Novels*, 6: 9.
60. Scott, *Antiquary*, pp. 149–50.
61. Scott, *Antiquary*, p. 32.
62. Scott, *Antiquary*, p. 33.
63. [Balfour], *The Genius of Caledonia*, p. 4, p. 5.
64. Scott, *Antiquary*, p. 134.
65. Camden, *Britannia*, xcii.
66. Scott, *Antiquary*, p. 242.
67. Scott, *Antiquary*, p. 66.
68. Tessone, 'Entailing the Nation', pp. 149–77.
69. Scott, *Antiquary*, p. 377.
70. The battle between the Earl of Mar (on behalf of the Regent Albany) and Donald Lord of the Isles was to prove indecisive (although sometimes victory was claimed by the Regent's historians).
71. Scott, *Antiquary*, p. 33.
72. Duncan, 'Late Scott', pp. 140–1.
73. Scott, *Antiquary*, p. 54.
74. Scott, *Antiquary*, p. 418.
75. Scott, *Antiquary*, p. 339; Dryasdust recurs in *Fortunes of Nigel* (1822), *Peveril* (1822), *Quentin Durward* (1823) and *Redgauntlet* (1824).
76. Scott, *Ivanhoe*, p. 22.
77. For the Norman Conquest see Duncan's introduction to Walter Scott, *Ivanhoe*, xiv.
78. Scott, *Ivanhoe*, p. 22.
79. Scott, *Ivanhoe*, p. 5.
80. Logan, *Runnamede*, p. 10.
81. Mackenzie, *Danish Massacre*, 1: 1, 1: 5.
82. Scott, *Ivanhoe*, xvi; for limits on this racial narrative see Sanders, '"Utter Indifference"?', p. 160. For usurpation see Wilt, *Secret Leaves*, p. 25.
83. Scott, *Ivanhoe*, p. 28.
84. Scott, *Ivanhoe*, p. 27.
85. Scott, *Ivanhoe*, p. 198.
86. For loyalty, class unrest and *Rokeby*, see Helen Phillips, 'Scott and the Outlaws', p. 126.
87. Scott, *Ivanhoe*, p. 58.
88. Scott, *Ivanhoe*, p. 245.
89. Charlotte Smith, *Minor Morals*, 2: 86.
90. Scott, *Ivanhoe*, p. 29.
91. Anon, *Edwy* 2: 137; the list of Norman crimes in Logan's *Tragedy* is even more substantial; there Normans are seen particularly as domestic violators (p. 5).
92. Scott, *Ivanhoe*, p. 233.
93. See Dyer, '*Ivanhoe*, Chivalry and the Murder of Mary Ashford', pp. 400–1; see also James Chandler, *England in 1819*, p. 11; McMaster, *Scott and Society*, p. 90.
94. A. M. Porter, *Knight*, 1: 7, 1: 24.
95. Scott, *Essay on Chivalry*, p. 88; Scott, *Ivanhoe*, p. 16.
96. Lockhart, *Life*, p. 623, for Scott's 1832 visit to Malta.
97. David Hume, *History of England*, 1: 403.

98. See Dibden, *Richard Coeur-De-Lion*. The French work had originally been written by Michel-Jean Sedaine.
99. Scott, *Ivanhoe*, p. 218.
100. Scott, *Ivanhoe*, p. 148. See Lincoln, *Walter Scott*, pp. 74–6 for a different interpretation of chivalric display in the novel.
101. Scott, *Ivanhoe*, p. 102, p. 463.
102. Rowlinson, *Real Money*, p. 59.
103. Scott, *Ivanhoe*, p. 7.
104. Ritson, *Robin Hood*, v.
105. Ritson, *Robin Hood*, vi.
106. A. M. Porter, *Knight*, 2: 195.
107. Scott, *Ivanhoe*, p. 316.
108. Schoenfield, 'Waging Battle', p. 71.
109. Scott, *Ivanhoe*, p. 235.
110. See Weinstein's edition of Scott's *St Ronan's Well*, pp. 442–3. References are to this edition unless otherwise stated.
111. 'Art. VIII. *St Ronan's Well*', *Monthly Review*, p. 61.
112. Scott, *St Ronan's Well*, ed. Lang, xvii.
113. Ferris, *The Achievement of Literary Authority*, p. 10.
114. Allen, 'Staging a Comeback', pp. 66–98.
115. Duncan, *Modern Romance*, p. 53; Burgess, *British Fiction*, pp. 186–234.
116. For generic instability see Rigney, *Imperfect Histories*, pp. 13–58; Mayer, 'The Illogical Status of Novelistic Discourse', pp. 911–38.
117. Scott, *St Ronan's Well*, ed. Lang, xvii.
118. Scott, *St Ronan's Well*, ed. Lang, xvii.
119. For Austen's novels and history, see Barchas, *Matters of Fact*, pp. 10–11.
120. Ferrier, *Marriage*, p. 11.
121. Scott, *St Ronan's Well*, p. 73.
122. Wollstonecraft, *Works*, 6: 13.
123. Wollstonecraft, *Works*, 6: 14.
124. Burke, *Reflections*, p. 121.
125. Scott, *St Ronan's Well* (1833), (ed. Lang), xiii.
126. Scott, *St Ronan's Well*, p. 390; Fiona Robertson, 'Romancing and Romanticism', p. 103.
127. Ferrier, *Marriage*, p. 4.
128. Scott, *St Ronan's Well*, p. 283.
129. Scott, *St Ronan's Well*, p. 282.
130. Scott, *St Ronan's Well*, p. 283.
131. Burgess, *British Fiction*, p. 226.
132. Scott, *St Ronan's Well*, p. 6.
133. Scott, *St Ronan's Well*, p. 342.
134. Scott, *St Ronan's Well*, p. 345.
135. Scott, *St Ronan's Well*, p. 345.
136. Scott, *St Ronan's Well*, p. 95.
137. Scott, *St Ronan's Well*, pp. 8–9.
138. See Weinstein's notes to Scott's *St Ronan's Well*, p. 382.
139. Scott, *St Ronan's Well*, p. 151.
140. Scott, *St Ronan's Well*, p. 155.
141. Scott, *St Ronan's Well*, p. 90.

142. Adam Smith, *Theory of Moral Sentiments*, p. 23; I. i. 5. 1.
143. Hayden, *Walter Scott*, p. 100.
144. Scott, *St Ronan's Well*, p. 185.
145. 'St. Ronan's Well', *British Critic*, (Jan 1824), p. 16.
146. David Chandler, 'Scott's *Saint Ronan's Well*', pp. 152–7.
147. Scott, *St Ronan's Well*, p. 365.
148. For the move towards a 'psychological case-study' see Irvine, 'Gender', p. 61.
149. David Hume, 'Of National Character'; see *Essays*, p. 206.
150. Scott, *St Ronan's Well*, p. 333, p. 40.

# Conclusion

Writing in an uncertain age of revolution, historical novelists of the late eighteenth and early nineteenth centuries struggled with both the meaning of history and the shape of the future. Even following Scott's creation of a tradition of transformation in the Waverley Novels, the motif of breakage and the apparent triumph of commerce remained disquieting. Although Thomas Carlyle argues that a healthy approach to the past is possible, in *The French Revolution* (1837) he offers a troubled reading of history as fundamentally pessimistic: 'the Event, the thing which can be spoken of, is it not in all cases, some disruption, some solution of continuity?'[1] Carlyle's dramatisation of history as tragedy is of course a product of the French Revolution itself but, as his allusion here to Edmund Burke suggests, it also reflects long-standing British anxieties about the management and desirability (or otherwise) of political change – for Burke, the aim of the 1701 Act of Settlement was to disguise any '[dis]solution of continuity'; but by 1837 it seemed to Carlyle that, at least within the discourse of history, such camouflage was impossible.[2]

Carlyle continues by suggesting that even 'a glad event' 'involves change, involves loss', but adds that glad events rarely form part of the narrative of history, which concerns itself with what 'befell', rather than what was 'done'.[3] Yet even as Carlyle imagines history as tragedy and breakage, the sheer number of occurrences suggests a more moderate model, that of gradual political change. Here the historical novel performed significant work. From the 1760s historical novels questioned the Stuart motif of return and interrogated the idea of ancient constitutionalism. The idea of a return to ancient rights could be used not only by the aristocracy against the monarchy but by more radical thinkers against an increasingly oligarchical parliament. As radicals probed the limits of the model and more conservative thinkers, like Reeve, struggled to contain its subversive potential, doubts about the effectiveness of the 'gothic' past as political standard grew. The fantasy of tradition in the form of static repetition was unsatisfactory. The alternative, a space outside the existing political order, the experiment of America, although repeatedly canvassed, seemed equally flawed. Burke's use of the rhetoric of chivalry in *Reflections* points to a third alternative. Stadial historians had seen chivalry as a marker of continuity between the stages they analysed and yet they posited it had also evolved. When Burke used the language of chivalry to distinguish between French breakage and British continuity, he facilitated radical historical novelists' access to stadial narratives of progress. The frauds of chivalry might be laid bare and yet the sensibility associated with the code could be the basis for a new political formation, as in Charlotte Smith's *Desmond*. Chivalry allowed the relationship between property, wealth and political power to be re-examined.

More moderate writers resisted or occluded the connection between property and wider political reform, imagining an attitudinal rather than a legislative change (in *Don Sebastian*, for instance, Anna Maria Porter imagines the moral reform of the nobility). Yet the stadial link between a society's manners, its economy and its governmental form that persists in such works has political implications. Thus, in *Marcus Flaminius* Ellis Cornelia Knight turns to the anti-individualistic, as she sees it, values of Roman Republicanism to underpin the social and political system. But even as legislative reform remains out of sight, her book acknowledges the connection between the mode of government, manners and labour. To return for a moment to Dominie Sampson's perplexity concerning his gradually changing garments in *Guy Mannering*, his new clothes suggest a greater respectability and prosperity; that is they signal a gradual shift in manners and economics. The third stadial term, governmental or political change is only suggested by the fact that it is the 'honest' lawyer Mac-Morlan who (strangely enough) manages the deception.[4] In other words, the virtual ubiquity of philosophical history ensures the possibility of governmental (as well as legal) alternation is implicitly present, even if the reader remains as unconscious of it as the hapless Dominie himself. However, in Scott's works it is not that the alternative models of change, inscribed in the earlier historical novel, vanish. It is rather that Scott enfolds more radical paradigms within an evolving stadial framework. In *Ivanhoe* even the radical alternative community has contact with the monarch. Political violence and the attempts to contain aggression within ritual are acknowledged and change is imagined as something that (half-reassuringly, half-alarmingly) has always already happened. The historical novel is a space in which ways to avoid the horrors of revolutionary breakage are repeatedly proposed, preparing the ground for a model of slow alteration.

Speaking about the ancient constitution, Bolingbroke asked: 'what need we any liberty but this?' Yet, as the over-persuasion of the rhetorical question suggests, the nexus of concerns and associations captured by the word 'liberty' did shift. Both Bolingbroke and Leland were concerned with the balance of power, Bolingbroke with Sir Robert Walpole's use of monarchical patronage and Leland with George III's potential for absolutism. But when Leland was writing, the threat of absolutism was less real. On the other hand, as Reeve's work bears testimony, concern with luxury and social mobility not only amongst the aristocracy but also amongst the lower orders was growing. Reeve's liberty consisted of a fixed social structure in which no rank would infringe on the prerogatives of another. All the same, in narratives of ancient liberties, where the primary scene of justice was the trial, an alteration was underway. Such set pieces had at first been focused on aristocratic identity as proof of property rights. Later, (as in Radcliffe's *Gaston de Blondeville*, for instance) such scenes of judgement reflected a wider concern with justice for those with less property and little status. Scott's trial by arms in *Ivanhoe*, dealing with the interpretation of a woman's intellectual inheritance, stands at the end of this tradition.

The association between property and power had been reinforced after the Act of Settlement. After 1710, legislation meant that 'knights of the shire' had to possess landed property worth £600 p.a. and burgesses £300 p.a.[5] As a result, 'the electoral system grew increasingly oligarchical' and fewer parliamentary seats were contested. A 1732 Act stipulated that JPs should possess land to the value of £100 (part of the context of Caleb's treatment by the magistrate in *Things As They Are*). The explicit link between land and power in the eighteenth-century British political system meant that the critique of chivalry could become a critique of system. The post-French Revolution historical novel only touches relatively lightly on the idea of 'liberty' as what Knight characterises as 'universal equality'; universal suffrage or the idea of working men as part of the machinery of government is not often broached except negatively. However, there is a broader sense, registered in *Montford Castle*, Edgeworth's 'Madame de Fleury' and even in the economic sufferings depicted in Porter's *Thaddeus of Warsaw*, that if property or earnings and the right to self-reproduction of the ordinary man were not considered, protest would follow: the political system needed to take these fundamentals of liberty into account. Unpicking chivalry from its sentimental associations, exposing its material underpinnings, Charlotte Smith's *Desmond* suggests that a redistribution of sympathy would lead to an extension of liberty.

The problem for William Godwin (even after he has moderated his initial suspicion of sentiment in *Political Justice*) is that sympathy itself is a potentially destabilising force. Liberty, that is, for Godwin, the independence of religion, politics and opinion, all supported by economic independence, is under threat from the hubris of leaders, from exclusionary sympathies, and from the hardening force of labour itself. For Edgeworth, however, liberty could be facilitated by the correct from of work – independence was associated with the market and an appropriate distance from the aristocratic body. The shift observable here is from a concern about the monarch as a risk to aristocratic property and power to an anxiety about the aristocracy's relationship to work, workers and the market. Coloured by general benevolence and rationality, aristocrats' sympathy for their labourers might operate as a safeguard to liberty; equally, their hubristic speculation might pose an economic and mortal threat.[6] Hostility to the role of the aristocracy in agrarian reform is redirected. In some sense, although commerce is connected with the possibility of greater independence, the aristocracy comes to operate in the historical novel as a figure for the potential harshness and exigencies of capitalism itself. Burney, for example, has the realisation that while work holds out a promise of independence, it also generates suffering: the tyranny of the market, the demands of business and debasement without payment all impinge on individual freedom. But, even as she makes a wider systemic critique, Burney's carelessly consuming upper ranks suggest the potential for hostility against the ruling classes. Hence a moderate writer like Jane Porter in *Thaddeus of Warsaw*, by having her chivalric hero experience hardship, tries to separate at least one virtuous aristocrat from economic blame.

Along with the issue of equality under the law, from the late 1780s the circulation of sympathy was also examined in the historical novel of the small nation. When dealing with Scotland, such novels raised the issue of monarchical (or political) regime change; they suggest that a nation's rulers should work for the prosperity and liberty of their subjects and should (at least culturally, and usually religiously) share some common ground with their subjects. In such works, the idea of the independent small nation works to defend the people against political oppression. Suggesting the shift to a more modern conception of nation, historical fictions focusing on Ireland test dynastic alliances on affective grounds; sentimental ties between nations are found to be under strain or (as in James White's *Earl Strongbow*) entirely absent. If the past marriage between Eva and Richard de Clare is flawed, so, White implies, is the current relation between England and Ireland. In the early historical novel history undercuts sentimental romance. It is only by moving romance to the present and bracketing historical strife by contemporary affect in an effective reversal of the historical novel that Sydney Owenson's first national tale is able to be somewhat more optimistic.

Even in the more radical amongst works the Union is usually given at least some token support. However, in more strongly pro-Union works sentiment is not so much redistributed between the classes, as Smith had envisaged, but redirected: 'liberty' is reattached to nation, and the passionate fight for national freedom overwrites the struggle for individual economic and political rights. Jane Porter's *The Scottish Chiefs* is a subtle example of some of the tensions at work here. In her 1828 preface to the novel she explains her aim is to distinguish between 'a true patriot' who 'establishes the liberty of his country, without infringing on the rights of others' and the 'pretender' 'who first founds a despotic empire over his own countrymen, and then leads them to put similar chains on their neighbours'.[7] The 'liberty of the nation' now subsumes more radical calls for individual political liberty, but such national sentiment does not lead to a contemporary call for Scottish independence. Instead, Wallace's struggle with England fuels Britain's resistance to Napoleonic imperialism. Still, Porter's novel reveals that nationalism itself poses a potential peacetime problem. When the country is at war, the sentiment of patriotism involves both the idea of common property in the nation and the suspension of the oppressor's law; radical concerns are thus redirected, becoming self-sacrifice on behalf of the freedoms of the properly functioning nation. But, when the defensive need is passed, such passions can be reread along radical lines. Therefore, while nationalist sentiment must be there, ready to be invoked, somehow such passions must also be contained. This sense is also registered in Porter's later historical fictions, where she attempts to create a kind of enclosed patriotic sublime: in *The Pastor's Fireside* (1815), she locates patriotism in relation to the domestic hearth, burning brightly but safely sheltered. But while, as Nicola Watson notes, such 'national romances' involve the redirection of sentiment to the nation, other historical novels are not so coy.[8] *Arville Castle*, for instance, suggests that sexual and sentimental bonds can unite conqueror and conquered in productive (and, unpleasantly, solely Caucasian) union. When dynastic ties are reimagined as affective and sexual ones, common to the people, the possibility of dubious reproduction through empire emerges.

Particularly between 1789 and 1814, the process described by the historical novel is one of de- and re-mystification. The radicals drew upon the materialities of history, drawing attention to the false admiration attached to chivalry and the shows of power. In Wollstonecraft's account, this supposedly more scientific approach to history would facilitate the political education of the people and encourage true progress for all. But such ideas were recuperated: in the work of, for example, the Porters, the (albeit modified) sensibilities of stadially inflected chivalry were re-attached to the nation. Equally, the idea of scientific history was reclaimed. For Hamilton, such an approach, facilitated by a clearer vision of the natural world, would in turn generate improved individual morality. In this type of narrative, the idea of the Christian duties of both ruler and people becomes more important than an emphasis on rights. Meanwhile, for West, the scientific vision of history was connected firmly with church and king. Science itself, while promising to record accurately what is there, becomes an instrument of patriotic mystification: in *The Loyalists* doctors and churchmen gain power over the gothic, superstitious and enthusiastic narratives that West associates with radical dissent. Not everyone, West suggests, can be trusted to investigate the truth. In this High Church formulation, laymen should have faith in their political and spiritual leaders. Nonetheless, in continuing the project of critiquing chivalry and in emphasising moral duty (although not with the egalitarian Christian emphasis of a Joseph Priestley or Richard Price), these writers internalise elements of the radical project.

These contradictory impulses, to mystify or to lay bare, to celebrate chivalry or expose the materialities of power, are registered in Carlyle's changing opinions of Scott. Reviewing Joanna Baillie's *Metrical Legends* (1821), Carlyle had remarked 'the fate of Wallace has been singularly bad, both in life and after it':

> We wish all this were remedied [. . .] THE WIZARD, if he liked, could image back to us the very form and pressure of those far-off times, the very life and substance of the strong and busy spirits that adorned it.[9]

In Scott Carlyle discovers a sense of character arising out of the violent and powerful circumstances of history, shaped by the density of material relations. Yet this sense of individual agency, the depiction of heroism in the face of historical force, requires a magical power. Scott projects 'spirits' that are not there. Later, Carlyle finds that the 'strong and busy' historical characters of the Waverley Novels do not seem to him as forceful as they once did: Scott generates too much of a sense of the inevitability of history that Carlyle finds so tragic in *The French Revolution*.[10] Along with this, Scott's apparent acceptance of capital, of the 'worldly', 'economical, material, of the earth earthy' increasingly troubles Carlyle, becoming a flaw in the novelist's personality.[11] Scott, who had once enchanted, now exposes. If the history historians write must in some way reflect the inevitable pains of the developing nation, the novelist, Carlyle occasionally suspects, surely has space for something more inspirational.

Thomas Carlyle argues that a truly 'great man' should 'have fire in him to burn up somewhat of the sins of the world'.[12] Without accepting either Carlyle's initial favourable reading of Scott or his later doubts, it is possible to argue that this fire, this resistance, is present in the historical novelists of the eighteenth and early nineteenth centuries. Largely opposing any narrative of history as abrupt change, they nonetheless, like Scott, saw the process of defining the relationship between past and present as profoundly important. Suspicious of the aristocracy, rejecting feudal ties, more radical writers emphasised the importance of economic independence, of the flow of feeling and finance. Yet, already contaminated by vested interests, the commercial present was also a site of speculative brutalities. Particularly when more moderate and conservative writers tackled the issues of property and commerce, they struggled against the seemingly unstoppable shift to market relations that came to worry Carlyle. While struggling to code political change, these novelists frequently resisted or problematised the rise of capital – it did not seem to them necessarily a given that, in the absence of the divine right of kings, the order that underpinned the state would be provided by the operations of the market. At the very least, their work suggests, such operations needed to be modified by another controlling principle. Negotiating the relationship between law, liberty and property while sometimes providing other foundations for the political order – in heroism, science or Christianity – these novelists fight in order to maintain a sense of agency in the face of political change.

Containing Carlyle's 'fire', the historical novel prepares the way for the 'great man' view of history.[13] While a conservative thinker like Clara Reeve promotes the inspirational effects of 'great men' of history in a relatively obvious way, more progressive thinkers were troubled by the tension between individual agency and historical force. In 'Of History and Romance' Godwin imagines fictionalised biography as a mode which might teach readers individually, bypassing the volatile effects of sympathy and enabling them to resist the pressures upon their independence. In contrast, Edgeworth attempts to develop associations in the individual mind that stimulate gratitude and social sensibility. The brain, whether of child or adult, becomes a space of intervention, undermining habit and possibly, therefore, the larger structures of social custom. In Edgeworth's work, the individual mind becomes the key site for safe political development. Yet there is also a sense of the strain and difficulty of pedagogical process. And if it was hard for ordinary individuals rationally to exercise agency against the determining force of circumstance, the idea of the 'hero' offered little help. Hamilton, exploring the impulses of a historical mind shaped by the manners of its day, asserts that the usual form of hero, egotistical, militaristic and destructive, is a 'pest'. Some more 'reasonable' approach to historical personality and to individual education is required to recreate society from the individual up.[14]

As the historical novel moves away from the idea of the (potentially mass) rational education proposed by Godwin and Wollstonecraft, towards the mass identification with the nation proposed by the Porters, the need to redefine the 'hero' sharpens. Like the idea of chivalry, it would have to be adjusted, not least because the personal revenge allowed by the code was at odds with the state's increasing monopoly on violence. *Don Sebastian* and *The Hungarian Brothers* teach the renunciation of power and the importance of mercy respectively. These were necessary for the hero, having identified with Nelson, Douglas or Percy, to return to everyday existence. Yet, as Porter experienced in relation to Sir Sidney Smith, the behaviour of even real-life heroes sometimes fell from the ideal.[15] In *The Scottish Chiefs* Wallace forms a substitute. If his character was 'frittered away to that of a fine gentleman', as Scott may have suggested, it was nonetheless an attempt to combine the Christian and heroic drives.[16] Wallace begins to perform the dual motions of nationalism, possessing the patriotic energy to fight, on the one hand, with the morality to avoid violence once the crisis is over, on the other. The hero must be capable of action and excusable inaction, conscious of moral agency at one point, and willingly subject to historical determinism (and the will of his rulers) at the next. In parallel with this, the historical novel both suggests that the suffering of the people should at least appear to be acknowledged and acted upon, and that it must be held at a distance, considered as something that the great pressures of history render largely unalterable. And these contradictory demands, developed in historical fiction, for action and inaction, for both a sense of individual moral agency and an acknowledgement of historical determinism, are part of what Scott's heroes inherit from earlier historical fiction.

Since the historical novel is where the competing demands of nation can be crafted and held in some sort of tension, the author by extension has the capacity to become a national hero. Conscious of this shaping function, Porter increasingly comes to see the author herself as a rival for any Nelson, Sir Sidney Smith, or General Kościuszko. In 1812, for example, Jane writes to her sister Anna Maria about a conversation she has had with a Mrs Dunscombe-Taylor. The woman tells Jane:

a gentleman whom I hold in the highest reverence, admires you more than I can tell you; and while he read over a letter of yours, in my presence, he shed tears, lamenting he had never seen you; but at every sentence you wrote exclaimed with emotion, <u>this is too much!, it is too much</u>! Indeed he seemed never weary of speaking of you . . . it is now many years ago, said she, 'it is General Kościuszko.'[17]

Although the letter that moved Kościuszko had in fact been written by Anna Maria Porter, a subtle transfer of heroism has taken place. As the book remains while the hero it honoured departs abroad, Jane becomes the central patriotic figure in the narrative, displacing even Kościuszko himself. But if Porter begins to intuit this, it is Scott and his authorial personae which ultimately bear that substantial weight. In reading Scott, Edgeworth insists, 'the whole tone of our minds is raised – for, thinking nobly of our kind, he makes us think more nobly of ourselves!'[18] Troubled by the way material substance of letters, portraits and seals bear false witness, Edgeworth desires authenticity. She also requires historical distance: in one episode in *Helen*, she encourages her characters to turn from contemporary illustrations to an older volume of caricatures so that at least the *'rat[s] political'* cannot be identified by name, only by type and tendency.[19] For Edgeworth, Scott's writing fulfils these contradictory demands. His words, for her, both guarantee and mediate the past. And yet, when Scott tackles the post-French Revolution debate concerning history, the tensions of the previous historical novel remain. The struggle between the chivalric and the material, the desire to veil and the need to strip bare, are found, wedged all together in single novels, captured, but not wholly contained, in ever more violent opposition.

## Notes

1. Carlyle, *The French Revolution*, p. 24.
2. Burke, *Reflections*, p. 102.
3. Carlyle, *The French Revolution*, p. 24.
4. Scott, *Guy Mannering*, p. 104.
5. Canon, *Parliamentary Reform*, p. 36.
6. See also Benger, *Memoirs*, 2: 113 for Elizabeth Hamilton's sentiments on the 'deep play of war and desolation' in which rulers indulge.
7. Jane Porter, *Scottish Chiefs*, p. 726.
8. For *Thaddeus* see Watson, *Revolution*, pp. 118–19.
9. Carlyle, 'Miss Baillie's Metrical Legends', pp. 402–3. For Carlyle's changing opinions of Scott, see Carlyle, *Two Notebooks*, p. 71, and Carlyle's appraisal of Scott in *The Westminster Review*, 'Sir Walter Scott', *Works*, 29: 54. See also Frye, 'Romancing the Past' and Richardson, 'Thomas Carlyle on Sir Walter Scott'.

10. Carlyle, *Critical and Miscellaneous Essays*, 4: 185–251.
11. Carlyle, *Critical and Miscellaneous Essays*, 4: 198.
12. Carlyle, *Critical and Miscellaneous Essays*, 4: 199.
13. I am indebted to Devoney Looser here, who makes a related point about Jane Porter, discussing her relationship with Sir Sidney Smith. Looser, 'The Great Man', p. 309.
14. Benger, *Memoirs*, 2: 113.
15. Looser, 'The Great Man', pp. 293–314.
16. Hogg, *Familiar Anecdotes*, p. 130.
17. Jane Porter to Anna Maria Porter, July [18–19] 1812, Bristol, MS, Jane Porter Papers POR1665, Huntington Library, CA.
18. Maria Edgeworth, *Helen*, 1: 267. The words are spoken by Granville Beauclerc.
19. Maria Edgeworth, *Helen*, 2: 229.

# Bibliography

Acton, Lord, John Emerich Edward, *Lectures on Modern History*, intro. John Neville Figges and Reginald Vere Laurence (London: Macmillan, 1906).

Allen, Emily, 'Staging a Comeback: The Remasculinization of the Novel', in *Theater Figures: The Production of the Nineteenth-Century British Novel* (Columbus: Ohio University Press, 2003), pp. 66–98.

Alliston, April, 'The Value of a Literary Legacy: Retracing the Transmission of Value through Female Lines', *Yale Journal of Criticism: Interpretation in the Humanities* 4 (1990), pp. 109–27.

Anderson, Benedict, *Imagined Communities: Reflections on the Origin and Spread of Nationalism*, rev. edn (1983; London: Verso, 1991).

Anon, *Arville Castle. An Historical Romance*, 2 vols (London: Crosby, 1795).

Anon, *Charles Dacres: Or, the Voluntary Exile. An Historical Novel, Founded on Facts*, 2 vols (Edinburgh: Moir, 1797).

Anon, *Edward de Courcy*, 2 vols (London: Minerva Press, 1794).

Anon, *Edwy, Son of Ethelred the Second: An Historic Tale; By a Lady*, 2 vols (Dublin: Rice; London: Robinson, 1791).

Anon, *Lady Jane Grey: An Historical Tale*, 2 vols (London: Minerva, 1791).

Anon, *The Monitor: Or, the British Freeholder, from August 9 1755 to July 3, 1756* (London: Scott, 1756).

Anon, *Montford Castle; Or the Knight of the White Rose. An Historical Romance of the Eleventh Century, Etc*, 2 vols (London: Crosby, 1795).

Anon, 'The Terrorist System of Novel Writing', *Monthly Magazine* 21.4 (August 1797), pp. 102–4.

Anon, *William of Normandy: An Historical Novel*, 2 vols (London: Axtell, 1787).

'Art. II. *Don Sebastian, or the House of Braganza, an Historical Romance* in Four Volumes, by Miss Anna Maria Porter', *The Critical Review. Series the Third* 18.4 (December 1809), pp. 356–63.

'Art. VII. *Tales of Fashionable Life*. By Miss Edgeworth', *Quarterly Review* (February/May) 1809, pp. 135–44.

'Art. VII. *Tales of Fashionable Life*', *Quarterly Review* (August 1809), p. 143.

'Art. VIII. *St Ronan's Well*. By the Author of "*Waverley*," "*Quentin Durward*," &c. 3 vols. Post 8vo. 1l. 11s. 6d. Boards', *Monthly Review* CIII (1824), pp. 61–75.

'Art. VIII. *Tales of Fashionable Life*', *Critical Review*, p. 191.

'Art. VIII. *Tales of Fashionable Life*', *London Quarterly Review* (June 1812), p. 330.

'Art. XIX. *The History of the Revolution of France*', *The Monthly Review, or, Literary Journal* 8 (1792), pp. 565–7.

'*Arville Castle. An Historical Romance. 2 vols. 12mo. 6s. Sewed. Crosby, 1796*', *The Critical Review, Or, the Annals of Literature* (London: Hamilton, 1796), p. 115.

Austen, Jane, *Emma*, ed. R. W. Chapman, 3rd edn (Oxford: Oxford University Press, 1933).

Baillie, Joanna, *Plays on the Passions*, ed. Peter Duthie (Peterborough, ON: Broadview Press, 2001).

[Balfour, Alexander], *The Genius of Caledonia: A Poem on the Threatened French Invasion* (Edinburgh: Symington, 1798).

Barbauld, Anna Laetitia, *The British Novelists: With an Essay and Prefaces, Biographical and Critical*, 50 vols (London: Rivington et al.; Edinburgh: Creech; York: Wilson, 1810).

Barchas, Janine, *Matters of Fact in Jane Austen: History, Location, and Celebrity* (Baltimore: Johns Hopkins University Press, 2012).

Batsaki, Yota, 'From Alchemy to Experiment: the Political Economy of Experience in Godwin's *St Leon: A Tale of the Sixteenth Century*', in Yota Batsaki, Subha Mukherji and Jan-Melissa Schramm (eds), *Fictions of Knowledge: Fact, Evidence, Doubt* (New York: Palgrave Macmillan; 2012), pp. 174–92.

Baxter, Denise Amy, 'Two Brutuses: Violence, Virtue, and Politics in the Visual Culture of the French Revolution', *Eighteenth-Century Life* 30 (2006), pp. 51–77.

Benger, Elizabeth, *Memoirs of the Late Mrs Elizabeth Hamilton, with a Selection from Her Correspondence and Other Unpublished Writings*, 2 vols (London: Longman, Hurst, Rees, Orme and Brown, 1818).

Bird, Benjamin, 'The Anxiety of Legitimacy in the Subject of the 1760s', *Romanticism* 12.3 (2006), pp. 189–99.

Bolingbroke, Henry St John, Viscount, *The Works of the Late Right Honourable Henry St. John, Lord Bolingbroke: With the Life of Bolingbroke by Dr Goldsmith*, 8 vols (London: Johnson et al., 1809).

Bolingbroke, Henry St John, Viscount, *Remarks on the History of England* (Basil: Tourneisen, 1794).

[Bowles, John], *A Protest against T. Paine's 'Rights of Man'*, 2nd edn (London: Longman, 1792).

Bowstead, Diana, 'Charlotte Smith's *Desmond*: the Epistolary Novel as Ideological Argument', in Mary Anne Schofield and Cecilia Macheski (eds), *Fetter'd or Free? British Women Novelists, 1670–1815* (Athens: Ohio University Press, 1986), pp. 237–63.

Brown, David, *Walter Scott and the Historical Imagination* (London: Routledge, 1979).

Burgess, Miranda, *British Fiction and the Production of Social Order, 1740–1830* (Cambridge: Cambridge University Press, 2000).

Burgess, Miranda, 'Courting Ruin: The Economic Romances of Frances Burney', *Novel* 28.1 (1995), pp. 131–53.

Burgess, Miranda, 'The National Tale and Allied Genres, 1770s–1840s', in John Wilson Foster (ed.), *The Cambridge Companion to the Irish Novel* (Cambridge: Cambridge University Press, 2006), pp. 39–59.

Burke, Edmund, *Reflections on the Revolution in France and on the Proceedings in Certain Societies in London Relative to that Event*, ed. Conor Cruise O'Brien (1790; Harmondsworth: Penguin, 1968).

Burney, Frances, *Journals and Letters*, ed. Peter Sabor and Lars E. Troide (London: Penguin, 2001).

Burney, Frances, *The Wanderer: Or, Female Difficulties*, ed. Margaret Anne Doody, Robert L. Mack and Peter Sabor (1814; Oxford: Oxford University Press, 1991).

Burrow, John, *A History of Histories: Epics, Chronicles, Romances and Inquiries from Herodotus and Thucydides to the Twentieth Century* (London: Penguin, 2009).

Butler, C., *The Age of Chivalry; Or, Friendship of Other Times: A Moral and Historical Tale, Abridged and Selected from the Knights of the Swan of Madam Genlis* (London: Peacock and Booker, 1799).

Butler, Marilyn, *Jane Austen and the War of Ideas* (1975; Oxford: Oxford University Press, 1987).

Butler, Marilyn, *Maria Edgeworth: A Literary Biography* (Oxford: Clarendon Press, 1972).

Camden, William, *Britannia, or A Chorographical Description of the Flourishing Kings of England, Scotland and Ireland, and the Islands Adjacent from the Earliest Antiquity*, ed. Richard Gough, 3 vols (London: Payne and Robinson, 1789).

Cameron, Kenneth Neill and Donald H. Reiman (eds), *Shelley and His Circle, 1773–1822*, 2 vols (Cambridge, MA: Harvard University Press).

Campbell, Thomas, *A Philosophical Survey of the South of Ireland* (London: Strahan and Cadell, 1777).

Campbell, Thomas, *Strictures on the Ecclesiastical and Literary History of Ireland* (London: Robinson, 1780).

Canon, John, *Parliamentary Reform 1640–1832* (Cambridge: Cambridge University Press, 1972).

Carlyle, Thomas, 'Miss Baillie's Metrical Legends', *New Edinburgh Review* 1 (October 1821), pp. 393–413.

Carlyle, Thomas, 'Sir Walter Scott', *The Collected Works of Thomas Carlyle*, 30 vols (New York: Scribner, 1898–1901).

Carlyle, Thomas, *Critical and Miscellaneous Essays*, 4 vols (Boston: Brown and Taggard, 1860).

Carlyle, Thomas, *The French Revolution*, intro. John D. Rosenberg (1837; New York: Modern Library, 2002).

Carlyle, Thomas, *Two Notebooks*, ed. Charles Eliot Norton (New York: Grolier Club, 1898).

Chandler, David, 'Scott's *Saint Ronan's Well* and Wordsworth's "Hart-Leap Well"', *Notes and Queries* 51.2 (2004), pp. 152–7.

Chandler, James, *England in 1819* (Chicago: University of Chicago Press, 1999).

Chaplin, Sue, 'Romance and Sedition in the 1790s: Radcliffe's *The Italian* and the Terrorist Text', *Romanticism: The Journal of Romantic Culture and Criticism* 7.2 (2001), pp. 177–90.

Chase, Bob, 'Walter Scott: A New Historical Paradigm', in Bill Schwartz (ed.), *The Expansion of England, Race, Ethnicity and Cultural History* (London: Routledge, 1996), pp. 92–129.

Clare, Lord, 'Lord Clare's Speech on a Motion of Address to the Lord Lieutenant', in N. Chapman (ed.), Vol. 4, *Select Speeches, Forensick and Parliamentary* (Philadelphia: Hopkins, 1807), pp. 205–68.

Clark, J. C. D., *Revolution and Rebellion: State and Society in England in the*

*Seventeenth and Eighteenth Centuries* (Cambridge: Cambridge University Press, 1986).

Colley, Linda, *Britons: Forging the Nation, 1707–1837* (1992; London: Vintage, 1996).

Collings, David, 'The Romance of the Impossible: William Godwin in the Empty Place of Reason', *ELH* 70.3 (2003), pp. 847–74.

Conway, Alison, 'Nationalism, Revolution and the Female Body: Charlotte Smith's *Desmond*', *Women's Studies* 24 (1995), pp. 395–409.

Corbett, Mary Jean, *Allegories of Union in English and Irish Writing 1790–1879: Politics, History and the Family from Edgeworth to Arnold* (Cambridge: Cambridge University Press, 2000).

Cordiner, Charles, *Remarkable Ruins and Romantic Prospects of North Britain with Ancient Monuments, and Singular Subjects of Natural History by the Rev. Charles Cordiner with Engravings by Peter Mazell*, 2 vols (1788; London: Taylor, 1795).

Coykendall, Abby, 'Gothic Genealogies, the Family Romance, and Clara Reeve's *The Old English Baron*', *Eighteenth-Century Fiction* 17 (2005), pp. 443–80.

Croker, John Wilson, *Quarterly Review* (April 1814), p. 124.

Cronin, Richard, *Paper Pellets: British Literary Culture after Waterloo* (Oxford: Oxford University Press, 2010).

Cross, Wilbur L, 'An Earlier Waverley', *Modern Language Notes* 17. 2 (1902), 88–90.

Crump, Justine, '"Turning the World Upside down": Madness, Moral Management and Frances Burney's *The Wanderer*', *Eighteenth-Century Fiction* 10.3 (1998), pp. 325–40.

Curthoys, Ann and John Docker, *Is History Fiction?* (Sydney: University of New South Wales Press, 2010).

Darby, Barbara, *Frances Burney, Dramatist: Gender, Performance and the Late Eighteenth-Century Stage* (Lexington: University Press of Kentucky, 1997).

[De Bruno, Louis], *Lioncel; Or, the Emigrant: An Historical Novel. Trans. By Louis de Bruno, a Native of the Banks of the Ganges*, 2nd edn, 2 vols (London: Stockdale, 1803).

De Genlis, [Stéphanie-Félicité], *The Knights of the Swan: Or, The Court of Charlemagne: A Historical and Moral Tale: To Serve as a Continuation to the Tales of the Castle: And of Which All the Incidents that Bear Analogy to the French Revolution Are Taken from History*, trans. The Rev. Beresford, 3 vols (London: Johnson, 1796).

De Groot, Jerome, *The Historical Novel* (Abingdon: Routledge, 2009).

Dibden, Thomas, *Richard Coeur-De-Lion. An Opera by General Burgoyne* (New York: Hobbs, 1831).

Dibdin, J. C., rev. Nilanjana Banerji, 'Henry Siddons', *Oxford Dictionary of National Biography*, <http://www.oxforddnb.com/view/article/16418> (last accessed 12 September 2013).

Dole, Carole M., 'Three Tyrants in *The Castle of Otranto*', *ELN* 26 (1988), pp. 26–35.

Dow, Gillian, 'Stéphanie-Félicité de Genlis and the French Historical Novel in Romantic Britain', *Women's Writing* 19.3 (2012), pp. 273–92.

[Du Bois, Edward], *St Godwin: A Tale of the Sixteenth, Seventeenth, and Eighteenth Centuries by Count Reginald De St. Leon*, 2nd edn (London: Wright, 1800).

Duncan, Ian, 'Late Scott', in Fiona Robertson (ed.), *The Edinburgh Companion to Sir Walter Scott* (Edinburgh: Edinburgh University Press, 2012), pp. 130–42.

Duncan, Ian, *Modern Romance and Transformations of the Novel: Gothic, Scott, Dickens* (Cambridge: Cambridge University Press, 2005).

Duncan, Ian, 'Scotland and the Novel', in Richard Maxwell and Katie Trumpener (eds), *Fiction in the Romantic Period* (Cambridge: Cambridge University Press, 2008), pp. 251–64.

Duncan, Ian, *Scott's Shadow: The Novel in Romantic Edinburgh* (Princeton: Princeton University Press, 2007).

Dyer, Gary, '*Ivanhoe*, Chivalry and the Murder of Mary Ashford', *Criticism* 39.3 (1997), pp. 388–408.

Edgeworth, Maria, *Belinda* (1801), ed. Siobhan Kilfeather, Vol. II of *The Novels and Selected Works of Maria Edgeworth* (London: Pickering and Chatto, 2003).

Edgeworth, Maria, *Castle Rackrent* and *Ennui*, ed. Marilyn Butler (London: Penguin, 1992).

Edgeworth, Maria, *Helen, a Tale*, 3 vols (London: Bentley, 1834).

Edgeworth, Maria, *Letters for Literary Ladies to Which Is Added a Letter on the Noble Science of Self-Justification* (London: Johnson, 1795).

Edgeworth, Maria, 'Madame de Fleury', *Tales of Fashionable Life*, vol. 10 of *Tales and Novels*, 18 vols (London: Baldwin and Cradock et al., 1833).

Edgeworth, Maria, and Richard Lovell Edgeworth, *Practical Education*, 2 vols (London: Johnson, 1798).

Ferguson, Adam, *An Essay on the History of Civil Society* (1767), 5th edn (London: Cadell, 1782).

Ferrier, Susan, *Marriage, A Novel* (Bampton: Three Rivers Books, 1984).

Ferris, Ina, *The Achievement of Literary Authority: Gender, History and the Waverley Novels* (Ithaca: Cornell University Press, 1991).

Ferris, Ina, 'The Irish Novel 1800–1829', in Richard Maxwell and Katie Trumpener (eds), *Cambridge Companion to Fiction in the Romantic Period* (Cambridge: Cambridge University Press, 2008), pp. 235–49.

Ferris, Ina, 'Pedantry and the Question of Enlightenment History: The Figure of the Antiquary in Scott', *European Romantic Review*, 13 (2002), pp. 199–205.

Ferris, Ina, *The Romantic National Tale and the Question of Ireland* (Cambridge: Cambridge University Press, 2002).

Ferris, Ina, 'Scott's Authorship and Book Culture', in Fiona Robertson (ed.), *The Edinburgh Companion to Sir Walter Scott* (Edinburgh: Edinburgh University Press, 2012), pp. 9–21.

Fieser, James (ed.), *Early Responses to Hume's* History of England, 2nd rev. edn, vol. 1, 2 vols (London: Thoemmes Continuum, 2005).

Foster, E. M., *The Duke of Clarence: An Historical Novel*, 4 vols (London: Minerva, 1795).

Foster, James R., 'The Abbé Prévost and the English Novel', *PMLA* 42 (1927), pp. 443–64.

Frye, Lowell T., 'Romancing the Past: Walter Scott and Thomas Carlyle', *Carlyle Studies Annual* 16 (1996), pp. 37–47.

[Fuller, Anne], *Alan Fitz-Osborne, an Historical Tale*, 2 vols (Dublin: Byrne, 1787).

[Fuller, Anne], *Alan Fitz-Osborne, Roman Historique, Traduit de l'Anglois* (Amsterdam and Paris: Briand, 1789).

[Fuller, Anne], *The Son of Ethelwolf: An Historical Tale*, 2 vols (London: Robinson, 1789).

Furniss, Tom, *Edmund Burke's Aesthetic Ideology: Language, Gender, and Political Economy in Revolution* (Cambridge: Cambridge University Press, 1993).

Gallagher, Noelle, *Historical Literatures: Writing about the Past in England 1660–1740* (Manchester: Manchester University Press, 2012).

Gamer, Michael, *Romanticism and the Gothic: Genre, Reception, and Canon Formation* (Cambridge: Cambridge University Press, 2000).

Garside, Peter, 'The Baron's Books: *Waverley* as a Bibliomanical Romance', *Romanticism* 14.3 (2008), pp. 245–58.

Garside, Peter, 'Popular Fiction and National Tale: Hidden Origins of Scott's *Waverley*', *Nineteenth-Century Literature* 46 (1991), pp. 30–53.

Garside, Peter, 'Scott and the Philosophical Historians', *Journal of the History of Ideas* 36 (1975), pp. 497–512.

Garside, Peter, 'Walter Scott and the "Common" Novel, 1808–1819', *Cardiff Corvey: Reading the Romantic Text* 3 (September 1999), <http://www.cf.ac.uk/encap/corvey/articles/cc03_n02.html> (last accessed 15 January 2015).

Gause, Artemis, 'White, James (1759–1799)', *Oxford Dictionary of National Biography*, <http://www.oxforddnb.com/view/article/29246> (last accessed 20 March 2015).

Gellner, Ernest, *Nations and Nationalism; New Perspectives on the Past*, 2nd edn, intro. John Breuilly (1983; Oxford: Blackwell, 2006).

Genlis, Stéphanie Félicité, *Knights of the Swan*, 2 vols trans. Beresford (London: Johnson, 1796).

Gibbons, Luke, *Edmund Burke and Ireland* (Cambridge: Cambridge University Press, 2003).

Godwin, William, *Caleb Williams*, ed. David McCracken (Oxford: Oxford University Press, 1982).

Godwin, William, *Collected Novels and Memoirs of William Godwin*, 8 vols (London: Pickering, 1992).

Godwin, William, *The Enquirer. Reflections on Education, Manners, and Literature. In a Series of Essays* (London: Robinson, 1797).

Godwin, William, *Enquiry Concerning Political Justice*, 3rd edn, 2 vols (London: Robinson, 1798).

Godwin, William, 'Of History and Romance' in William Godwin, *Things as They Are; Or, the Adventures of Caleb Williams*, ed. Maurice Hindle (London: Penguin, 2005), pp. 359–74.

Godwin, William, *Political Justice*, ed. Mark Philp, vol. 3, *Political and Philosophical Volumes of William Godwin*, 7 vols (London: Pickering, 1993).

Godwin, William, *St Leon*, ed. Pamela Clemit (Oxford: Oxford University Press, 1994).

Goode, Mike, 'Dryasdust Antiquarianism and Soppy Masculinity: The Waverley Novels and the Gender of History', *Representations*, 82 (2003), pp. 52–86.

Gores, Steven John, *Psychosocial Spaces: Verbal/Visual Readings of British Culture, 1750–1820* (Diss. University of Wisconsin, 1991).

Graves, Richard, *Plexippus; Or, the Aspiring Plebeian* (London: Dodsley, 1790).

Green, Sarah, *The Private History of the Court of England*, ed. Fiona Price (1808; London: Pickering and Chatto, 2011).

Grenville, William, '5th March 1783, Fifteenth Parliament of Great Britain: third session (5 December 1782 to 16 July 1783)' in vol. 9, *Parliamentary Register 1780–1796: The Parliamentary Register of History of the Proceedings and Debates of the House of Commons* (5 December 1782 to May 1783), pp. 395–7.

Hamilton, Elizabeth, *Translations of the Letters of a Hindoo Rajah*, ed. Pamela Perkins and Shannon Russell (1796; Peterborough, ON: Broadview, 1999).

Hamilton, Elizabeth, *Memoirs of the Life of Agrippina, the Wife of Germanicus*, 3 vols (London: Robinson, 1804).

Hamilton, Elizabeth, *Memoirs of Modern Philosophers*, ed. Claire Grogan (1800; Peterborough, ON: Broadview, 2000).

Harding, Russell, *David Hume: Moral and Political Theorist* (Oxford: Oxford University Press, 2007).

Hayden, John O., *Walter Scott: The Critical Heritage* (Abingdon: Routledge, 1970).

Hazlitt, William, '35. Hazlitt and the Spirit of the Age', *New Monthly Magazine*, 4 (April 1824) in John O. Hayden (ed.), *Walter Scott* (Abingdon: Routledge, 1970), pp. 279–89.

[Hazlitt, William], '*The Wanderer: Or Female Difficulties*. A Novel by Madame D'Arblay', Edinburgh *Review, or Critical Journal*, vol. 24 (November 1814 to February 1815), pp. 320–38.

Hewitt, Regina, *Symbolic Interactions: Social Problems and Literary Interventions in the Works of Baillie, Scott, and Landon* (Lewisburg: Bucknell University Press, 2006).

Hibbert, Christopher, *George III: A Personal History* (Harmondsworth: Penguin, 1998).

Hilbish, Florence May Anna, *Charlotte Smith, Poet and Novelist (1749–1806)*, DPhil thesis (Philadelphia: The University of Pennsylvania, 1941).

Hill, Bridget, *The Republican Virago: The Life and Times of Catharine Macaulay, Historian* (Oxford: Clarendon Press, 1992).

Hobsbawm, E. J., *Nations and Nationalism since 1780: Programme, Myth, Reality* (Cambridge: Cambridge University Press, 1990).

Hodson, Jane, *Language and Revolution: Burke, Paine, Wollstonecraft* (Aldershot: Ashgate, 2007).

Hogg, James, *Familiar Anecdotes of Sir Walter Scott* (New York: Harper, 1834).

Home, John, *Douglas A Tragedy* (Edinburgh: Hamilton and Balfour, 1757).

Hume, David, *Enquiries Concerning Human Understanding and Concerning the Principles of Morals*, ed. L. A. Selby-Bigge and P. H. Nidditch, 3rd edn (1777; Oxford: Clarendon Press, 1975).

Hume, David, *Essays Moral, Political and Literary*, ed. Eugene F. Miller, 3rd edn (1777; Indianapolis: Liberty Fund, 1985).

Hume, David, *History of England from the Invasion of Julius Caesar to the Revolution of 1688* (1754–1762), foreword William B. Todd, 6 vols (1778; Indianapolis: Liberty Fund, 1983).

Hume, Robert D., 'Introduction', in *Longsword, Earl of Salisbury, An Historical Romance*, by Thomas Leland (New York: Arno Press, 1974), i–xxiii.

Hunt, Lynn, 'The Rhetoric of Revolution in France', *History Workshop* 15 (1983), pp. 78–94.

Hurd, Richard, *Letters on Chivalry and Romance* (London: Millar; Cambridge: Thurlbourne and Woodyear, 1762).

Hurd, Richard, *Moral and Political Dialogues: Being the Substance of Several Conversations between Divers Eminent Persons of the Past and Present Age; Digested by the Parties Themselves, and with Critical and Explanatory Notes by the Editor* (London: Millar; Cambridge: Thurlborne and Woodyer, 1759).

Irvine, Robert P., 'Gender and the Place of Culture in Scott's St Ronan's Well', *Scottish Studies Review*, 2.1 (2001), pp. 46–64.

Jameson, Frederic, *The Seeds of Time* (New York: Columbia University Press, 1994).

Jasper, Collin, 'A Poetics of Dissent; or, Pantisocracy in America', *Theory and Event* 10.1 (2007), <http://muse.jhu.edu/journals/theory_and_event/v010/10.1jager.html> (last accessed 12 March 2015).

Johnson, Claudia, *Equivocal Beings: Politics, Gender and Sentimentality in the 1790s* (Chicago: University of Chicago Press, 1995).

Johnson, Claudia, *Jane Austen: Women, Politics and the Novel* (Chicago: University of Chicago Press, 1988).

Johns-Putra, Adeline, '"Blending Science with Literature": The Royal Institution, Eleanor Anne Porden, and *The Veils*', *Nineteenth-Century Context* 33.1 (2011), pp. 35–52.

Johns-Putra, Adeline, 'Eleanor Anne Porden's *Coeur de Lion* (1822): History, Epic and Romance', *Women's Writing* 19.3 (2012), pp. 350–71.

Johnston, Arthur, *Enchanted Ground: The Study of Medieval Romance in the Eighteenth Century* (London: Athlone Press, 1964).

Jones, Chris, *Radical Sensibility: Literature and Ideas in the 1790s* (London: Routledge, 1993).

Kahn, Madeleine, 'Hannah More and Ann Yearsley: A Collaboration across the Class Divide', *Studies in Eighteenth-Century Culture* 25 (1996), pp. 203–23.

Kamps, Ivo, *Historiography and Ideology in Stuart Drama* (Cambridge: Cambridge University Press, 2009).

Kasmer, Lisa, *Novel Histories: British Women Writing History, 1760–1830* (Lanham, MD: Fairleigh Dickinson University Press, 2012).

Kavanagh, Thomas M., *Enlightenment and the Shadows of Chance: The Novel and the Culture of Gambling in Eighteenth-Century France* (Baltimore: Johns Hopkins University Press, 1993).

Kelly, Gary, 'Clara Reeve, Provincial Bluestocking: From the Old Whigs to the Modern Liberal State', in Nicole Pohl and Betty A. Schellenberg (eds), *Reconsidering the Bluestockings* (San Marino: Huntington Library, 2003), pp.105–25.

Kelly, Gary, *English Fiction of the Romantic Period, 1789–1830* (London: Longman, 1989).

Kelly, Gary, *Varieties of Female Gothic*, 6 vols (London: Pickering and Chatto, 2002).

Kelly, Gary, *Women, Writing, and Revolution 1790–1827* (Oxford: Clarendon, 1993).

Kendrick, T. F. J., 'Sir Robert Walpole, the old Whigs and the Bishops, 1733–1736: A Study in Eighteenth-Century Parliamentary Politics', *The Historical Journal* 9 (1968), pp. 421–45.

Kent, John, *Wesley and the Wesleyans: Religion in Eighteenth-Century Britain* (Cambridge: Cambridge University Press, 2002).

Ketton-Cremer, R. W., *Horace Walpole: A Biography* (Ithaca: Cornell University Press, 1966).

Kidd, Colin, *British Identities before Nationalism: Ethnicity and Nationhood in the Atlantic World, 1600–1800* (Cambridge: Cambridge University Press, 1999).

King, Edward, *Essay on the English Constitution and Government* (1767), in [Tobias George Smollett], *The Critical Review or, Annals of Literature* 22 (1766), pp. 362–4.

Klancher, John, 'Godwin and the Genre Reformers: On Necessity and Contingency in Romantic Narrative Theory', in Tilottama Rajan and Julia M. Wright (eds), *Romanticism, History and the Possibilities of Genre* (Cambridge: Cambridge University Press, 1998).

Klancher, John, 'Godwin and the Republican Romance', in Marshall Brown (ed.), *Eighteenth-Century Literary History: An MLQ Reader* (Durham: Duke University Press, 1999), pp. 68–86.

Knight, E[llis] Cornelia, *Marcus Flaminius; Or, a View of the Military, Political and Social Life of the Romans; In a Series of Letters from a Patrician to His Friend*, 2nd edn, 2 vols (1792; London: Cadell and Davies, 1808).

Knox, Kevin C., 'Lunatick Visions: Prophecy, Signs and Scientific Knowledge in 1790s London', *History of Science* 37.4 (1999), pp. 427–58.

Kramnick, Isaac, *Bolingbroke and His Circle: The Politics of Nostalgia in the Age of Walpole* (Ithaca: Cornell University Press, 1992).

Labbe, Jacqueline, *The Romantic Paradox: Love, Violence and the Uses of Romance 1760–1830* (Basingstoke: Macmillan, 2000).

Lang, Andrew, intro. *Waverley* by Walter Scott (London: Nimmo, 1892).

Larrissy, Edward, *The Blind and Blindness in Literature of the Romantic Period* (Edinburgh: Edinburgh University Press, 2007).

Lee, Sophia, *The Recess: Or, A Tale of Other Times*, ed. April Alliston (Lexington: University Press of Kentucky, 2000).

Lee, Sophia (trans.), *Warbeck: A Pathetic Tale. Translated by the Author of* The Recess, [by François Thomas Baculard d'Arnaud], 2 vols (Dublin: Colbert, 1786).

Lee, Yoon Sun, *Nationalism and Irony: Burke, Scott, Carlyle* (New York: Oxford University Press, 2004).

Leerssen, J. Th., 'Fiction, Poetics and Cultural Stereotype; Local Colour in Scott, Morgan, and Maturin', *Modern Language Review* 86 (1991), pp. 273–84.

Lefebvre, Georges, *The French Revolution: From Its Origins to 1793* (London: Routledge, 2001).

Leland, Thomas, *A Dissertation on the Principles of Human Eloquence: With Particular Regard to the Style and Composition of the New Testament* (London: Johnston, 1764).

Leland, Thomas, *A History of Ireland from the Invasion of Henry II, with a Preliminary Discourse on the Ancient State of that Kingdom*, 3 vols (Dublin: Marchbank, 1773).

Leland, Thomas, *Longsword, Earl of Salisbury: An Historical Romance*, 2 vols (Dublin: Faulkner, 1762).

Leland, Thomas (trans.), *The Orations of Demosthenes: Pronounced to Excite the Athenians against Philip, King of Macedon*, 2 vols (1754; London: Whittaker et al., 1819).

Lewis, Jayne Elizabeth, '"Ev'ry Lost Relation": Historical Fictions and Sentimental Incidents in Sophia Lee's *The Recess*', *Eighteenth-Century Fiction* 7 (1995), pp. 165–84.

Lincoln, Andrew, *Walter Scott and Modernity* (Edinburgh: Edinburgh University Press, 2007).

Lockhart, J. G., *The Life of Sir Walter Scott* (London: Dent, 1906).

Loeber, Rolf, Magda Loeber, with Anne M. Burham, (eds), *A Guide to Irish Fiction, 1650–1900, An Electronic Version of A Guide to Irish Fiction, 1650–1900* (Dublin: Four Courts P, 2006), <http://www.lgif.ie/authorDetails. action?authorId=1170> (last accessed 22 March 2015).

Logan, *Runnamede, A Tragedy* (London: Robinson; Edinburgh: Creech, 1784).

Lokke, Kari, 'Charlotte Smith's *Desmond*: The Historical Novel as Social Protest', *Women's Writing* 16.1 (2009), pp. 60–77.

'*Longsword*', *Critical Review* 13 (March 1762), pp. 252–7.

Looser, Devoney, *British Women Writers and the Writing of History 1670–1820* (Baltimore: Johns Hopkins University Press, 2000).

Looser, Devoney, 'The Great Man and Women's Historical Fiction: Jane Porter and Sir Sidney Smith', *Women's Writing* 19.3 (2012), pp. 293–314.

Lukács, Georg, *The Historical Novel* (1937), trans. Hannah and Stanley Mitchell (London: Merlin Press, 1962).

Mack, Ruth, 'Horace Walpole and the Objects of Literary History', *ELH* 75.2 (2008), pp. 367–87.

Mack, Ruth, *Literary Historicity: Literature and Historical Experience in Eighteenth-Century Britain* (Stanford: Stanford University Press, 2009).

[Mackenzie, Anna Maria], *Danish Massacre: An Historic Fact*, 2 vols (London: Minerva, 1791).

Mackenzie, Anna Maria, *Feudal Events or, Days of Yore*, 2 vols (London: Minerva, 1800).

[Mackenzie, Anna Maria], *Monmouth: A Tale, Founded on Historic Facts*, 3 vols (London: Lane, 1790).

[Mackenzie, Anna Maria], *Mysteries Elucidated: A Novel*, 3 vols (London: Minerva Press, 1795).

Mackenzie, Anna Maria, *Swedish Mysteries; Or, the Hero of the Mines*, 3 vols (London: Minerva Press, 1801).

Macpherson, James, *The Poems of Ossian and Related Works*, ed. Howard Gaskill (Edinburgh: Edinburgh University Press, 1996).

MacQueen, John, *The Rise of the Historical Novel* (Edinburgh: Scottish Academic Press, 1989).

'The Magic Banner; Or, Two Wives in a House', *Monthly Mirror* 2 (1796), p. 119.

Manning, Susan, 'Antiquarianism, the Scottish Science of Man, and the Emergence of Modern Disciplinarity', in Leith Davis, Ian Duncan, and Janet Sorensen (eds), *Scotland and the Borders of Romanticism* (Cambridge: Cambridge University Press, 2004), pp. 57–76.

Marx, Karl, *Grundrisse: Foundations of the Critique of Political Economy*, trans. Martin Nicolaus (London: Penguin, 1973).

Marx, Karl, *Survey From Exile*, in David Fernbach (ed.), *Political Writings*, vol. 2 (Harmondsworth: Penguin, in association with *New Left Review*, 1973).

Maxwell, Caroline, *Alfred of Normandy: Or, the Ruby Cross, An Historical Romance*, 2 vols (London: Seale, 1808).

Maxwell, Richard, 'The Historical Novel', in Richard Maxwell and Katie Trumpener (eds), *The Cambridge Companion to Fiction in the Romantic Period* (Cambridge: Cambridge University Press, 2008), pp. 65–87.

Maxwell, Richard, *The Historical Novel in Europe, 1650–1950* (Cambridge: Cambridge University Press, 2009).

Maxwell, Richard, 'Phantom States: *Cleveland, The Recess*, and the Origins of Historical Fiction,' in Margaret Cohen and Carolyn Dever (eds), *The Literary Channel: The Inter-National Invention of the Novel* (Princeton: Princeton University Press, 2002), pp. 151–82.

Maxwell, Richard, 'Pretenders in Sanctuary', *Modern Language Quarterly: A Journal of Literary History* 61 (2000), pp. 287–358.

Mayer, Robert, 'The Illogical Status of Novelistic Discourse: Scott's Footnotes for the Waverley Novels', *ELH* 66.4 (1999), pp. 911–38.

McCracken-Flesher, Caroline, *Possible Scotlands: Walter Scott and the Story of Tomorrow* (Oxford: Oxford University Press, 2005).

McGeough, Jared, 'Unlimited Questioning: The Literary Anarchism of William Godwin', *Studies in the Literary Imagination* 45.2 (2012), pp. 1–25.

McLean, Thomas 'Jane Porter, Edmund Kean, and the Tragedy of Switzerland', *Keats-Shelley Review* 25.2 (2011), pp. 147–59.

McLean, Thomas, 'Nobody's Argument: Jane Porter and the Historical Novel', *Journal for Early Modern Cultural Studies* 7.2 (2007), pp. 88–103.

McMaster, Graham, *Scott and Society* (Cambridge: Cambridge University Press, 1981).

Mee, Jon, '"The Uses of Conversation": William Godwin's Conversable World and Romantic Sociability', *SiR* 50.4 (2011), pp. 567–90.

'Memoirs of Sir Roger de Clarendon', *Critical Review* 2nd ser. 10 (March 1794), p. 281.

Mhunghaile, Lesa Ní, 'Anglo-Irish Antiquarianism and the Transformation of Irish Identity, 1750–1800', in David A. Valone and Jill Marie Bradbury (eds), *Anglo-Irish Identities, 1571–1845* (Cranbury: Associate University Press, 2008), pp. 181–98.

Miles, Robert, 'The Gothic and Ideology', in Diane Long Hoeveler and Tamar Heller (eds), *Gothic Fiction: The British and American Traditions* (New York: MLA, 2003), pp. 58–65.

Millikin, Anna, *Corfe Castle; Or, Historic Tracts. A Novel*, 2 vols (Cork: Haly, 1793).

Millikin, Anna, *Eva, an Old Irish Story* (Cork: Connor, 1795).

Mohr, Hans Ulrich, 'The Picturesque: A Key Concept of the Eighteenth Century', in Frederick Burwick and Jurgen Klein (eds), *The Romantic Imagination: Literature and Art in England and Germany* (Amsterdam: Rodopi, 1996), pp. 240–85.

Monod, Paul Kléber, *Jacobitism and the English People 1688–1788* (Cambridge: Cambridge University Press, 1989).

Moore, Dafydd, '"Caledonian Plagiary": The Role and Meaning of Ireland in the Poems of *Ossian*', in Ben Dew and Fiona Price (eds), *Historical Writing in Britain 1688–1830: Visions of History* (Basingstoke: Palgrave, 2014), pp. 92–108.

Moretti, Franco, *Graphs, Maps, Trees: Abstract Models for Literary History* (London: Verso, 2005).

Morris, David B, 'Gothic Sublimity', *New Literary History* 16 (1985), pp. 299–319.

Mowl, Timothy, *Horace Walpole: The Great Outsider* (London: Murray, 1996).

Muir, Edwin, *Scott and Scotland: The Predicament of the Scottish Writer* (London: Routledge, 1936).

Murry, Ann, *Mentoria; or the Young Ladies Instructor: In Familiar Conversations on Moral and Entertaining Subjects*, 8th edn (1778; London: Dilly, 1796).

Myers, Victoria, 'William Godwin and the *Ars Rhetorica*', *SiR* 41.3 (2002), pp. 415–44.

Nordius, Janina, '*Gustavas Vasus* in a Gothic Mirror: Anna Maria Mackenzie's *Swedish Mysteries*', *Moderna Språch* 101 (2007), pp. 9–22.

Nordius, Janina, 'A Tale of Other Places: Sophia Lee's *The Recess* and Colonial Gothic', *Studies in the Novel* 2002 (34), pp. 162–76.

'Obituary of Eminent Persons, *Gentleman's Magazine* 60.2 (July 1790), p. 669.

O'Brien, Karen, *Narratives of Enlightenment: Cosmopolitan History from Voltaire to Gibbon* (Cambridge: Cambridge University Press, 1997).

O'Brien, Karen, *Women and Enlightenment in Eighteenth-Century Britain* (Cambridge: Cambridge University Press, 2009).

O'Halloran, Clare, *Golden Ages and Barbarous Ages: Antiquarian Debate and Cultural Politics in Ireland c.1750–1800* (Cork: Cork University Press, 2004).

O'Halloran, Clare, 'Irish Re-Creations of the Gaelic Past: The Challenge of Macpherson's Ossian', *Past and Present* 124 (1989), pp. 69–95.

O'Halloran, Sylvester, *An Introduction to and a History of Ireland* (Dublin: Fitzpatrick, 1803).

Owenson, Sydney, Lady Morgan, *Florence Macarthy: An Irish Tale*, 4 vols (London: Colburn, 1818).

[Owenson, Sydney], Lady Morgan, *O'Donnel; A National Tale*, 3 vols (London: Colburn, 1815).

Owenson, Sydney, Lady Morgan, *The Wild Irish Girl; A National Tale* (1806), ed. Kathryn Kirkpatrick (Oxford: Oxford University Press, 1999).

Paine, Thomas, *Political Writings*, ed. Bruce Kuklick (Cambridge: Cambridge University Press, 2000).

Percy, Thomas, *Reliques of Ancient English Poetry* (1765; London: Dent 1906).

Perovic, Sanja, 'The French Revolutionary Calendar: Time, History and the Revolutionary Event', *Journal of Eighteenth-Century Studies* 35.1 (2012), pp. 1–16.

Phillips, Helen, 'Scott and the Outlaws', in Helen Phillips (ed.), *Bandit Territories: British Outlaws and Their Traditions* (Cardiff: University of Wales Press, 2008), pp. 119–42.

Phillips, Mark Salber, *Society and Sentiment: Genres of Historical Writing in Britain, 1740–1820* (Princeton: Princeton University Press, 2000).

Pittock, Murray G. H., 'Scott as Historiographer: The Case of Waverley', in J. H. Alexander and David Hewitt (eds), *Scott in Carnival* (Aberdeen: Association for Scottish Literary Studies, 1993).

Pocock, J. G. A., 'The Origins of Study of the Past: A Comparative Approach', *Comparative Studies in Society and History* 4 (1962), pp. 209–64.

Pocock, J. G. A., *Virtue, Commerce, and History: Essays on Political Thought and History, Chiefly in the Eighteenth Century* (Cambridge: Cambridge University Press, 1985).

Porter, Anna Maria, *Don Sebastian, or, the House of Braganza. An Historical Romance*, 4 vols (London: Longman et al., 1809).

Porter, Anna Maria, *The Hungarian Brothers*, 3rd edn, 3 vols (1807; London: Longman, Hurst, Rees, Orme, and Brown, 1814).

Porter, Anna Maria, *The Hungarian Brothers*, Standard Novel Edition vol. 11 (1807; London: Coburn and Bentley, 1832).

Porter, Anna Maria, *The Knight of St. John, A Romance*, 2 vols (Philadelphia: Thomas, 1817).

Porter, Jane, letter to Anna Maria Porter, 20 February 1820, MS, Jane Porter Papers POR1781, Huntington Library, CA.

Porter, Jane, letter to Anna Maria Porter, 24 February 1820, Brighton, MS, Jane Porter Papers POR1782, Huntington Library, CA.

Porter, Jane, letter to Anna Maria Porter, July [18–19] 1812, Bristol, MS, Jane Porter Papers POR1665, Huntington Library, CA.

Porter, Jane, letter to Robert Ker Porter, 23 September 1821, Long Ditton, Surrey, MS, Jane Porter Papers, POR2045, Huntington Library, CA.

Porter, Jane, *The Scottish Chiefs, A Romance*, ed. Fiona Price (1810; Peterborough, ON: Broadview Press, 2006).

Porter, Jane, *Thaddeus of Warsaw*, intro. Jane Porter, Standard Novels 4 (1803; London: Colburn and Bentley; Edinburgh: Bell and Bradfute; Dublin: Cumming, 1831).

Porter, Sir Robert Ker, 'Buonaparte Massacreing Fifteen Hundred Persons at Toulon', Brown University Library Centre for Digital Scholarship Digital Collections FrBH 1794–9 mf1a <http://library.brown.edu/cds/repository2/repoman.php?verb=render&id=1130155700437506&view=showmods> (last accessed 25 March 2015).

Pownall, General, *An Antiquarian Romance, Endeavouring to Mark a Line, by Which the Most Ancient People, and the Processions of the Earliest Inhabitancy of Europe, May Be Investigated* (London: John Nichols, 1795).

[Prévost d'Exiles, Antoine François], *The Life and Entertaining Adventures of Mr. Cleveland, Natural Son of Oliver Cromwell, Written by Himself*, 5 vols (London: Astley, 1734).

Price, Fiona, '"A Great Deal of History": Romantic Women Writers and Historical Fiction', *Women's Writing* 19.3 (2012), pp. 259–72.

Price, Fiona, 'Making History: Social Unrest, Work and the Post-French Revolution Historical Novel', in Ben Dew and Fiona Price (eds), *Historical Writing in Britain 1688–1830: Visions of History* (Basingstoke: Palgrave, 2014), pp. 145–61.

Price, Richard, *A Discourse on the Love of Our Country*, 2nd edn (1789; London: Cadell, 1790).

Priestley, Joseph, *An Appeal to the Public, on the Subject of the Riots in Birmingham*, part 2 (London: Johnson, 1792).

Priestley, Joseph, *The History and Present State of Electricity, with Original Experiments* (1767), 2nd edn (London: Johnson and Davenport, 1767).

Priestley, Joseph, *Lectures on History and General Policy* (London: Tegg, 1826).

Punter, David, *The Literature of Terror: A History of Gothic Fictions from 1765 to the Present Day* (London: Longman, 1996).

Radcliffe, Ann, *Gaston de Blondeville or, the Court of Henry III keeping Festival in Ardenne*, ed. Frances Chiu (Chicago: Valancourt, 2006).

Rajan, Tilottama, *Romantic Narrative: Shelley, Hays, Godwin, Wollstonecraft* (Baltimore: Johns Hopkins University Press, 2010).

Rancière, Jacques, *Proletarian Nights: The Worker's Dream in Nineteenth-Century France* (1981; London: Verso, 2012).

'The Recess', *Critical Review* 55 (March 1783), p. 233.

'The Recess', *Monthly Review* 75 (August 1786), pp. 134–5.

Reeve, Clara, *Destination: Or, Memoirs of a Private Family*, 3 vols (London: Longman and Rees, 1799).

Reeve, Clara, *Memoirs of Sir Roger de Clarendon*, 3 vols (London: Hookham and Carpenter, 1793).

Reeve, Clara, *The Old English Baron: A Gothic Story*, ed. James Trainer (1778; Oxford: Oxford University Press, 1977).

Reeve, Clara, *The Progress of Romance, through Times, Countries, and Manners; With Remarks on the Good and Bad Effects of It, on Them Respectively; In a Course of Evening Conversations*, 2 vols (Colchester: for the author by Keymer; [London]: Robinson, 1785).

Rendall, Jane, '"The Grand Causes which Combine to Carry Mankind Forward": Wollstonecraft, History and Revolution', *Women's Writing* 4 (1997), pp. 155–77.

Richardson, Thomas C., 'Thomas Carlyle on Sir Walter Scott', *Carlyle Society Papers* 6 (1992–3), pp. 27–38.

Rigney, Ann, *Imperfect Histories: The Illusive Past and the Legacy of Romantic Historicism* (Ithaca: Cornell University Press, 2001).

[Ritson, Joseph], *Robin Hood: A Collection of All the Ancient Poems, Songs and Ballads Now Extant Relative to that Celebrated English Outlaw: To Which Are Prefixed Historical Anecdotes of His Life*, 2 vols (London: Egerton and Johnson, 1795).

Robertson, Fiona, *Legitimate Histories: Scott, Gothic and the Authorities of Fiction* (Oxford: Clarendon, 1994).

Robertson, Fiona, 'Romancing and Romanticism', in Fiona Robertson (ed.), *The Edinburgh Companion to Sir Walter Scott* (Edinburgh: Edinburgh University Press, 2012), pp. 93–105.

Robertson, John, 'Universal Monarchy and the Liberties of Europe: David Hume's Critique of an English Whig Doctrine', in Nicholas Phillipson and Quentin Skinner (eds), *Political Discourse in Early Modern Britain* (Cambridge: Cambridge University Press, 1993), pp. 349–73.

Robertson, William, *History of the Reign of the Emperor Charles V* (1769), 3 vols (Dublin: Whitestone et al., 1777).

Robertson, William, *The History of Scotland during the Reigns of Queen Mary and of King James VI. Till His Accession to the Crown of England. With a Review of the Scottish History Previous to that Period; And an Appendix Containing Original Papers*, 14th edn, 2 vols (London: Cadell, 1794).

Rogers, Katharine M., 'Inhibitions on Eighteenth-Century Women Novelists Elizabeth Inchbald and Charlotte Smith', *Eighteenth-Century Studies* 11.1 (1997), pp. 63–79.

Rooney, Morgan, *The French Revolution Debate and the British Historical Novel, 1790–1814: The Struggle for History's Authority* (Lanham, MD: Rowman & Littlefield, 2013).

Rousseau, Jean-Jacques, *Emile: Or on Education* (1762), trans. and intro. Allan Bloom (London: Penguin, 1991).

Rowlinson, Matthew, *Real Money and Romanticism* (Cambridge: Cambridge University Press, 2010).

Rudé, George, *The Crowd in the French Revolution* (Oxford: Oxford University Press, 1959).

Rudé, George, 'Prices, Wages and Popular Movements in Paris during the French Revolution', *Economic History Review* NS 6.3 (1994), pp. 246–67.

Rudé, George, 'La Taxation populaire de mai 1775 à Paris et dans la région parisienne', *AHFR* 143 (1956), pp. 139–79.

Samson, John, 'Politics Gothicized: The Conway Incident and *The Castle of Otranto*', *Eighteenth-Century Life* 10 (1986), pp. 145–58.

Sanders, Andrew, '"Utter Indifference"?: The Anglo-Saxons in the Nineteenth-Century Novel', in Donald Scragg and Carole Weinberg (eds), *Literary Appropriations of the Anglo-Saxons from the Thirteenth to the Twentieth Century* (Cambridge: Cambridge University Press, 2000), pp. 157–73.

Sanderson, William A., *A Compleat History of the Lives and Reigns of Mary Queen of Scotland, and of Her Son and Successor, James the Sixth, King of Scotland* (London: Moseley, Tomlins, and Sawbridge, 1656).

Schmidt, Claudia M., *David Hume: Reason in History* (University Park: Penn State University Press, 2003).

Schoenfield, Mark, 'Waging Battle: Ashford v. Thornton, *Ivanhoe* and *Legal Violence*', *Prose Studies* 23 (2000), pp. 61–86.

Scott, A., Citizen and Hairdresser, *Plain Reasons for Adopting the Plan of the Societies Calling Themselves the Friends of the People, and Their Convention of Delegates, as Copied from the Works of Mr Thos Paine. In a Serious Address to the Citizens of Edinburgh* (Edinburgh: John Balfour, 1793).

Scott, Walter, *The Antiquary*, ed. Nicola Watson (1816; Oxford: Oxford University Press, 2002).

Scott, Walter, *Essay on Chivalry* (1818) in *Essays on Chivalry, Romance, and the Drama* (Edinburgh: Cadell, 1834), pp. 1–126.

Scott, Walter, *Guy Mannering*, intro. Jane Millgate, ed. Peter Garside (1815; Harmondsworth: Penguin, 2003).

Scott, Walter *Ivanhoe*, ed. Ian Duncan (1819; Oxford: Oxford University Press, 2008).

Scott, Walter, *Lives of Eminent Novelists and Dramatists*, rev. edn Chandos Classics (London: Warne; New York: Scribner, Welford and Armstrong, n.d.).

Scott, Walter, *Quentin Durward*, ed. Susan Manning (1823; Oxford: Oxford University Press, 1992).

Scott, Walter, *St Ronan's Well*, ed. Andrew Lang (Boston: Dane Estes, 1894).

Scott, Walter, *St Ronan's Well*, ed. Mark Weinstein (Edinburgh: Edinburgh University Press, 1995).

Scott, Walter, *Waverley; Or, 'Tis Sixty Years Since*, ed. Claire Lamont (1814; Oxford: Oxford University Press, 1986).

Seaman, L. C. B., *Victorian England: Aspects of English and Imperial History, 1837–1901* (London: Routledge, 2002).

Shaftesbury, 3rd Earl of, Anthony Ashley Cooper, *Characteristics of Men, Manners, Opinions, Times* (1711), ed. Lawrence E. Klein, Cambridge Texts in the History of Philosophy (Cambridge: Cambridge University Press, 1999).

Shaw, Philip, 'Walter Scott: The Discipline of History', in *Waterloo and the Romantic Imagination* (Basingstoke; New York: Palgrave Macmillan, 2002), pp. 35–66.

Shields, Juliet, *Sentimental Literature and Anglo-Scottish Identity, 1745–1820* (Cambridge: Cambridge University Press, 2015).

Siddons, Henry, *William Wallace: Or, the Highland Hero. A Tale, Founded on Historical Facts*, 2 vols (London: Wilkie, 1791).

Smith, Adam, *Theory of Moral Sentiments*, ed. D. D. Raphael and A. L. Macfie (Oxford: Clarendon Press, 1976).

Smith, Charlotte, *Desmond*, ed. Antje Blank and Janet Todd (Peterborough, ON: Broadview Press, 2001).

Smith, Charlotte, *Ethelinde or the Recluse of the Lake*, 5 vols (London: Cadell, 1789).

Smith, Charlotte, *Minor Morals, Interspersed with Sketches of Natural History, Historical Anecdotes, and Original Stories*, 2 vols, 2nd edn (London: Sampson Low, 1799).

Smyth, Jim, 'Wolfe Tone's Library: The United Irishmen and "Enlightenment"', *Eighteenth-Century Studies* 45 (2012), pp. 423–35.

'*The Son of Ethelwolf*', *Allegemeine Literatur-Zeitung* 82 (March 1792), p. 650.

'*The Son of Ethelwolf: An Historical Tale*', *Monthly Review* 81 (September 1789), pp. 239–40.

'*St. Ronan's Well*', *British Critic*, vol. 22 (January 1824), pp. 16–26.

Stevens, Anne H., *British Historical Fiction before Scott* (Basingstoke: Palgrave, 2012).

Stevens, Anne H., 'Tales of Other Times: A Survey of British Historical Fiction 1770–1812', *Cardiff Corvey: Reading the Romantic Text* 7 (December 2001), <http://www.cf.ac.uk/encap/corvey/articles/cc07_n03.html> (last accessed 3 September 2010).

Sweet, Rosemary, *Antiquaries: The Discovery of the Past in Eighteenth-Century Britain* (London: Continuum, 2004).

Tacitus, *The Agricola* and *The Germania*, trans. and intro. H. Mattingly, rev. trans. S. A. Handford (London: Penguin, 1970).

Tarling, Barbara, '"The Slight Skirmishing of a Novel Writer": Charlotte Smith and the American War of Independence', in Jacqueline Labbe (ed.), *Charlotte Smith in British Romanticism*, The Enlightenment World 5 (London: Pickering and Chatto, 2008), pp. 71–86.

Tessone, Natasha, 'Displaying Ireland: Sydney Owenson and the Politics of Spectacular Antiquarianism', *Eire-Ireland: A Journal of Irish Studies* 3/4 (2002), pp. 169–86.

Tessone, Natasha, 'Entailing the Nation: Inheritance and History in Walter Scott's *The Antiquary*', *Studies in Romanticism* 51.2 (2012), pp. 149–77.

Thame, David, 'Cooking up a Story: Jane West, Prudentia Homespun, and the Consumption of Fiction', *Eighteenth-Century Fiction* 16 (2004), pp. 217–42.

Thuente, Mary Helen, 'Lady Morgan's Beavoin O'Flaherty: Ancient Irish Goddess and Enlightenment Cosmopolitanism', *New Hibernia Review* 16.2 (2012), pp. 33–53.

Tompkins, J. M. S., 'James White, Esq: A Forgotten Humourist', *The Review of English Studies* 3.10 (1927), pp. 146–56.

Trumpener, Katie, *Bardic Nationalism: The Romantic Novel and the British Empire* (Princeton: Princeton University Press, 1997).

Tytler, W., *An Inquiry, Historical and Critical, into the Evidence against Mary Queen of Scots. And an Examination of the Histories of Dr. Robertson and Mr Hume, with Respect to that Evidence*, 3rd edn (Edinburgh: Drummond; London: Owen, Dilly, Cadell, Richardson and Urquhart, and Wilson, 1772).

Von Ranke, Leopold, 'Autobiographical Dictation' (November 1885), in Roger Wines (ed.), *Leopold von Ranke: The Secret of World History; Selected Writings on the Art and Science of History* (New York: Fordham University Press, 1981).

Von Ranke, Leopold, 'Introduction', to *History of the Latin and Teutonic Nations* in Roger Wines (ed.), *Leopold von Ranke: The Secret of World History; Selected Writings on the Art and Science of History* (New York: Fordham University Press, 1981).

Wall, Cynthia, 'The Castle of Otranto: A Shakespeareo-Political Satire?' in Lorna Clymer and Robert Mayer (eds), *Historical Boundaries, Narrative Forms: Essays on British Literature in the Long Eighteenth Century* (Newark: University of Delaware Press, 2007), pp. 184–98.

Wall, Cynthia, '"Chasms in the Story": Sophia Lee's *The Recess* and David Hume's *History of England*', in Rivka Swensen and Elise Lauterbach (eds), *Imagining Selves: Essays in Honor of Patricia Meyer Spacks* (Newark: University of Delaware Press, 2008), pp. 21–40.

Wallace, Tara Ghosal, 'Rewriting Radicalism: Wollstonecraft in Burney's *The Wanderer*', *Eighteenth-Century Fiction* 24.3 (2012), pp. 487–508.

Walpole, Horace, *The Castle of Otranto: A Gothic Story*, ed. W. S. Lewis, intro. Emma Clery (Oxford: Oxford University Press, 1998).

Walpole, Horace, *Memoirs of the Reign of King George the Third*, ed. G. F. Russell Barker, 4 vols (New York, 1894).

Walpole, Horace, *The Yale Edition of Horace Walpole's Correspondence*, ed. W. S. Lewis et al., 48 vols (Oxford: Oxford University Press, 1937–83).

Walpole, Horace and Thomas Park, *A Catalogue of the Royal and Noble Authors of England, Scotland, and Ireland: With Lists of Their Works*, vol. 5 (London: John Scott, 1806).

Watkins, John, *Representing Elizabeth in Stuart England: Literature, History, Sovereignty* (Cambridge: Cambridge University Press, 2002).

Watson, Nicola J., *Revolution and the Form of the British Novel 1790–1825: Intercepted Letters, Interrupted Seductions* (Oxford: Clarendon Press, 1994).

Watt, James, *Contesting the Gothic: Fiction, Genre and Cultural Conflict, 1764–1832* (Cambridge: Cambridge University Press, 1999).

Wein, Toni, *British Identities, Heroic Nationalisms, and the Gothic Novel, 1764–1824* (Basingstoke: Palgrave Macmillan, 2002).

Wein, Toni, 'Tangled Webs: Horace Walpole and the Practice of History in *The Castle of Otranto*', *ELN* 35 (1998), pp. 12–22.

West, Jane, *Alicia de Lacy: An Historical Romance*, 4 vols (London: Longman, 1814).

West, Jane, *Letters Addressed to a Young Man, on His First Entrance into Life, Adapted to the Peculiar Circumstances of the Present Times*, 3 vols (London: Longman and Rees, 1801).

West, Jane, *The Loyalists: An Historical Novel*, 2nd edn, 3 vols (London: Longman, Hurst, Rees, Orme and Brown, 1812).

West, Jane, *The Refusal*, 3 vols (London: Longman, Hurst, Rees and Orme, 1810).

Wheeler-Manwaring, Elizabeth, *Italian Landscape in Eighteenth-Century England: A Study Chiefly of the Influence of Claude Lorrain and Salvator Rosa on English Taste, 1700–1800* (New York: Russell, 1965).

Whitaker, John, *Gibbon's History of the Decline and Fall of the Roman Empire, Volumes IV, V, VI Reviewed* (London: Murray, 1791).

White, Daniel E., *Early Romanticism and Religious Dissent* (Cambridge: Cambridge University Press, 2006).

White, James, *The Adventures of John of Gaunt, Duke of Lancaster*, 3 vols (London: Crowder for Robinson, 1790).

White, James, *The Adventures of Richard Coeur de Lion*, 3 vols (London: Evans, 1791).

[White, James], *Earl Strongbow; Or, the History of Richard de Clare and the Beautiful Geralda*, 2 vols (Dublin: Byrne, White, Wogan et al., 1789).

Whitehouse, John, *Poems: Consisting Chiefly of Original Pieces* (London: Blyth, 1787).

Wikborg, Eleanor, 'Political Discourse versus Sentimental Romance: Ideology and Genre in Charlotte Smith's *Desmond* (1792)', *English Studies* 6 (1997), pp. 522–31.

[Wilkes, John], ed. *The North Britain; From No. 1 to No. 46 Inclusive* (London: Bingley, 1769).

'William Wallace', *The Critical Review, or Annals of Literature* 3 (1791), p. 235.

Williams, Ioan, ed. *Novel and Romance 1700–1800: A Documentary Record* (London: Routledge, 1970).

Wilt, Judith, *Secret Leaves: The Novels of Walter Scott* (Chicago: University of Chicago Press, 1985).

Wollstonecraft, Mary, *Political Writings: A Vindication of the Rights of Men; A Vindication of the Rights of Woman; An Historical and Moral View of the French Revolution*, ed. Janet Todd (Oxford: Oxford University Press, 1994).

Wollstonecraft, Mary, *The Works of Mary Wollstonecraft*, ed. Janet Todd and Marilyn Butler, 7 vols (London: Pickering, 1989).

Womersley, David, *Gibbon and 'The Watchmen of the Holy City': The Historian and His Reputation, 1776–1815* (Oxford: Oxford University Press, 2002).

Wood, Lisa, 'Bachelors and "Old Maids": Anti-Revolutionary British Women Writers and Narrative Authority after the French Revolution', *Tulsa's Studies in Women's Literature* 22 (2003), pp. 81–9.

Wood, Lisa, '"This Maze of History and Fiction": Conservatism, Genre, and the Problem of Domestic Freedom in Jane West's *Alicia De Lacy*', *English Studies in Canada* 23 (1997), pp. 125–39.

Wood, Paul, *Science and Dissent in England, 1688–1945* (Aldershot: Ashgate, 2004).

Wright, Angela, *Britain, France and the Gothic, 1764–1820* (Cambridge: Cambridge University Press, 2013).

Wright, Angela, 'Scottish Gothic', in Catherine Spooner and Emma McEvoy (eds), *The Routledge Companion to Gothic Literature* (New York: Routledge, 2007), pp. 73–82.

Wright, Julia M., '"The Nation Begins to Form": Competing Nationalisms in Morgan's *The O'Briens and the O'Flahertys*', *ELH* 66.4 (1999), pp. 939–63.

Yearsley, Ann, *The Royal Captives: A Fragment of Secret History*, 4 vols (London: Campbell, 1795).

Zaptka, Francis, 'Jane Porter's Kościuszko', in James S. Pula, M. B. Biskuski and Thomas J. Napierkowski (eds), Selected Essays from the 5th Anniversary International Congress of the Polish Institute of Arts and Sciences of America, *Heart of the Nation: Polish Literature and Culture* 3, East European Monographs 390 (1993), pp. 165–79.

# Index

Royal Society, the, 150
Rudé, Georges, 88

Saint Edmund, 29
Sanderson, William, *A Complete
    History*, 63
science, 13, 19, 76–7, 89, 130, 136,
    140, 149–65, 173, 175, 178, 179,
    183, 189–90, 193, 199
Scotland, 5, 18–19, 99, 101–10, 117,
    128, 129, 145–7, 174, 180, 191,
    199, 210
Scott, James, Duke of Monmouth,
    105–8
Scott, Walter
    *Antiquary*, 13, 19, 105, 172–83,
        184, 185, 186, 190–1, 193–4,
        197–202
    *Castle Dangerous*, 70, 182
    *Essay on Chivalry*, 187
    *Guy Mannering*, 3, 76, 199, 208
    *Ivanhoe*, 14, 19, 44, 53, 170, 172,
        183–91, 193, 196–8, 199, 200–2,
        208, 209
    *Letters on Demonology*, 13
    *Lives of Eminent Novelists*, 35
    *Quentin Durward*, 44, 164
    'Rokeby', 185
    *St Ronan's Well*, 108, 172, 173,
        191–202
    *Waverley*, 1–3, 16, 18, 44, 46, 99,
        106, 136, 170–1, 174, 191
Sebastian I, King of Portugal, 141
Second Barons' War, 48
Second Partition of Poland, 124
September Massacres, 92
Seven Years War, 36, 70
Shakespeare, William, 191, 199
Sheridan, Richard Brinsley, 114
Siddons, Henry, *William Wallace*, 101,
    108–10, 118, 128
Smith, Adam, 21n, 50, 96n, 106, 108,
    198
Smith, Charlotte
    *Desmond*, 7, 12, 17, 50, 71–7, 80,
        84, 90, 92, 159, 171–2, 175–6,
        183, 191–2, 208–9
    *Ethelinde*, 70, 81, 121, 134, 143, 192
    *Letters of a Solitary Wanderer*, 182
    *Minor Morals*, 150–1, 186
Smith, Sidney, 214
Society for Constitutional Information,
    39, 44
Society of Antiquarians, the, 150

Society of United Irishmen, the, 117
Spenser, Edmund, 65, 110, 114
Staël, Madame de, *Corinne*, 12
Stevens, Anne H., 6, 11, 16, 132n
Stewart, Dugald, 152, 155
Stuarts, the, 10, 31–2, 38–9, 65, 92,
    105, 128, 181, 188
Sweet, Rosemary, 150

Tacitus, 118
'Terrorist System of Novel Writing',
    69
Teutoburg Forest, battle of, 84, 119
Tompkins, J. M. S., 114–15
trade *see* commerce
Trumpener, Katie, 5, 99, 104

Union, the, 2, 5, 6, 18, 19, 99–130,
    136, 145, 181, 211

von Ranke, Leopold, 164–5

Wales, 18, 99, 129
Walker, Joseph Cooper, *Historical
    Memoirs of the Irish Bards*, 127
Walpole, Horace, 17, 31, 38–9, 47, 48,
    53–4, 86
    *Castle of Otranto*, 5, 6, 12, 25, 26,
        31–5, 112–13
Walpole, Robert, Sir, 9, 24, 26, 29, 35,
    59, 209
War of the Second Coalition, 137
War of the Third Coalition, 137
Watson, Nicola, 128, 174, 211
Watt, James, 102–3, 112
Wein, Toni, 15, 26, 31
West, Jane, 2, 3, 19, 121, 172, 173,
    179, 201
    *Alicia de Lacy*, 164
    *A Gossip's Story*, 138, 157
    *Letters Addressed to a Young Man*,
        157–9, 161, 171
    *The Loyalists*, 151, 157–65, 174,
        176, 178, 190, 199, 212
    *The Refusal*, 12, 178
    *A Tale of the Times*, 157, 198
White, James
    *The Adventures of John of Gaunt*,
        113, 117
    *The Adventures of Richard Coeur-de-
        Lion*, 113, 159
    *Earl Strongbow*, 13, 102, 105,
        112–15, 132n, 179, 185, 210
Whitehouse, John, *Poems*, 68